Family Life

Domestic Roles and Social Organization

Graham Allan

Basil Blackwell

© Graham Allan 1985

First published 1985

Basil Blackwell Ltd
108 Cowley Road, Oxford OX4 1JF, UK

Basil Blackwell Inc.
432 Park Avenue South, Suite 1505,
New York, NY 10016, USA

British Library Cataloguing in Publication Data

Allan, Graham
Family life, domestic roles and social organization.
1. Family — Great Britain
I. Title
306.8'5'0941   HQ613
ISBN 0-631-14286-X
ISBN 0-631-14287-8 Pbk

Library of Congress Cataloging in Publication Data

Allan, Graham A.
Family life.

Includes index.
1. Family. 2. Social structure. 3. Domestic relations.
I. Title.
HQ734.A43   1985   306.8'5   85-3888
ISBN 0-631-14286-X
ISBN 0-631-14287-8 (pbk.)

Typeset by Getset (BTS) Ltd, Eynsham, Oxford
Printed in Great Britain by The Bath Press, Avon

Contents

Acknowledgements

This book has grown out of various lecture series I have given on the sociology of the family at the University of Southampton over the last few years. I owe the students on these courses a debt for all the criticisms they have made and the ideas they gave me. I would also like to thank colleagues in the Department of Sociology and Social Administration at Southampton for the support they provided, particularly Professor John Martin and Professor John Smith who, as Heads of Department, made available the resources needed for producing the book.

I am grateful to the following publishers for permission to reproduce copyright material: George Allen and Unwin for tables from *Middle-Class Couples* by Stephen Edgell; Basil Blackwell for tables from *The Sociology of Housework* by Ann Oakley; Family Policy Studies Centre for a table from *Crisis or Challenge? Family Care, Elderly People and Social Policy* by Chris Rossiter and Malcolm Wicks; Macmillan (London and Basingstoke) for a table from *Trends in British Society Since 1900* edited by A. H. Halsey; Routledge and Kegan Paul for tables from *The Symmetrical Family* by Michael Young and Peter Willmott.

I am especially grateful to Sue Allan, Graham Crow, Joan Higgins and Jenny Mason for the encouragement and help they have given me. Amongst other things, they all read the typescript and made suggestions and comments which improved it a good deal. In their own rather different ways, 'Mortis', Nick and Chrissie also provided inspiration. Finally, but by no means least, I would like to thank Pam Roberts who has typed all the different drafts of the book quickly and accurately, no matter how unreasonable the deadline I requested. If it was not for her effort and commitment the book would have taken far longer to complete than it did. I owe her a great deal for all the work she put into it.

1

Introduction

Of all our social institutions, the family is probably the one about which the most contradictory images abound. On the one hand, home and family are often seen as a haven from the harsh realities of the outside world. They are taken to be the natural location of our most meaningful, intense and rewarding attachments and experiences. Certainly our relationships with our spouses and children are generally accepted as being the most important we create and our commitment to them provides the ultimate justification for a good deal of what we do. Marriage itself continues to be almost the sole 'rite de passage' our society has for indicating adulthood and is as popular a state as it ever has been. Not withstanding the incidence of divorce, parents continue to want their children to marry, settle down and have children of their own. It is not just that the parents' job is somehow done once this is achieved but that many see a stable and happy family existence as the major goal of life itself. Similarly, contemporary marriage is often portrayed as qualitatively better than marriage in previous times — more equal, more caring, more companionate, or whatever.

Yet at the same time as all this, the modern family is regularly portrayed as being in quite a serious state of decline. Unlike times past when family members could rely on each other to meet the contingencies of everyday life, we are told that contemporary families are incapable of providing the collective support and sustenance that used to be their hallmark. Not only has family life become privatized and isolating, with each household living out its existence trapped in its own little box, but, perhaps more importantly, family relationships are less stable and apparently less caring. Evidence of the breakdown of traditional family values and solidarity appears all around us. The rising divorce rate, the level of domestic violence, the neglect of the elderly, the number of 'latch-key' children, the frequency of extra-marital affairs, and so on all indicate how family organization is currently being undermined. Equally many broader social problems are traced back to these changes in family patterns. For instance, amongst the young, mugging, vandalism and the rise of other juvenile crime, together with discipline problems in school, are typically thought to be caused by family disorganization. It is pertinent here that the then Home Secretary's immediate response to the inner city riots of 1981 was to consider legislation to make parents responsible for their children's criminal activities.

The contradictions and ambiguities in our everyday views about the family are not particularly surprising. Such views are not objective descriptions of family life *per se*, but rather attempts to account for and explain the social tendencies and trends we perceive to be occurring in our society. We select out and emphasize this element or that as necessary from the disparate range of ideas we hold about family life without worrying too much about their internal consistency. In doing this, present experience is often interpreted against a somewhat idealized background. As with notions of community, reference to the happy past, be it the past of 50 years ago or 250 provides a framework which allows today's problems to be understood.

But equally of course, our experience of family life is itself changing. Being the main location of social and physical reproduction, the family is not static but alters with changes in the material and cultural basis of the wider society. Certainly in comparison with previous eras, there is currently more variation and variability in people's family circumstances. In a sense family life has become less predictable. Whereas even a generation ago it was quite sensible to analyse domestic circumstances in terms of a 'family cycle' — implying a more or less consistently structured set of stages through which families passed from marriage to death — it is far less so now. In particular, increases in divorce, single-parent and reconstituted families and changes in married women's employment patterns have resulted in a far greater diversity in the experiences of families and made the family cycle empirically much messier.

This is not to argue that family and domestic experiences are random and no longer patterned. Clearly they are still systematically structured, especially with respect to the relationships between the genders and the generations. But the changes — real and imagined — which there have been do raise various issues and questions. Has the family become privatized and cut off from the wider community? If so, what implications does this have for husbands and wives, for children and the elderly? Is marriage breaking down or is it, on the contrary, becoming stronger through being a more democratic and rewarding relationship? Have changes in wives' employment patterns affected domestic organization and family relationships? What are the consequences of higher divorce rates?

How are children affected by parental separation and divorce? Are the old being neglected by their families? And so on.

The aim of this book is to throw some light on questions and issues like these. By drawing on recent (and some not so recent) sociological research, it attempts to analyse contemporary patterns of family and domestic life. In particular, it is concerned with showing how the organization of family life is structured by the broader social and economic contexts within which families operate. As the title indicates, a major part of this involves uncovering the way in which the division of tasks and responsibilities between the genders within the home is both shaped by and shapes the divisions and inequalities that occur outside it. This is a main theme that recurs throughout the book.

The book is intended as an introduction to these issues. It is written for those who would like to know more about the contribution sociology can make to our understanding of family life rather than for the expert, and so does not assume very much prior knowledge or reading. Specifically, it is hoped that the book will prove helpful to those studying sociology in some formal capacity — as undergraduates or possibly at A level or as part of their training for social work, health visiting or some other profession — and to people who simply wish to know more about the sociology of the family. As with all such texts, some topics have been covered more thoroughly than others and some neglected altogether, in line with the author's interests. None the less, the purpose of the book is to provide a useful and reasonably comprehensive introduction to the sociological analysis of family life.

Chapter 2 is concerned with the relationship between the family and other organizations in society. It looks at the role that the contemporary family plays and the extent to which it is becoming socially marginal. It also attempts to show how the internal patterning of family life is shaped by the demands that external organizations make of it. The consequences of this internal division of labour within families is analysed in Chapter 3. Building on the argument of the previous chapter, it examines how the routine demands of domesticity shape the experiences of women as wives and mothers and limits the opportunities open to them. Chapter 4 focuses on the idea that family life is becoming privatized. It examines the growth of 'home-centredness' and the impact this has on leisure patterns and sociable activity. Chapter 5 is concerned with the nature of contemporary marriage, and particularly the degree to which this tie remains one of inequality. It looks at different ways of measuring marital equality and links the structure of marriage to factors lying outside the domestic sphere. The next three chapters examine issues over which there is currently a good deal of social concern. Chapter 6 analyses contemporary patterns of marriage break-up and divorce. Following the analysis in the previous chapters, it is particularly concerned with the effect divorce has for female life styles. Chapter 7 focuses on the elderly and the consequences their increasing number has for family life. It analyses the part that daughters especially play in caring for the elderly and the impact this has on their lives. It also examines the extent to which current community care policies are likely to affect the caring that families/daughters provide. Chapter 8 is concerned with assessing the impact that unemployment has on family life. It looks particularly at the way in which unemployment affects the division of tasks and responsibilities within the home and concludes that, contrary to some popular views, the basic structure of marriage and family life specified in the previous chapters is reinforced rather than undermined by it. By way of conclusion, the final chapter examines briefly how different state policies impinge on family life. In line with the rest of the book, it is concerned mainly with showing how recent policies presuppose and consequently help sustain gender based divisions in domestic organization.

2

The Family in Society

This chapter is concerned primarily with the part played by the family in present-day society. It seeks to locate the family within the social structure by examining the links that exist between it and other social institutions. To do this it will analyse the manner in which these other institutions make use of relationships based on kinship and the degree to which the demands they make shape the organization of family life. Such concerns have been central in the development of family sociology and have also generated much popular debate. The single most dominant viewpoint is that with industrialization the family gradually became less important in social life. To use a theatrical analogy, whereas once it occupied a position centre stage, involved in most of what was going on, the family is now found somewhere near the wings, not altogether unimportant but away from much of the action. Part of this process is seen to involve the shift from large extended families to the smaller nuclear ones now so' common.

The sociological perspective that most fully embodies this view of the family becoming more peripheral is the American 'loss of function' approach, which itself reflects much popular folk-wisdom. The essential argument is that with technological change and increasing specialization various activities once associated almost exclusively with the family — including economic, health and welfare, and educational ones — have been taken over by institutions newly created specifically for these pur- poses. As a result the bonds that previously held the wider extended family together were broken so that the family became denuded, struc- turally peripheral and potentially disorganized.

In its grosser forms, this picture of family life is clearly suspect, not least for its portrayal of previous family patterns. Firstly, Laslett and his colleagues have shown that there is little evidence that extended family households ever existed outside the aristocracy prior to industrialization

(Laslett, 1969; Laslett and Wall, 1974). Certainly the image of three-generational families typically co-operating and caring for one another is illusory as very few people ever lived long enough to become grand-parents. Early death made such extended families an impossibility for the great majority. Indeed, as Anderson (1971) has argued, three-generation families actually developed as a consequence of industrialization rather than being destroyed by it.

Equally, it is possible to question the extent to which families ever performed some of the activities supposedly taken away from them by the creation of new institutions and organizations. For example, most families were ill-equipped to meet extensive health and welfare needs effectively. The care they could give their sick was limited by the poor material conditions of the home, and of course by their lack of effective medical knowledge. Similarly, however wide the definition of the family used, kin could do little by way of providing insurance against illness or unem-ployment − even if they had wished to − as their collective resources were usually too small. In Britain the state has recognized this for well over 350 years, however inadequate its consequent provision may be adjudged to have been. Again it is questionable whether families had an educational as distinct from a socializational function. Most of the knowledge imparted in schools was simply not available to the majority of people. Ignorant parents could hardly teach their children the academic disciplines which are the hallmark of formal systems of education. If, on the other hand, educational functions are taken to include socialization ones, then the proposition is simply wrong. Families are more involved than ever in socializing their children, not least because changing educational provision has helped extend the period during which children are deemed to be socially and economically dependent. Similarly one can question the extent to which families ever engaged in collective recreational pursuits. The image of family soirées this conjures up could hardly have been typical of the majority of people's leisure activities, given the material conditions that prevailed prior to this century. Indeed one of the ideas to be discussed in a later chapter is the exact opposite of this: that the home has become a more central focus in people's lives as increased prosperity and tech-nological innovation have improved its ambience.

Talcott Parsons: the structurally isolated conjugal family

While the more simplistic forms of the 'loss of function' and 'family breakdown' thesis are questionable, more sophisticated analyses, like that provided by Talcott Parsons, warrant fuller consideration. Parsons is in agreement with other writers that the family no longer performs some of the functions it once did, but he sees this change in a rather more positive light than some. He is sceptical of the claim that family life is becoming disorganized and, in line with his wider theoretical speculations, argues instead that a process of specialization and differentiation has occurred. Essentially, whereas in more primitive societies kinship dominates social life in the sense that 'there are few concrete structures in which participation is independent of kinship status' (Parsons 1956, p. 9), in industrial society a process of differentiation has resulted in non-kinship units (such as business firms, churches, schools, trade unions, professional associations, etc.) playing a far larger part. This process 'inevitably entails "loss of function" on the part of some or even all of the kinship units . . . [leading to] the reduction of the importance in our society of kinship units other than the nuclear family' (1956, p. 9). For Parsons this differentiation is not to be seen in terms of a breakdown of the family, but rather in terms of its increased specialization. The result of this specialization is that society is more exclusively dependent on the family for the performance of a small number of crucial functions, specifically those relating to the generation and maintenance of human personality. Indeed Parsons (1956, p. 16) alludes to the family being a 'factory' in which human personalities are produced at two levels: firstly through the primary socialization of children so that they become competent members of society, and secondly through the stabilization of adult personalities by their incorporation and commitment to ties of marriage and parenthood. In order to perform these functions adequately, the family is itself internally differentiated, according to Parsons, with the two spouses having specialized and distinct roles. The husband tends to be the more instrumental of the two in terms of decision-making as well as income provision, while the wife's role is predominantly expressive. Her task is to succour the other family members and provide for their emotional well-being. He, if you like, brings the raw materials to the family factory, while she beavers away inside its walls creating the finished product of human personality.

The similarities between Parsons's views and earlier functionalist theories are apparent. Nevertheless Parsons's use of the more subtle concept of differentiation marks his perspective off from formulations that refer merely to loss of function or the family's breakdown, the more so as he is as much concerned with the consequent integration of the differentiated parts as with the process of differentiation itself. This is evident in the following passage where he explains what he means by differentiation: 'Differentiation refers to the process by which simple structures are divided into functionally differing components, these components becoming relatively independent of one another, and then recombined into more complex structures in which the functions of the differentiated units are complementary' (Parsons, 1962, p. 103). For the present purposes the important issue is the way in which the differentiated family structure which Parsons identifies fits in with other societal institutions in contemporary industrial society.

Parsons characterizes the differentiated form of family typical of modern industrial society as 'the structurally isolated conjugal family'. There is some ambiguity about exactly what Parsons means by this concept. The conjugal family can be defined as a co-residing married couple with or without dependent children. (Following Harris and Stacey (1969) the term 'nuclear family' will here refer to the conjugal family in which there are dependent children). The term 'structural isolation' is more complicated and has consistently been misunderstood. Parsons is not here referring to 'social isolation' in the usual sense of the amount of contact that there is between different kin. On the contrary he recognizes that there is always likely to be contact between at least some categories of non-conjugal kin. Rather what Parsons is referring to is the far greater importance attached in our kinship system to the obligations we owe to our conjugal family than to those due to other kin. As an illustration, it is clearly in the nature of nuclear families as defined above that they disappear as the children of the family become adult. Kinship obligations do not disappear at this point − parents do not stop caring for their now adult children, nor siblings for one another − but the intensity of their obligations is weakened. Normally, for instance, they no longer form a residential or an economic unit together. So we have some obligations and duties towards non-conjugal kin, but these are usually secondary to our obligations and duties to conjugal family members. It is the latter who are given priority. To put this another way, in comparison to many non-Western societies, our kinship system is marked by the relative absence of any rules encouraging the formation of wider kin groupings, such as clans, lineages or other forms of 'extended family'.

The benefits of the absence of such rules in an industrial society are essentially two-fold in Parsons's view. Firstly, because according to his scheme the conjugal family contains only one main income earner, it does not discourage occupationally induced geographical mobility. Such mobility, which Parsons takes to be characteristic of industrial society, would be hindered if the domestic kin group contained more than one income earner needing to find work simultaneously in the new location. Secondly, Parsons points out that typically the family and economic institutions are premised on quite different sets of values. The former are based on criteria which are ascriptive − a consequence of birth − and particularistic − to do with the particular qualities and needs of the individual involved. The latter are achievement-oriented and universalistic — applying a given set of rules or procedures to all equivalent cases, irrespective of any personal commitment. While these latter values are the dominant ones in society, potential conflict is generally avoided by the two spheres being kept separate. From the Parsonian perspective, the structurally isolated nuclear family plays its part in this as it contains only a single link between the two systems, that being the main income earner. In other words, while there are significant (and sociologically interesting) exceptions (Allan, 1982), kin do not normally play roles opposite one another in economic institutions, and consequently the economic system continues to operate largely unruffled by ascriptive, particularistic considerations of family solidarity. The significance of the structural isolation of the nuclear family for Parsons is summarized succinctly by Harris in the following passage:

> Major conflict is therefore avoided by *two* types of segregation. The nuclear family is cut off from *wider kin* in the sense that the most stringent ties are confined within it, and because its members do not perform economic roles opposite one another it is also segregated from the *economic system* except for the husband. In this way intrusion of family values into the sphere of work is avoided and work values do not disrupt the solidarity of the family. (Harris, 1983, p. 58; emphases in original)

Eugene Litwak: the modified extended family

Parsons's formulation of the structural isolation of the nuclear family has been criticized by numerous authors, many of whom use empirical evidence from kinship studies to demonstrate that the contemporary family is not socially isolated from other kin. However as Parsons never made such a claim, these criticisms are of little substance. A more adequate criticism is provided by Eugene Litwak who developed the concept of 'modified extended family', though as we shall see Litwak's theories are not as contrary as he supposes to Parsons's views (Litwak 1960a, 1960b, 1965; Litwak and Szelenyi, 1969). The form of family found in contemporary society is, according to Litwak, neither an isolated nuclear/conjugal one nor an extended one in the classical sense. Rather it lies somewhere in between. In particular, while it is certainly true that household structure is predominantly nuclear/conjugal rather than extended, and that individual conjugal families are largely autonomous, it is not true that there is little support or assistance flowing between related families. The classical notion of extended families as a residential and economic unit made up of nuclear family sub-units does not apply, but equally every kinship study published has shown that aid and exchanges routinely flow between non-conjugal kin. Litwak intends the concept 'modified extended family' to convey his image of a non-residential network of kin who are available to provide one another with a range of services and help at times of need.

Some such informal organization is necessary in an industrial society according to Litwak for reasons very similar to those which have led other theorists to argue that the family is losing its functions: because of the dominance in such societies of specialized, legal-rational bureaucracies. The classical advantages of bureaucracies are that they encourage uniformity of response, impartiality and expertise to develop. This makes them highly suitable for solving standard and more or less predictable contingencies. The other side of the coin though, Litwak argues, is that they are less able to handle idiosyncratic, non-regular issues which inevitably affect every individual as an individual. No matter how all-embracing and efficient bureaucracies become, they will rarely be able to satisfy all a person's requirements and needs precisely because they are universalistic rather than particularistic. Litwak's thesis is that to function to maximum advantage, bureaucracies often require the simultaneous presence of a primary group which acts particularistically in handling the peculiar problems of the individual at a given point in time. Normally the primary group that acts in this way is, Litwak asserts, the modified extended family, though in a later paper he argues that friends, neighbours and kin can each best perform distinct 'primary group' tasks (Litwak and Szelenyi, 1969).

Some examples will make the relationship between the activities of bureaucracies and primary groups clearer: health, education, and care of the elderly, all of which are supposed to have been removed from the family's orbit according to the 'loss of function' thesis. In the field of health care it is obvious that we now have a range of organizations and bureaucracies responsible for health that did not exist to any extent before this century. Hospitals, clinics, health centres and their like have flourished, as have the numbers of medical and paramedical workers and the specialized services for dealing with specific conditions. In Britain, medical provision is dominated by the National Health Service, a massive bureaucracy that seeks to ensure that everyone in the country receives adequate medical care. And yet when episodes of illness are examined, it is quite clear that health services do not act alone. Not only do most of us spend relatively little time in hospital receiving specialist nursing, but when we are ill our use of medical organizations is normally restricted to a brief visit to the doctor and the exchange of a prescription for medicine. The rest of our recovery to health is normally handled by our families, and mainly by wives and mothers acting in a non-specialist, non-professional basis. Certainly without the great bulk of nursing care they provide, our medical bureaucracies would be unable to cope.

Equally with education, a wide range of institutions and specialists have developed over the last hundred years or so. The amount of time children spend in full-time education has continued to rise since the first compulsory primary schooling in 1871. Not only has the minimum school leaving age gradually been increased from 11 to 16, but as importantly there has been societal encouragement for children to remain in education even longer, either full-time or part-time, at university or college, to acquire knowledge and expertise that will better equip them individually and the society generally. While it is no surprise that educational opportunities are seized differentially on a class basis − given that one of the educational system's functions is to sort people out into occupational strata − educationalists have asserted for many years that a chief factor influencing educational success is family background. In essence, though as bureaucracies educational institutions make a wide range of information and knowledge available, educational potential appears only to be fulfilled if the more intimate and personal primary group of the family fosters the desire to learn by providing the necessary encouragement and support.

Finally if we turn to care of the elderly, we can again recognize that despite the growth of specialized organizations, a great deal of the care the elderly receive comes from their families, and in particular their daughters. The great increase there has been in the number of elderly people, especially over the age of 75, has resulted in many more specialized services being provided. Some of these are medical or para-medical − geriatric wards, chiropody and ophthalmic services − others are social − sheltered housing, meals on wheels, social services. All of them appear to be stretched to the limit constantly, hardly capable of meeting the demands made of them. Yet the situation would be far worse if families were not augmenting these services to the elderly. Research continues to demonstrate that professional, non-familial provision is usually only called on when either there is no family to care for the elderly person or when the elderly person is too debilitated to be cared for by the family in an adequate manner. The advantage of familial over professional care is of course precisely that identified by Litwak. The family is able to react to the specific needs of its elderly members in a particularistic fashion. It can ensure the relative well-being of the elderly with the minimum possible disruption to their independence and autonomy, especially if it can call on professional services as required for assistance. The costs to other family members may be large, as will be discussed in Chapter 7, but there is little doubt that the family group can react to the requirements of its elderly members in a more satisfactory and humane manner than any bureaucratically organized, universalistic institutions.

Modified elementary families?

It is in such ways then that Litwak sees the relationship between societal institutions on the one hand and the modified extended family on the other. The former can handle uniform, predictable occurrences, while the latter, acting particularistically, can best deal with personal, individual contingencies. Thus rather than being opposed forms of social organization, they are in reality complementary. Litwak's formulation can be seen to have three major strengths. Firstly, and perhaps most importantly, it recognizes that the family is not becoming functionless in the sense of having its social importance limited to one or two residual activities – tension management and socialization, say. Rather the family and the help and assistance its members offer one another is central to society, for its actions as a primary group help many of the more formal organizations and institutions to fulfil their goals. Far from being peripheral, the family is involved in quite a wide range of activities, including health care, education, social welfare and economic provision. 'However', as Litwak argues, 'in each of these areas it contributes only part to the achievement of goals. The other part is contributed by the formal organization' (Litwak, 1965, p. 294).

Secondly, Litwak's ideas are interesting because of their recognition that the family operates as a network in which a range of services are exchanged between the individual members. The family in this view is not best seen as a fixed group, be it residentially, economically or politically defined, but as a collection of individuals who can draw on one another and use each other as resources in a co-ordinated fashion as and when the occasion demands. As much as anything else, it is this informal provision of reciprocated services covering a range of activity that Litwak is trying to convey by the concept 'modified extended family'.

The third advantage of Litwak's model is in a sense the culmination of the other two: it is the recognition that bureaucratic organizations cannot satisfy all the contingencies people face. His emphasis on the need for primary groups/networks in an industrial society, as well as for more formal associations, is a point that is too often forgotten by writers intent on demonstrating the declining importance of communal activities generally and family life in particular. Such primary relationships are not some kind of unnecessary luxury in modern society, but rather are crucial in one form or another to its functioning. In emphasizing the significance of informal relationships, Litwak has provided a much needed corrective.

However while Litwak's thesis provides a useful framework, it is not beyond criticism. To start with, his conceptualization is not the rebuttal of Parsons's theories that he supposes. Parsons made two essential points. Firstly, the individual's primary, though not sole, responsibility is to his conjugal family. And secondly, in contemporary society family and bureaucratic organizations are based on quite separate values, the former on particularistic and ascriptive ones, the latter on universalistic and achievement oriented ones. Litwak's ideas contradict neither of these points. Indeed as Harris (1969; 1983) notes, the main thrust of his argument that there is an interdependence between the modified extended family and bureaucratic institutions in the achievement of their goals depends entirely on the second of Parsons's claims here. It is precisely because the family is particularistic that it can satisfy idiosyncratic and personal requirements in a way that fits in with the universalistically operating bureaucracy. Thus far from contradicting Parsons, Litwak is merely building upon his premise, albeit in an important and illuminating fashion.

Equally Litwak does not negate Parsons's first contention: that the individual's overriding obligation is to his or her conjugal family. If Parsons had argued that only this obligation was honoured, then Litwak would certainly be contradicting him, but this is not Parsons's claim. Other responsibilities and duties are recognized, and are ignored only when they conflict with those to one's conjugal family. On the other hand, Parsons actually tells us very little about the content of our obligations either to our conjugal family or to other kin. Litwak at least attempts to specify to some degree this content by examining the empirical operation of family life under given circumstances, and as a result portrays the workings of kinship networks in contemporary society more effectively than Parsons.

A more important issue than the compatibility of Parsons's and Litwak's views is the extent to which the family-based primary network that Litwak rightly identifies as central to the operation of industrial society is in fact best characterized as a 'modified extended family'. There are two related points behind this questioning: one, the extent to which any non-conjugal kin are normally involved in the activities bureaucratic organizations alone cannot handle; and two, the degree to which the term 'extended', be it modified or not, overemphasizes the actual range of such kin who provide support for the conjugal family.

If we accept the proposition that some primary group or network is required to help many of the more formal bureaucracies achieve their objectives, exactly who are the members of this group? It is certainly arguable that in many cases it is in fact the conjugal family. Consider again the examples of health care and education discussed above. Whilst recognizing that family encouragement and orientation are significant factors in educational achievement, the family group whose encouragement is central and whose orientation needs to be aligned with that of the school is normally the nuclear one. The material, cultural and ideological provision of the home, and the influence of parents, and possibly older siblings, are what counts. Other kin, especially grandparents, may in some instances also be influential in encouraging children to value educational development, but usually it is parents who activate such desires. Equally with health care, most of the routine nursing and other unofficial care that our health services depend on is done by the conjugal family, especially wives and mothers. When a member of the conjugal family falls ill, that family usually manages to cope without calling on the services of other kin. On some occasions other kin may give assistance. Grandmothers in particular are likely to provide help if possible when the mother herself is ill, or when she works and the grandmother does not, or for specific predictable episodes like confinement (Hubert, 1965). Usually, though, such assistance is not required as the conjugal family uses its own resources to cope. The issue here then is not that the family fails to perform the activities Litwak claimed for it, nor even that non-conjugal kin play no part. It is rather that the primary group or network operating in many of the contexts Litwak discusses need not necessarily be a group any wider than the conjugal family. Often it is, either consistently or on occasion, depending on the activities in question. Indeed in some instances it clearly must be, as with the care of the elderly. But it is not inevitably so. The conjugal family is in this sense a viable organization, well adapted to cope with many of the daily contingencies it faces. The important point to recognize is that this unit can, as necessary, normally call on the assistance of other kin who do not reside within it. The kin group does in this sense operate as a network in which different services are exchanged depending on need and resources available. Crucially, though, this does not mean that these kin are routinely required. Their strength lies in the fact that they are there ready to be called on, even though normally it is not necessary to do so.

The second point to consider here is just who are the kin that can be called upon in this way. Is it possible to specify more precisely who belongs to the 'modified extended family'? The difficulty with the concept, as with the more general term 'extended family', is that in principle all kin could be included. There can be an indefinite progression. Indeed one could argue that Litwak has paid insufficient attention to contemporary kinship studies, especially those such as Firth's (Firth, 1956; Firth, Hubert and Forge, 1970) or Williams's (1963) which concern themselves with the total kin universe. These studies show that while the range of kin known about by any individual is generally large − varying from seven to 388 in Firth's study of middle-class kinship (Firth et al., 1970, p. 159) − the numbers who are in Firth's terms 'effective' kin is much smaller. Effective kin are those with whom people are involved in an 'active social relation', so that 'the recognition of the relationship has some effect, however minimal, on the social life of the informant' (1970, p. 195). On average Firth's respondents had 20 effective kin, about one third of their known living kin. Effective kin themselves can be separated into intimate and peripheral kin. By intimate kin, Firth means 'those with whom contact tended to be purposeful, close and frequent, and the set of persons involved tended to be described by our informants in such terms as "immediate family circle"' (1970, p. 156). It is presumably these whom Litwak would see as forming the primary group that supports the individual. While the boundaries are not precise, it is clear that intimate kin are normally only a minority of the effective kin category, and consequently contain a small proportion of an individual's acknowledged kin universe. More important than numbers though is who these kin actually are. The enormous majority of them are primary kin, i.e. members of the individual's elementary family of origin or elementary family of procreation − his or her parents, siblings, spouse and children. Secondary kin, i.e. those related to the individual by more than one genealogical link, are on the whole far less significant. Apart from grandparents and grandchildren, secondary kin do not figure greatly in the organization of people's daily lives (see Firth, 1956; Firth et al., 1970; Williams, 1963).

In other words the personnel involved in the 'modified extended family' is likely to be almost exclusively limited to primary kin. It is primary kin to whom the individual is likely to turn at times of need and who will routinely be involved in the round of daily events. Certainly the research literature contains little evidence to suggest that secondary kin act in the manner of Litwak's modified extended family. Indeed it would seem that it is mainly direct descendants who do act in this way. Adult children normally turn to their parents for help before their siblings, and of course it is adult children who cater and care for elderly parents. Siblings help each other out on occasion, for example with childcare or by passing on clothes or furniture. Occasionally too particular siblings may regard one another as best friends and consequently rely on each other a good deal for a variety of purposes (Allan, 1977). Generally, though siblings are involved rather less in each other's lives than parents and adult children. This is the central bond.

The consequence of the two considerations discussed here is not a denial of Litwak's argument that kin-based primary networks are of great significance in industrial society, but rather a questioning of whom these groups involve. Litwak is right to indicate that conjugal families use their kin as resources, but in the process perhaps unintentionally overemphasizes the 'extendedness' of the kin who are so used. By and large, as one goes through the activities he mentions be they health, education, financial assistance, care for the elderly or what have you, the primary group or network involved seems, aptly, to be primary kin, and in particular though not exclusively direct descendants. Consequently rather than terming the unit he identified the 'modified extended family', Litwak might have more accurately labelled it the 'modified elementary family'. Clearly Litwak used the former term because it symbolized his rejection of claims that kinship is of little significance in contemporary society, but in many ways the latter term gives a clearer indication of the extent of kinship involvement for the majority of people.

Families or females? The creation of domestic roles

So, from this discussion we can see that when individuals and families face idiosyncratic problems and difficulties of one sort of another, they often draw upon (non-conjugal) primary kin to cope with them. Yet at the same time it needs emphasizing that life is not entirely haphazard, so that many of the demands made on the family by the outside organizations and agencies it co-ordinates with are routine and regular. In this they affect the ordinary domestic unit, the conjugal family, rather more than any wider kin network. But they do so in a particular way, for as Parsons argued, a major outcome for the domestic group of the growth in specialized institutions was pressure for its own internal differentiation with husband and wife having separate responsibilities and spheres of activity. This internal differentiation has very important implications for the sort of theory Litwak produced. In discussing the role that the 'modified extended family' plays in industrial society, the tendency is to see the family as a unit, an integral entity, and consequently to ignore the important divisions within it. The same of course applies equally to alternative concepts such as the 'modified elementary family' suggested above. However the 'families' that are being referred to in such theories are often not families in this sense at all. Rather they are almost invariably the wives, mothers and sisters of such families, for it is mainly female time that is taken up and female effort that is required in meeting the demands of non-domestic agencies. In other words the demands made on the family by external organizations are largely met by women in their specialized capacity of housewives and mothers. They can provide the services they do in the manner Litwak describes because, as a consequence of the differentiation of roles within families, their time as housewives and mothers is apparently free both in terms of availability and cost. This point is central to contemporary family organization and is worth developing at some length.

At issue here is the way in which a particular form of family life developed as the demands made by external agencies − be these to do with production, education, health, welfare or whatever − altered. To put this another way, even though, as Laslett (1969, 1974) shows, household composition has remained surprisingly constant over the last 400 years, this does not mean that the 'content' of domestic life − the relationships and activities it incorporates − is equally unchanged. The thing we term 'the family' − and even to talk of it in this way makes it appear overly fixed and static − is modified and moulded as other elements of the social mosaic of which it is part themselves alter. Even while apparently performing the same ageless functions − such as caring for, protecting and socializing its members − the specific manner in which the family achieves these is not historically constant. The calls made upon it, the way its members behave and react, the detailed performance of family living − these things all alter as the society itself is gradually transformed by its own tensions, contradictions and innovations (see Donzelot (1980) for a fascinating discussion of such processes in France).

Arguably, from this perspective, the most significant change in domestic and family life since the early period of industrialization has been the emergence of the contemporary housewife role, a role the majority of women fill part or full time for a large portion of their lives. In other words it is not simply that the demands of the developing industrial economy affected the nature of domestic obligation and necessary household tasks, but more importantly that the organization of family relationships was shaped by various social and economic factors that collectively encouraged a specific gender-based division of domestic responsibility whereby men/ husbands have been assigned the prime responsibility of income provision and women/wives that of carer and servicer. Because this conventional domestic division of labour is so much part of the everyday assumptions people make about marriage, there is a tendency to see it almost as a natural arrangement rather than a socially created one which developed in response to structural pressures emanating from other changes in society. While it may well be the case that females have been primarily responsible for domestic tasks throughout our civilization, it is patently untrue to suggest that the particular constellation of tasks now subsumed under the role of 'housewife' are historically universal. The contemporary housewife role is one which developed as a consequence of changes brought about by industrialization over the last 200 years or so. Indeed it is arguable that in this respect industrialization affected work within the home as much as that outside it.

A major factor in the creation of the housewife role was the removal of the great bulk of married women from paid employment by the end of the last century. Clearly this could happen only to the extent that husbands began to be paid wages sufficiently large to support their families. This in turn depended in large measure on the increased efficiency and productivity of industrial output which enabled a greater proportion of the population to be 'unproductive' in this narrow sense. Not surprisingly, this pattern became established first among middle-class wives, whose husbands could afford to have them run the marital home full-time. Only towards the end of the nineteenth century did a similar pattern emerge in most working-class homes. As Pinchbeck (1969) shows, prior to this paid work was essential for many working-class wives as their husbands' wages were often below household subsistence level. However by the turn of the century, the majority of working-class husbands were earning enough to provide for the essential requirements of their families. This did not apply uniformly though as a number of husbands continued to receive wages too low to keep their families at even a basic level of comfort. In these families wives still needed to supplement their husbands' incomes in one way or another. Large families dependent on a single wage earner were especially likely to experience marked poverty, just as they are today (Land, 1978). Overall though, the creation of the so-called 'family wage' by the beginning of the twentieth century made the development of the full-time housewife role possible. While increased productivity need not inevitably have produced an ideology of the family wage and resulted in the absence of most married women from formal employment, this was one of its main effects. By 1901 only 10 per cent of married women were officially employed outside the home, though a good number of others contributed to household income informally by, for example, taking in lodgers or doing cleaning and washing on a casual basis (Scott and Tilly, 1975; Davidoff, 1979; Pahl, 1984). This pattern of married women's formal employment did not alter significantly in peace time until just before the second half of the century.

Related to the increased industrial productivity that enabled married women to work full time in the home were improvements to the domestic environment that led to modifications in the content of housework. Improvements in housing standards, reductions in overcrowding, the separation of residential areas from industrial grime, the increased facilities within the home including, especially, the routine provision of hot water systems and electrical power, the development of domestic machinery for laundering and cleaning, the improved knowledge of health hazards and their prevention, all meant that in this century homes could be kept to a much improved standard of cleanliness. Equally the development of inexpensive, easily laundered clothing and the ready availability of relatively cheap, nutritious food has resulted in a far higher level of personal hygiene and physical health for large sections of the population than was possible before this century. Prior to these changes, it would have been quite impossible to maintain the home and its personnel in the fashion now expected. In this sense the work demanded of the housewife in meeting these recently developed expectations is genuinely novel, unknown to most classes previously. Such factors, which can be labelled broadly environmental, were important in shaping contemporary ideas about appropriate domestic standards, and consequently in creating the housewife role as it has come to be defined.

As will be discussed in Chapter 4, these material changes in domestic conditions have fostered an image of the home as a place of relaxation and self-fulfilment in contrast to the harsh realities of the work place. Somewhat ironically for the housewife, the two spheres appear to be antithetical and in opposition to one another. Yet in reality their separation is not so clear-cut, for the demands of paid work continue to mould family life and the work that housewives do. At its most obvious, the hours that people are employed, the time they spend travelling or away from home, the shift system in operation, and the character of the work − its mental or physical arduousness − weave a pattern that imprints itself on the daily routine that is family life. If weekends are the time for the family, it is precisely because the rest of the week cannot be. The working week is the dominant component and domestic organization clearly reflects this in such areas as the timing of meals, the periods the family spends together and the general rhythm of family life. Far from being unrelated to production, the family, and especially the housewife, arrange their schedules around the requirements of employment (Finch, 1983).

As recent analyses of the housewife role have shown (Seccombe, 1974; Molyneux, 1979), the family and economic productions are also linked because of the role that domestic labour plays in sustaining an individual's ability to work. Essentially the argument here is that people's capacity for work depends on their variable physical, cultural and emotional requirements being regularly met. In principle such provision could be socialized with many of these needs being provided communally, as indeed some are. In practice, given the variation that inevitably exists between workers, in terms of their social circumstances and individual preferences, these services are likely to continue to be provided within the domestic group, which in terms of adaptability and satisfaction of more or less idiosyncratic desires has all the advantages over large-scale communally organized provision that Litwak analysed. Given this and the other pressures for a domestic division of labour, a separation of primary responsibilities between husband and wife with the latter's services sustaining her husband's capacity for employment, seems rational and continues today even though many wives now also make a significant contribution to household income.

The implication of the above argument is that having a division of labour in which one category of household member — wife/mother — services the others is to the benefit of industrial capitalism. As well as ensuring that workers are adequately rejuvenated for each new day's work, such a division of labour commits workers more fully to their work through the need to provide financially for their families. Certainly it is apparent that employers and the state have collectively encouraged this division by disadvantaging wives in the labour market and limiting their opportunities for employment. However, even granting these points, there remains the question 'Why women?' or more specifically 'Why married women?', for it is by no means self-evident that increased productivity necessitated the removal of married women as such from employment. To put this another way, there seems little in the 'logic of capitalism' that requires a division of labour based upon either gender or marriage.

Instead it can be argued that the creation of the housewife role has benefited men/husbands as much if not more than capitalism. In other words, excluding married women from employment can be understood as a strategy men pursued, notably through their developing trade union movement, to further specifically male interests. It did this in two principal respects. Firstly, while much was (and still is) made of the need to protect women, a major consequence of their exclusion was to limit competition for jobs, thereby increasing male wage rates not just for those with families but for all men (Barrett and McIntosh, 1980). Secondly, as Delphy (1984), amongst others, has argued, the unpaid servicing that wives now provide improved men's standards at relatively little cost to them. Though dressed up in the language of love and partnership, housework, precisely because it is unpaid, places wives in a subordinate position, making them economically and socially dependent on their husbands. The ramifications of this dependence will be discussed more fully in later chapters. The important point to recognize here is that the routine organization of domestic labour developed socially rather than naturally. It was the result of economic and political considerations rather than biological ones.

Further pressure for a gender-based division of responsibility within families arose from the changing position of children in our society.

Essentially, since industrialization there has been a gradual transformation in the way that children and childhood are socially defined, and consequently in the responsibilities parents have towards them. While the process started much earlier (Ariès, 1962), this century has seen the continuing separation of the world of childhood from the activities and contingencies of adult life. The extension and redefinition of this apparently crucial stage of personal development has had practical, financial and emotional repercussions on family life. In essence, while there has been a reduction in the average number of children women bear — from around 3.5 at the turn of the century to slightly over 2 now — the increased freedom this promised has been countered in many respects by what can be termed the changed 'qualitative' requirements of childcare.

One of the most important factors in encouraging the modern view of childhood has been the continual extension of educational provision. Whatever else they might do, schools demarcate childhood experience from adult life. They are an institutional expression of this separation, of the non-adult, dependent status of those who are required to attend them. Thus the regular raising of the minimum school-leaving age, from 11 at the turn of the century to 16 at the present time, should not be seen simply as an attempt to meet the labour force requirements of an increasingly complex industrial state, nor even as a political strategy for coping with unemployment by reducing the available labour supply. Rather it reflects and reinforces a general belief that to be ready to face the physical, emotional and even intellectual demands of the adult world, individuals need a longer and longer apprenticeship. They need to be kept in a social context that will protect them from harsh reality and allow them to develop properly and fully into competent adults.

Other state provision is equally suggestive of our consciousness of the special needs of children. For example a good deal of social service provision is directed at the welfare of children. Equally, recent housing legislation, such as the 1977 Homeless Persons Act, together with guidelines like those issued by the gas and electricity authorities, emphasize that children should not suffer from inadequate provision as a consequence of adult deeds. Most signficant, too, is the way that the law recognizes that children need to be treated in their own peculiar fashion. In contrast to previous eras when children as young as seven were hung for petty offences (Pinchbeck and Hewitt, 1973), the state now recognizes a minimum age of criminal responsibility and deals with cases involving children in special juvenile courts whose powers are designed specifically to meet the supposed best interests of minors.

Such changes as these in society's treatment of and expectations about childhood could not, of course, have occurred without affecting domestic life, the principal arena in which childhood is organized. As Harris argues (1977), in some respects the family can be seen as becoming increasingly child-centred, in extreme cases pathologically so with children almost suffocating from the pressure of it all. But while these developments have affected the family as a unit, they have done so principally by reinforcing the gender divisions within marriage and emphasizing the need for a primary carer. The educational system provides a clear indication of this. While a child spends only a minority of his or her time in school, the school has priority over the timing of its demands for the child's attendance. Given that education is provided collectively and universalistically, i.e. bureaucratically, this is necessarily so. As a consequence the family has to fit around the requirements of the school system and be flexible enough to cope with its demands. These include a relatively short working day, and long, irregular holidays. They also include periods of 'malfunctioning', when either the school is closed, for example because of direct or indirect industrial action, or the child cannot attend, generally because of illness. As a result the family's domestic organization is necessarily ordered in a fashion that allows it to cater to the demands of schooling.

Again, then, these factors have helped reinforce a domestic division of labour in which women, this time as mothers, routinely find themselves cast in the role of carer. Buttressed by the different forms of maternal deprivation theory that have proved so irrepressible and by deeply held convictions that women are naturally suited to this type of work, the reality of the economic and occupational system make it rational in individual families for the male to be the principal income earner, leaving the female to assume primary responsibility for childcare and to fit her remaining activities, including paid work, around this one. Of course husbands assist to differing degrees in these tasks, depending on their attitudes and their other commitments, but routinely it remains the wife's responsibility. As Comer notes, 'the hand of motherhood lies heavier on women now than ever before' (1974, p. 142).

Finally in this section, it can be recognized that welfare and health care make demands of family time which also encourage this form of domestic organization. Aside from caring for children when they fall sick, family members often need to co-ordinate their efforts at a later stage in order to care satisfactorily for elderly parents. Once again it is females, this time as daughters, who bear most of the brunt of such care, and who consequently have to organize other aspects of their lives to fit in with these obligations. If this does not require giving up paid work, either because their parents do not need constant attention/supervision like children or because daughters have already retired by the time their parents need extensive caring, it can none the less impose quite severe constraints on the amount of genuinely free time such women have. The need to visit, shop for, clean for and nurse elderly parents cannot but take its toll on people who themselves are some way removed from the first flush of youth, or for that matter middle age. Indeed, however inappropriate or unfair it may seem, given current demographic trends, an increasing number of women face a 'retirement' spent caring for their very elderly parents.

The point here is that while state provision for the elderly has increased, so too has their number. In the great majority of cases, as the elderly gradually become less able to care for themselves, it is their families — if they have them — who step in, more or less adequately, to minister appropriate aid. The theory is that the state supports them in this by providing services that relieve the pressure on the caring families. It is debatable whether this happens in actual fact. Often the process appears to operate in reverse. Given the limited resources available, the state in practice intervenes where there is no family capable or willing to accept the responsibility their elderly impose. Indeed the fact that resources for the elderly are continually kept at full stretch could be interpreted as a means by which the state minimizes its own contribution by maximizing the effort and commitment required of individual families, irrespective of the emotional, physical and financial costs to them (see Chapter 7).

The shaping of the family

This chapter has been concerned with the relationship between the family and other forms of social organization. It has focused on the extent to which the contemporary family is institutionally separate and removed from other spheres of activity. It is quite clear that family and kinship ties do not dominate the organization of society, as they do in some non-industrial societies. As we have seen only primary kin are of much consequence in family life, and even then it needs to be recognized that they are not central in most non-domestic areas of activity. It is equally true though that the family as a functioning unit or network is not discrete from all the other activities that make up social life. This, of course, is not a surprising conclusion, for on reflection the family is too important an institution not to be integrated with others. Indeed the only type of society in which it is conceivable that the family would not be institutionally integrated is a simple peasant one in which each homestead provided entirely for its own needs. Such a subsistence society is clearly the opposite of the organic type prevailing now.

The argument of this chapter, then, has been that any perception of the contemporary family being institutionally separate and isolated from non-domestic organization misrepresents reality twice over. Not only do many non-familial organizations within contemporary society rely to differing degrees upon the family acting as a supportive network in the manner Litwak discussed, but equally their demands in turn encourage particular patterns of domestic life. The historically specific pattern that has emerged with industrialization is one which involves a high degree of role specialization between spouses. In the first half of this century especially, a social context developed in which it seemed 'natural' for individual families to rely on one income, leaving the other spouse free not only to service family members but also to service the increasing demands being made on the family by non-domestic organizations of one sort or another. It appeared equally 'natural', given the nature of the tasks involved and the inequalities of the labour market, that that spouse should be the wife, the majority of whom consequently become entirely dependent, financially if not in other ways, on their husbands. Such a domestic division of labour has come to be taken for granted and is now embodied in one way or another in much social life, including the state's domestic policies, despite consequent changes in wives' patterns of employment.

So while Litwak's formulation linking family and bureaucratic activities is a useful starting point, it is deficient in not emphasizing sufficiently the degree to which many of the demands external agencies make on the family are met by one specialist domestic 'servicer', the wife/mother of the family. The requirements of the other organizations that depend on family co-operation encourage and help sustain a domestic division of labour in which husbands' and wives' responsibilities are differentiated, with domestic provision and co-ordination being in the latter's court. Thus the relationship between the family and external organizations depends not only on factors like the particularistic values of the family, but more crucially on its internal division of labour which assigns some individuals – wives and mothers – the unpaid responsibility of servicing others. In this respect Parsons's analysis may be judged more adequate than Litwak's, though it remains unsatisfactory in that it discounts the economic and social inequalities that this division of labour entails.

3

Women, Marriage and Housework

In the last chapter, it was argued that the form which family and domestic life takes is shaped by its relationship with other organizations and institutions within the society. Even if household structure did not change very much with industrialization, the content of family life did as the social and economic environment of which it was part became more complex and differentiated. The most important consequence for domestic life was the absence of most married women from formal employment and the subsequent creation of a more specialized carer/servicer role than had existed previously. Instead of contributing directly to family income, her role now became that of maximizing the family's well-being through the management of the housekeeping, and the co-ordination of domestic activity to meet the requirements of the various non-domestic organizations that impinged on the family.

Yet while this 'housewife' role was clearly the dominant one for most married women during the first part of this century when only some 10 per cent of married women were officially employed, the changes in employment patterns that have occurred since would make it seem less so now. As shown in Table 3.1, by 1951 around a fifth of all wives were employed in some form or other, a figure which increased to two-fifths by 1971 and since has gradually edged up to close on 50 per cent:

Table 3.1 Percentage of married women employed

	1911	1931	1951	1971	1981
All married women	10	10	22	42	47
Married women under 60	n.a.	n.a.	n.a.	49	57

Sources: Wainwright, 1978; Census, 1971, 1981

Even though these wives are not all employed full time, they are clearly contributing to household income in a way their mothers and grandmothers did not. As such, solely portraying them as housewives responsible for co-ordinating and managing the home while their husbands provide the necessary income would appear inadequate. Just as the housewife role developed with the changing occupational requirements of an earlier era of industrialization, so inevitably it will be modified and altered in various ways by the fresh circumstances and opportunities of a later period, and by the consequent demands these make on domestic organization.

Yet there is at the same time an evident continuity in the division of domestic responsibilities between husbands and wives. Despite their increased rates of employment, wives/mothers retain the primary responsibility for servicing and caring for their families. The detailed performance of this role has undoubtedly changed, not just because of employment trends but also with improved housing and more advanced domestic technology. None the less the expectation that wives and mothers take responsibility for most of the cooking, washing, cleaning and other routine housework, while husbands provide the necessary income remains a central feature of most domestic organization. While many husbands offer their wives some degree of help at least with the more interesting aspects of childcare and housework, this is not the same as being jointly responsible for it. Responsibility continues to be defined as primarily female. Consequently whatever employment wives are involved in tends, especially after the birth of children, to be seen by themselves and others as less crucial than their domestic role, and is consequently fitted around the demands this makes on them, notwithstanding their contribution to household income.

The argument to be developed in this and the following chapters is that the division of labour within the home whereby females are assigned the main responsibility for domestic functions and males that of securing an adequate income is pervasive and consequently central to the analysis of family life. It is pervasive especially in its impact on women, and is so in two distinct senses. Firstly, because domestic organization is routinely premised on this division, the housewife role is one that the great majority of women perform for much of their lives. Not only are most women full-time housewives for some years — usually the earlier ones in their marriage which may well be the most formative in creating the ground-rules of the relationship — but as importantly they continue at later stages in the family cycle to combine its demands with their other interests and commitments, including employment. But secondly, the trinity of wife/mother/housewife is pervasive in that it structures the opportunities and experiences of most married women and usually dominates their social identity. This is because their role within the home limits the freedom they have outside it and helps sustain their social and economic dependence on their husbands. In other words, what at first glance is simply a convenient and sensible division of tasks turns out on closer inspection to be an unequal relationship which systematically constrains the options most wives find open to them. For these reasons analysing the situation of women as housewives is necessary for an understanding of contemporary family life.

Marriage and family formation

Before delving into these issues more thoroughly it is worth providing some pointers as to women's domestic involvement by considering contemporary patterns of marriage, child-rearing and employment. For marriage, two basic trends have been apparent over this century. Firstly, the proportion of people ever marrying has increased, and secondly, people are tending to marry at a younger age. The first of these points can be illustrated by considering the total proportion of the population who had married at least once by the time they reached middle age. As can be seen from the third column of Table 3.2 the proportion of men in the age group 35−44 who had married in 1981 is some five points more than the equivalent figure for 1901. This, though, is more than matched by the increase in the proportion of females in this age group who had married. Whereas in 1901 nearly a fifth of these women had not married, in 1981 only one in every 17 remained single.

Table 3.2   Proportion of the population ever married in specified age groups in England and Wales

| | 20−24 | | 35−44 | |
	Males	*Females*	*Males*	*Females*
1901	17.4	27.4	84.2	81.5
1931	13.9	25.8	87.5	80.6
1951	23.7	48.2	88.0	86.3
1971	36.8	60.3	89.1	92.8
1981	25.2	46.3	89.7	94.3

Source: Annual Abstract of Statistics, vols. 88, 117, 120

This table also illustrates the trend there has been towards younger marriages. It can be seen that at the turn of the century about one in four women and one in six men in the age group 20–24 had been married. In 1951 these figures were approximately one in two and one in four respectively, but by 1971 over three-fifths of women and a third of men in these age categories had married. To put this another way, the average age at which people first married fell by about two and a half to three years between the 1930s and the 1970s (Leete 1979, p. 13). As can be seen this trend has been reversed in the 1970s as the average age at first marriage has increased. In the period 1971 to 1982 the median age of a first marriage rose from 22.0 to 23.6 for females and from 23.4 to 24.3 for males. In part though this may be countered by the number of people who are cohabiting with one another before or outside marriage. Reliable data on this topic are scarce, but the indications are that there has been quite a radical change in this. For example it is estimated that some 4 per cent of those couples entering first marriage between 1966–70 had previously lived together. This proportion increased steadily throughout the 1970s, so that by 1977 to 1979 nearly a fifth of those marrying for the first time had previously cohabited, on average for slightly less than a year. (A far higher proportion — about 60 per cent — of those entering a second marriage between 1977 and 1979 had previously lived together, and for a slightly longer period on average (Brown and Kiernan, 1981).) To some extent then, the increase in age at marriage can be seen as a shift from formal to informal union, with people beginning cohabitation at much the same age.

Along with these changes in marriage there have been major shifts in child-bearing patterns. Currently at least one child is born in some 90 per cent of all first marriages. As importantly, since the beginning of this century the average number of children born in families has decreased, and so consequently has the period of time between the birth of first and last child. An indication of the fall in average family size that occurred in the first part of this century is given in Table 3.3. As can be seen, each successive cohort produced fewer children on average, though the biggest change was for women marrying in the first 20 years of the century, with the average family size for women marrying in 1921 being about two-thirds that of women marrying in the first ten years of the century. While women marrying in the 1950s and 1960s had slightly larger families, overall average family size has remained somewhere between 2 and 2.5 children for first marriages since the 1920s.

Table 3.3   *Mean family size by year of marriage — England and Wales*

	1900–9	1911	1921	1931	1941
All women under 45 at marriage	3.53	2.96	2.32	2.01	1.98
Women 20-24 at marriage	3.60	3.16	2.54	2.25	2.15

Source: Halsey, 1972, p. 55.

Table 3.4　Birth intervals in months

	Marriage to first birth England and Wales	1st to 2nd birth (UK)	2nd to 3rd birth (UK)
1972	22	31	39
1974	26	32	39
1977	30	33	42
1979	30	33	44

Source: Britton, 1980

As well as having smaller families, women have also tended to have them earlier in their marriage, though again there are fluctuations in spacing from one cohort to the next. In general, close on 90 per cent of couples complete their families within ten years of marriage. One indication of this is given in Table 3.4, which provides details of the average interval between successive births for recent years. While the figures need to be treated with some caution, taken together with the dominant trend towards small families they do suggest that child-bearing is typically completed in somewhat less than a decade even for three-child families, notwithstanding the slight increase there has been in birth intervals in recent years.

Figure 3.1 Length of stages of family cycle for successive marriage cohorts 1860–1950　Source: Hole and Pountney, 1971

The overall significance of these changes, together with increases in life expectancy, is illustrated in Figure 3.1. Here it can be seen that the major consequence of fewer children being born earlier in the marriage is that the wife (and for that matter her husband too) have a greatly extended period without young children in the family. Women marrying between the ages of 20 and 24 in 1950 will on average be about 45 when their youngest child reaches the age of 15, and are expected to have some 30 years of life ahead of them. By comparison, women marrying at that age in 1900 would have been approximately 50 by the time their last child reached 15 and could expect to live for less than 20 years more. While these changes in family structure are not the only factors involved, they have in practice given married women somewhat greater freedom from purely domestic labour and indirectly facilitated their greater participation in paid employment during the second half of this century.

As noted earlier, well over half of all married women under 60 are now employed compared with some 25 per cent a generation ago (see Table 3.1). Yet the continuing impact of domestic responsibilities on these employment patterns is reflected in the amount of part-time employment undertaken. In 1951 there were slightly more than 0.78 million part-time women workers. This increased to 3.5 million in 1981, over 3 million of whom were married. Indeed in 1982 over 50 per cent of all employed wives were employed part-time. The advantage of part-time work is of course that it can more readily be combined with domestic and childcare commitments. As indicated in Table 3.5, the level of wives' involvement in the labour force varies inversely with the presence of dependent children in the home, though the general trend is for increased part-time employment throughout the family cycle.

Table 3.5 *Percentage of women not employed (ne), employed part-time (pt) and employed full-time (ft) by age of youngest child*

	0–4			5–9			10+			None		
	ne	pt	ft	ne	pt	ft	ne	pt	ft	ne	pt	ft
1973	75	18	7	40	42	18	33	37	30	31	17	52
1982	75	19	6	43	44	13	31	44	25	35	18	47

Source: General Household Survey, 1982

Housework as work

The way in which domestic and childcare activities shape women's experiences can now be considered more fully. As Oakley (1974; 1976) has shown in her influential study of housewives, the most appropriate way of doing this is to treat housework as a particular form of work and analyse its economic and social characteristics. By contrasting these characteristics with those typically applying to employment, the implications of the conventional division of labour within the home can be seen more clearly.

Work, as many commentators of different social and political persuasions have emphasized, is central to much human activity. Through work, individuals become incorporated into a set of social relationships that shape their consciousness, give meaning to their lives and integrate them into mainstream society. This theme is expressed succinctly by David Lockwood in the following passage:

> Without doubt in modern industrial society the most important social conditions shaping the psychology of the individual are those arising out of the organization of production, administration and distribution. In other words the 'work situation'. For every employee is precipitated by virtue of a given division of labour, into unavoidable relationships with other employees, supervisors, managers or customers. The work situation involves the separation and concentration of individuals, affords possibilities of identification with and alienation from others, and conditions feelings of isolation, antagonism and solidarity. (1958, p. 205)

In our society paid work can be seen to incorporate the individual into society at a variety of levels. More than any other activity, it symbolizes, both for the individual and for others, his or her full participation in and membership of society, even if the work done provides few satisfactions in its own right. Economically, the ability to earn income, to have money of one's own, is itself a 'good' which marks a person off from those who are merely dependent and rely on the efforts of others directly or through the state for their upkeep. Irrespective of whether the work done is defined as socially useful — and with a little effort most forms of paid work can be — the very fact of employment signifies the individual's status as an autonomous and competent member of society. Equally the growth of trade unionism and of professional associations of different sorts has resulted in the great majority of workers being included in organizations which are institutionally incorporated into the political and economic fabric of the society.

However, most importantly, as the quotation from Lockwood suggests, employment incorporates people socially by involving them in an active set of social relationships. These relationships with work-mates and colleagues, with superiors and subordinates, with customers, patients, clients or what have you, result in the individual worker being socially integrated to a degree to which those outside employment are often not. Work, in other words, provides individuals with regular and routine opportunities for interaction and sociability with others, often in the course of work activities themselves but also in rest breaks from work. The significance for individual workers of such relationships has long been recognized by industrial and occupational sociologists, and of course, following the work of Mayo at the Hawthorne plant, led to the development of the human relations school of managerial control (Smith, 1975). Equally the significance of work-place interaction is highlighted in studies of unemployment and retirement (Hill et al., 1973; Jahoda et al., 1972; Marsden and Duff, 1975; Sinfield, 1981; Parker, 1982; Shanas and Streib, 1965). These studies illustrate how the camaraderie and involvement of work-based relationships is missed by those affected. Disengagement from these relationships and the absence of any equivalent structural basis for creating similar ties, is frequently experienced as a major disadvantage of their situation by both the retired and the unemployed.

Essentially these claims for the significance of work relate to employment, i.e. to paid work. Clearly in a society like ours with its high division of labour, employment generates many distinct patterns of work organization and performance. Yet equally these distinct patterns are generally premised on and shaped by similar underlying parameters which arise from the basic principles of work organization normally found in systems of industrial capitalism and which give employment its special value. Three are of particular significance here:

1 the distribution of material rewards is rooted in the wage form so that the individual workers receive income for fulfilling specified functions within production;
2 the separation of work from non-work with clear and self-evident boundaries of time and space distinguishing the spheres;
3 the socialization of work so that the majority of workers are dependent on co-ordinating their work with that of others.

In contrast, the major form of unpaid work in our society — housework/childcare — cannot be so readily characterized by these parameters. Indeed it does not fit at all cosily into this portrayal of work, as it does not involve the worker in the economic or social relationships that (so-called) 'real' work does. Indeed from the perspective of employment, this work seems similar to leisure in some respects, notably in its location and the extent to which the worker is free to control its timing. None the less, in Lockwood's sense, it is the domestic work situation that we need to examine if we are to understand at all adequately the social experiences of most women. As has already been argued, domestic responsibilities are primary for the majority of mothers and wives, and far more central to their social identity than employment. So by treating domestic labour as a particular form of work and analysing its social and economic organization in some detail, we can begin to see how women's lives are patterned and understand better the operation of family life. Three aspects of the organization and nature of housework are particularly relevant here: the degree of autonomy it entails; the fact that it is unpaid; and its privatized nature (Oakley, 1974). The implications and consequences of each of these factors will be analysed in turn. Following this there will be a discussion of the specific experiences and circumstances of mothering as distinct from housework. While the arguments made are applicable to all housewives/mothers, the focus will initially be on those who do this work full time. As the discussion proceeds, the impact of employment on domestic work will be considered.

Autonomy

Unlike most other workers housewives neither have an employer nor are party to an employment contract – unless one chooses to see their husbands and their marriage contract in this light. The housewife does not sell her labour power to others and is consequently not bound by time schedules or the requirements of task co-ordination in quite the same way most paid workers are. She is apparently freer to organize her work as she thinks best, to suit her own purposes and provide herself with the most satisfaction. In addition there are few standarized tasks organized by others that she needs to perform. Indeed the standard to which she fulfils her tasks and the tasks she takes to be the more crucial are to some measure of her own choosing. Consequently the routines a housewife develops can be modified more or less frequently to a greater or lesser degree to fit in with whatever opportunities for other forms of activity present themselves. Thus domestic labour is far more autonomous than most forms of labour; the worker is less bound by restrictions placed on her by others and is consequently freer to structure her work day as she pleases. It is this aspect of the work which surveys have shown housewives most appreciate (Gavron, 1966; Oakley, 1974). It is this aspect also which allows husbands to deprecate the amount of effort and commitment domestic labour entails in arguments and discussions about the relative contribution each spouse makes to the household.

Yet, as Oakley notes, the autonomy that housewives have is in many ways less real than it appears, at least in its consequences. She captures this well in suggesting that the housewife 'is "free from" rather than "free to'': the absence of external supervision is not balanced by the liberty to use time for one's own ends' (1976, p. 92). There are a number of reasons why the apparently autonomous nature of housework is misleading. Firstly, the ultimate responsibility for housework lies with the housewife. Not doing a task today normally means doing it tomorrow. The work may be postponed for short periods but usually it cannot be cancelled. This applies especially to childcare, meal production, washing and essential housecare. The housewife may arrange the timing of these tasks to suit other purposes, but while doing so she is aware that in the final event she will be responsible for them.

Secondly, while the housewife is not bound by work schedules or the need for co-ordination to the same degree as many industrial workers, she is certainly not entirely free from such constraints. As the arguments in Chapter 2 suggest, the demands of her family's working day limit her too. In particular the constant, regular provision of meals seven days a week can structure her arrangements as effectively as 'clocking on' requirements do paid workers (Land, 1978). Similarly the need to organize children for school and to be present on their return limits flexibility. In addition, with gentle encouragement from their husbands, many housewives feel it their duty to have the housework done and the house clean and tidy for their husband's return. Piles of washing and dirty dishes are thought by many to be unrequired intrusions into the domestic comfort of husbands as well as being indicators that the wife is not coping adequately with her tasks − possibly through spending too much time on more trivial activities. Such factors as these do provide a structure to the scheduling of domestic work and consequently limit the actual autonomy the housewife has.

Thirdly, the degree of autonomy is limited by the varied nature of the work. In particular, while it may be the case that housework, and especially dusting and cleaning, may be hurried or left partly undone in order to create time for other activities, this is not so with childcare. In particular, not only is it felt wrong for mothers to curtail the amount of time they spend with their children, but the growth of ideologies of childhood emphasize that young children especially need as much directed attention as it is possible to give them if they are to prosper educationally in later years. In consequence there is some pressure on mothers to spend the time they save by rushing their other tasks on their children. What they manage to gain on the roundabouts of their work, they are expected to use, almost literally, in pushing the swings!

A fourth factor that limits the actual freedom of housewives is captured in the old adage that a housewife's work is never done. This is true partly by its nature but also, equally importantly, as a consequence of its social organization. Because the work is so varied, involving meal preparation, childcare and cleaning, because there are no absolute standards set, and because the work is repetitive, never being done once and for all, in a quite literal sense the work can never be completed. It is like painting the Mersey Tunnel or the Forth Bridge. Once you get to the end, it is time to return to the beginning and start all over once again. Freshly laundered articles quickly become soiled; dust begins to settle as soon as it is swept away; children and husbands quickly sully newly tidied living areas. Perfection can be achieved only for so long as the focus of that perfection is not used for the purpose it was created.

Domestic work is never finished in the second, organizational sense that the housewife has no fixed hours. Unlike industrial workers who sell their labour power for a fixed period of time, the housewife cannot watch the clock in the sure knowledge that work will soon be over. There is no formal end to the working day. It has no beginning, it has no end − it is merely a continuing set of tasks that need doing more or less adequately. This is indicated in part by the actual number of hours housewives work, though accurate statistics on this are difficult to obtain. This is partly because housework does not involve a standard work day, but mainly because the divide between 'work' and 'non-work' is often ambiguous. One obvious instance is where a mother is visiting friends or relatives with her children. She remains responsible for them but is unlikely to regard herself or be seen by others as 'working' during this time. None the less the estimates that have been produced show, with few exceptions, that over the course of the seven-day week, the housewife's hours are normally far longer than those of industrial workers. In one of the best-known estimates produced, the Chase-Manhatten Bank calculated that the average American housewife spent 99.6 hours each week doing some twelve different jobs. British studies have produced slightly lower estimates but still ones which are far higher than the average hours full-time employees spend at work. Oakley (1974), for example, calculated that the 40 house-wives she studied spent an average of 77 hours a week on housework and childcare. This ranged from a mere 48 hours by the one respondent who was also employed full time to 105 hours per week. Over 60 per cent of her sample spent between 70 and 89 hours on domestic work each week. This did not include 'baby-sitting' periods when children were asleep unless the respondent was actually engaged in other domestic tasks. Thus, if any-thing, it underestimates the amount of time the housewife is 'on call' and responsible for her family's welfare.

All in all it can be seen that while housewives appear to have a good deal of freedom and autonomy in their work, this is in practice illusory, especially when there are young children in the family or others, like the elderly, in need of extensive care. While the housewife may within limits arrange her time to facilitate social activities of a non-domestic nature, the contingencies of the work, its demands and conditions, give her rather less freedom overall than that available to non-domestic workers. Many employed workers are unable to arrange their work as they may like, but they at least know their working week is limited, and that when the hooter or bell sounds their work is finished.

Absence of pay

The second feature of domestic work that marks it off from 'real' work is a crucial one − the absence of pay. There is no employer or employment contract but equally there is no wage at the end of the day. Instead the domestic worker, especially though by no means only the full-time one, is dependent for the income she has access to on the wage or salary her husband receives from his employment. For the full-time housewife, the only exception to this is the child benefit, a politically contentious issue for this very reason. Importantly, this economic dependence on the main 'bread winner', like other economically unequal relationships, is transformed by a variety of subtle and not so subtle means into a social dependence as well. It is certainly arguable that the marriage relationship can never approach equality until wives have the same access to resources as their husbands, a theme which lay behind the early support in the women's movement for wages for housework (Dalla Costa, 1972).

Many couples would deny that their marriage relationship is one of economic inequality. There is a strong theme in contemporary culture that marriage is a relationship of love and equality. In comparison with the past, marriage is held to be more democratic with both partners having the right to an equal say in the way in which household resources are utilized. Certainly it would be churlish to argue that there has been no change, or indeed that husbands are not more open than in the past about the amount of money they earn. Yet despite these changes and the growth of ideologies of equality, and despite wives themselves denying the salience of such arguments (at least in general terms), the wife/domestic worker − husband/wage earner relationship remains one of economic dependence.

Clearly the full-time housewife relies on the income provided by the wage earner for her means of subsistence. Her task is to transform a portion of that wage into the highest standard of living she can for the whole domestic unit. Thus the money she receives from her husband, the housekeeping money, is not a wage. It is not money for her to spend freely on herself as she will, but money to be spent on the needs and comforts of the household. Equally, as we have seen, it is not money exchanged for a specified amount of labour power. The housekeeping is not reward for achieving a particular standard, nor for working for a given period of time. Nor, importantly, is her dependence on her husband equivalent to his dependence on his employer. A wife's relationship with her husband is self-evidently more complex than that typical of employer − employee relationships. It contains affective, domestic, sexual, companionate, sociable and welfare elements amongst others, and consequently cannot be reduced to an economic relationship in the way that most wage labour can be. However this does not mean that economic dependence plays no part. It does − essentially because income earned outside the home is thought ultimately to be the property of the person who is employed to earn it.

This acceptance that the wage belongs to the wage earner because she/he is the one who does the work that most obviously generates it is deeply rooted in British and other capitalist societies. Income is obtained by individuals − rather than family units − fulfilling negotiated obligations to an employer outside the domestic unit. The contract is thus between the employer and an individual who receives wages in return for satisfying the former's requirements. Irrespective of what goes on outside work, income would not be received unless the employed worker was so employed. Equally, provided the worker remains employed, she/he will receive the standard income whatever his or her domestic situation is. Being married or unmarried, with or without children will not affect the amount the work is worth in the market-place, though of course tax allowances will affect the amount actually received.

A husband's wage thus appears independent of his domestic background and unaffected by any contribution from his wife who is in the position of· being supported by her husband. The flaw in this kind of argument, as many writers have recently pointed out, is that wives contribute to the workers' ability to earn by providing for their domestic needs (Seccombe, 1974; Molyneux, 1979; Rushton, 1979). If the worker were to satisfy these through the market his actual spending power, or real wage, would be markedly reduced. However because the housewife's domestic services are free in the sense that no price is put upon them, her contribution to the family's economy is largely hidden. The money received into the household through the wage appears to be totally independent of the work done within it.

While many full-time housewives assert in the abstract that they do fully contribute in this way to the domestic economy and that therefore they should be viewed as equal partners with their husbands, their actions tend to suggest otherwise. In particular, as Pauline Hunt (1978) has emphasized, housewives' expenditure patterns demonstrate an acceptance of the view that husbands have a greater right to any income after payment for necessities. They are freer to spend on personal requirements than their wives who often feel a moral obligation to place themselves last and provide extras for their husbands and children instead. The point here is that unlike the wage earner who normally feels free to spend whatever money he has left after paying for necessities, including housekeeping, without too much reference to the rest of the domestic group, the full-time housewife rarely feels she has any money of her own. It is all subsumed under housekeeping and is really for the family as a whole and not herself individually. This applies as much to any money she might save through particular efforts she makes as to regular weekly expenditure. As P. Hunt cogently argues:

> Since homemaking is seen and experienced as personal service, rather than as productive labour, it does not seem to be a 'real' job warranting remuneration and this gives rise to the houseworker's guilt about spending money on herself. The houseworker's claim to a share of the wage is on the whole made not as a co-worker, but as a member of the family consumption collective. (1978, p. 561)

Hunt points out that such definitions of individual and household income are found irrespective of the way in which the distribution of finances are organized in the household. Whether or not a set amount is put aside for housekeeping, whether husband or wife pays bills, whether bank accounts are joint or single, the housewife tends to save and 'make do' on her own requirements in comparison to those of other family members. Its root lies in the acceptance by all that the husband's wage is more his than theirs. Husbands may reinforce this tendency — 'Good grief! You can't need more money. Where's it all gone to?' — by making it difficult for their wives to ask for or demand more. Yet such control appears to need exerting only infrequently. The relationship is structured sufficiently tightly to ensure that these assumptions about resources are only rarely questioned. Indeed the housewife is in something of a double bind here. On the one hand, her job is to stretch the family's resources as far as possible. On the other, her duty is to care properly for her husband and children and provide them with the best. Inevitably the result of this contradiction is not only that many housewives spend a disproportionate amount of time trying to save a small amount here or find a bargain there, but that they make do by spending less on themselves than on the others in the family unit.

Of course the position is somewhat different in those families where the wife, as well as caring for the home, is employed outside it. Like their husbands, these wives are likely to see the money they earn as more their own to spend as they decide. The consequences of wives working will be discussed shortly, but three points should be mentioned here. Firstly, few wives earn as much as their husbands, consequently their income tends very much to be seen as secondary and relatively unimportant in the family's economy. Secondly, some of the income they earn is spent on items that allow them to combine paid work with their domestic obligations. And thirdly, many women feel a degree of guilt for the supposed 'sacrifices' their families have to suffer as a consequence of their employment, so think that the money they earn should rightfully go towards compensating their families rather than being spent on personal luxuries. Later in the chapter we shall return to how and why such images of wives' earnings are sustained.

Privatization

Industrialization involved the separation of home and production, continuing modifications to definitions of male and female potentiality, and the creation of fully domestic roles for wives. While the number and proportion of married women in employment has increased dramatically in recent years, the separation of housework from income-producing activities remains. So too has the basic unit of domesticity. If few men would emulate one of the miners in Dennis, Henriques and Slaughter's ethnography of Ashton and throw their evening meal on the fire if it was cooked by someone other than their wife, (1969, p. 182) the expectation still remains that domestic services are provided separately for each family. Indeed with the exception of some childcare activities, few domestic tasks are undertaken communally. Logically and technologically there are no apparent reasons why domestic work should be organized in this fashion. The history of other forms of work shows a trend towards a greater division of labour and increased co-operation in work, but this has not been echoed with housework and domestic tasks which remain essentially privatized.

Indeed during this century, and especially since the end of the Second World War, technological and economic changes have increased the extent to which domestic labour is privatized. In particular radical improvements in the size and facilities of housing units and the increased availability of electrical appliances to aid domestic work have had a marked effect on the organization of the housewife's day. The performance of her tasks is rather less public than it once was. For example, improvements in housing standards have reduced the extent to which different households have to share basic facilities like taps, stoves and toilets. Increases in relative wealth and storage facilities have lessened the need for frequent shopping.

Washing and laundering are far less likely to take place in public wash-houses or launderettes but are done instead in the privately owned washing machine. Socially, these changes are of course highly desirable, reflecting the increased standard of living that industrialization creates. No one, least of all housewives, would wish to see the clock put back. Domestic innovations have reduced the arduousness of housework and, while not affecting the amount of time spent on tasks, have increased its quality and whatever intrinsic satisfaction is obtained from it. On the other hand it has simultaneously resulted in domestic work becoming more privatized, thus reducing the opportunities housewives have for interaction with one another while working. Tasks that once involved a public or communal element no longer do so, so the housewife is trapped to a greater extent in her more comfortable and convenient domestic setting, getting on in private with her more sophisticated though equally time-consuming work. The only parts of her job that of themselves involve interaction with others are elements of her childcare role and shopping, though with the growth of large supermarket complexes, the latter too has become less frequent and more anonymous than previously.

A major outcome of the privatized character of contemporary domestic labour is the physical and psychological isolation experienced by many full-time housewives. Clearly there are differences in the degree to which they are affected, but research studies have consistently found that most housewives do feel isolated for quite significant portions of their time (Gavron, 1966; Oakley, 1974; Hobson, 1978). The absence of adult company and sociability for much of the day appears regularly to be the most dissatisfying aspect of housework. One writer who emphasizes this is Dorothy Hobson who provides some illuminating illustrations. One respondent, who lived in a high-rise flat, described her situation as follows:

> I usually just sit on me own. It's not very often anyone ever comes y'know. It's very rare anybody ever comes.. . . When I had Shane he was good company y'know, me first baby. He was quite a lot of company and I just used to talk to him from when he was very tiny. I used to think he understood but I don't suppose he did (laughs) but he was just like a bit of company, somebody to talk to.. . . Before I had him I used to talk to the cat (laughs) and I'm sure that cat used to understand (laughs).

Another of Hobson's respondents reported how at one time she was driven to looking out of her flat at the cars below 'just for something to do' (1978, pp. 86–7). While these examples are extreme and exacerbated by both respondents living in high-rise blocks of flats, they do, as Hobson notes, accurately reflect the depths of the loneliness housewives can experience.

What is important to recognize is that such isolation is not caused by personal idiosyncrasies, but is a consequence of the organization of domestic work in our society. As we have noted housework of itself provides little opportunity for interaction with others. The work in the main occurs behind closed doors, in a private and solitary setting. This contrasts markedly with other forms of work in which the activity is almost inevitably social as well as economic. The performance of most jobs requires interaction with others, and nearly all involve communal sociability in rest and eating breaks. In comparison the housewife cannot take such episodes for granted, having almost to conjure up excuses for similar interaction. Admittedly other workers are also isolated on monotonous tasks for much of their working day, but as Goldthorpe et al. (1969) have shown, they can rationalize their experiences by an instrumental orientation in which they see themselves as trading part of their life − their working hours − for relatively high wages that provide increased satisfaction outside of work. Housewives of course cannot justify their work experiences in this way as they receive no pay. Nor, as noted earlier, can they rejoice in the end of the workday like other workers for their work is not scheduled in this fashion. Their relief comes, in theory, only when their husbands return, though his needs, shaped by his own daily work experience, are likely to be rather different from his wife's. Frequently he is unable or unwilling to provide the sociable sustenance she requires, being, as she full well knows, only slightly interested in the domestic trivia that dominate her working life.

We can also note here that the privatized nature of housework means that when sociable interaction with others does occur it tends to be defined in a significantly different fashion from that which occurs in paid employment. With this latter, episodes of sociability are incorporated into the work by its nature. Participating in them, be it in breaks or while working, does not reflect in any way on the performance of the work task. Because of their apparent autonomy and the solitary nature of their work, this is not so for housewives. If they interact with others, it is normally through choice rather than as a direct concomitance of their work. Even when childcare is involved, it is for many incongruous to define sitting at home chatting with friends or relatives as work since it is so clearly 'non-work' in both setting and content. In the absence of clearly specified tasks or hours, the housewife cannot demonstrate that such episodes of sociability do not interfere with her work, and is consequently always open to the unfair attack that they indicate just how soft her work life really is. 'I wish *I* could sit around having coffee with my mates all day.'

Mothering

So far this chapter has focused principally on the work situation of full-time housewives. Before going on to discuss the impact of employment on these patterns, it is worth developing a topic that so far has remained implicit — the experiences specific to mothering. This is warranted because though the generalized role of housewife may encompass both childcare and housework, the actual tasks and activities associated with the two areas are discrete and often contradictory. In particular there is an evident opposition between the end product of housework — order — and the demands which young children make. Until recently though mothering attracted relatively little interest from sociologists. Much has been written on the range of factors that affect children's development and well-being, but little on the actual work involved in mothering or on the rewards or difficulties it entails. In addition the research that has been published — for example, Gavron (1966), Oakley (1974; 1980), Ginsberg (1976), Backett (1982) and Boulton (1983) — has focused specifically on families with quite young children. As a result there is very little information on the impact that adolescents, for instance, have on their mothers' (or fathers') lives.

Two points made earlier are worth reiterating here. Firstly, childhood is quite central to most people's perceptions of family life. The 'normal' family is almost automatically taken to be one in which there are dependent children, even though only a minority of families are actually like this at any particular time. This itself reflects broader changes in our image of childhood. As discussed in Chapter 2, to a greater degree than ever before childhood is seen as a special stage of development in which children need protection, understanding and stimulation if they are to mature adequately. Schooling is the institutional expression of this, but it is parents who carry the main responsibility. As a consequence family life has become more child-centred, routinely being organized to meet the perceived needs of children whose achievements in turn provide parents with much satisfaction.

The second point to emphasize is that catering for children and servicing their needs are tasks not borne equally by both parents. The responsibility for childcare is very much a female one, so that changes occurring in the social position of children have had far more effect on mothers' life-styles than fathers'. Even though fathers are now somewhat less distant figures than they once were, they remain peripheral in terms of everyday responsibility. Notwithstanding 'considerable attempts to create and sustain a belief in [father's] greater involvement' (Backett, 1982, p. 369), it is mothers who actually do the caring and who 'carry a heavy responsibility in being accountable for their children's health, their intelligence and performance at school, the clothes they wear and their general development' (Antonis, 1981, p. 70).

As already mentioned, the research literature on mothering is limited. One of the fullest and most interesting analyses is provided by Boulton (1983) who interviewed 50 mothers with pre-school children, half from middle-class backgrounds and half from working-class ones. While this sample is small, the results of her research tie in well with other writing on mothering, (e.g. Gavron (1966); Oakley (1974); Comer (1974)), so the issues she develops are likely to be ones commonly experienced by most mothers with young children. A basic distinction Boulton makes is between the feelings mothers have about their day-to-day involvement with their children − the pleasures and frustrations childcare involves − and the broader meaning and purpose attached to motherhood. The first of these will be considered most fully here as it relates closely to the issues raised in the previous discussion of housework.

The feature that most dominates mothers' experience of caring for pre-school children is the degree of responsibility they have for them. Given the way that childcare is organized in our society, for most mothers this responsibility is total. In effect, the job of mothering young children involves a constant and continuing obligation to be present throughout each and every day, with relatively little help or relief, to meet the child's myriad requirements. It is in Boulton's phrase a 'responsibility without bounds' (1983, p. 78) in terms of the activities − caring, cleaning, comforting, amusing and so on − and the time involved. This total responsibility − being fully in charge of a developing individual who is entirely dependent on your love and care − is a major source of satisfaction for many mothers. At the same time, it can also be experienced as extremely irritating and constraining. Indeed these latter feelings are virtually inevitable given the very nature of young children. So, for example, finding fresh means of amusing them given their short attention span, watching over them constantly to make sure they are not up to anything harmful, coping with their limited powers of expression and their inability to appreciate other people's needs, can all make mothering frustrating and time-consuming. The constancy of the responsibility was expressed well by one of Boulton's respondents:

There are times when I feel like saying 'I will feed you twice as much today so tomorrow I can just have a break.' Before, I could say, 'The fridge really needs to be cleaned, but I can leave it.' With children they need feeding when *they* need feeding. Their nappies have to be washed every day. It's as simple as that. When they cry, you can't say, 'Well, I'll see you in an hour.' That is what hits you: the fact that it's seven days a week, twenty-four hours a day, and *they* make the rules. (1983, p. 69; emphases in the original)

Similarly one of Oakley's respondents said: '. . . but there's times when I feel if you went out for an afternoon, twice a week, just you, you'd be much better the other times. I find you're tied hand and foot every minute of the day . . . Sometimes all you want is for somebody to just take that baby for a hour off you. You do' (1980, pp. 139–40).

In line with the earlier discussion of housework, the constant and overriding responsibility each mother has for her own young children severely curtails the social opportunities open to her. As various writers have pointed out, their social being becomes wrapped up and submerged by their mothering which dominates other aspects of their lives in a way that few other roles do (Oakley, 1974; Comer, 1974; Boulton, 1983). There are at least three strands to this. Firstly, as the quotes given above suggest, within the home mothers looking after young children can rarely do what they want to do or get on with their own activities, no matter how small. Whenever they try to do so, they are likely to be disrupted by a child wanting to join in or getting up to mischief elsewhere. Even a simple task like making a phone call loses some of its appeal if children are climbing all over you to say something into the mouthpiece or are busy emptying the vegetable rack all over the kitchen floor. For many, the situation is symbolized by what must be the ultimate invasion — not even being able to go to the toilet when you want to without children banging on the door clamouring to get in.

A second way in which the mothering role imposes itself is by shaping the range of social ties that can be developed. Many of the issues applying here were raised in the previous section on 'privatization' and do not need rehearsing again. The main point to make is that most of the social contacts mothers have are with people in a similar situation to themselves, i.e. other mothers, if only because they fit more readily in with the peculiar rhythm of childcare and housework. While such relationships can be very supportive and rewarding, they do tend to reinforce the identity of 'mother'. To begin with, children are usually present during any contact, making demands and disrupting discussion. As importantly, the conversation is likely to be dominated by childcare and other domestic matters as this is the world they occupy and share in common. As a result, such relationships are likely to reinforce the domestic boundaries of a mother's life, marking off her experiences as quite different from others more integrated in the 'outside' world. They are often perceived, especially by middle-class mothers, as providing little fresh stimulation and doing little to counter their feelings of mental stagnation. Domesticity rules − but not so OK.

The third sense in which caring for young children dominates a mother's social identity stems from a combination of the other two. It concerns the feelings that many mothers have that constant childcare erodes their individuality and robs them of any sense of freedom. It was put well by another of Boulton's respondents:

> You give up a lot. I think you give up individuality. In that you are a *mother* with young children, you tend to remain as a mother rather than yourself. But it's very difficult to have an identity of your own, when you have so many people, not relying on you but *needing* you. So you tend to have to consider everyone else before you consider yourself and what *you* want to do. And it's very hard. (1983, p. 96. Emphases in original)

The various factors discussed above exacerbate this absence of any independent identity. For example, finding the time and energy to undertake outside pastimes and projects does not come easily when so many other things need doing, when child-minding or baby-sitting has to be organized, and when in any case you are feeling worn out by the time the children are eventually settled in bed. On top of this, joining in with others − even if there is the opportunity − is made the harder by the lack of confidence that comes from being 'just a mother/housewife' and the feeling that compared to everyone else you have little to offer. In these ways the 'mother' identity becomes dominant, effectively reinforcing itself by limiting participation in other spheres that might result in its being challenged.

Given these and the other factors discussed earlier in the chapter, it is hardly surprising that a significant proportion of mothers do not really enjoy the daily routine of caring for their young children. On the other hand, as Boulton's research shows, a good proportion of mothers do get a great deal of pleasure from it. Of Boulton's working-class mothers 56 per cent felt positively about the everyday tasks of childcare, as did 40 per cent of her middle-class respondents (1983, p. 57). In addition, the great majority (88 per cent) of the working-class mothers in this study found that their children could be quite rewarding companions. They enjoyed playing with them, for spells at least, and, once the children were a bit older, chatting to them about the day's happenings. While these claims must be seen in the light of the mothers' relative isolation − remember Hobson's respondent quoted earlier who said her cat was good company − they none the less indicate the slightly different perspectives working-class and middle-class mothers in Boulton's study had towards childcare, for only a quarter of the latter enjoyed their children's companionship in the same way. Also of interest here is the way the mothers regarded playing with their children or otherwise entertaining them. The working-class mothers tended to join in with games and the like because they actually wanted to do so. Conversely they stopped once they no longer enjoyed it or lost interest. The middle-class mothers, on the other hand, neither looked for nor found much satisfaction from play activities in themselves, perceiving them more as a duty − something that needed to be undertaken irrespective of their own feelings because it was beneficial for the child's development. In this respect too then, the working-class mothers tended to regard their children as more companionable than their middle class counterparts did.

Middle-class mothers were more likely to find satisfaction from the sense of meaning and direction that their children gave their lives. This longer-term perspective was fuelled in numerous ways. Knowing that you are indispensable to your children; that they love and trust you unconditionally; seeing them gradually develop and progress, learning new skills and coping with new situations; receiving praise for their (and your) achievements; all provide a source of satisfaction that can help to counter the inherent frustrations of day-to-day childcare. As Harris (1977) argues, current ideologies suggest that children are to some degree their parents', and especially their mothers', 'creations', so that mothers can take some pride in their children's steady development as it in part reflects on their own performance as mothers and provides them with an indication of their own value and worth. In Boulton's (1983) research two-thirds of the middle-class respondents felt like this as did half the working-class mothers. As one of Oakley's respondents put it:

> Yes, I like [looking after my child]. I'd rather be at home with the child than at work − or doing anything else I could think of . . . I expected to find it rewarding, but not quite as much as it is . . . Just the whole thing of seeing a person developing and somebody learning right from nothing to do things and *be* − and the amount of influence you have on this for good or for bad. (1974, p. 173; emphasis in original)

So from this it is evident that mothering can entail various levels of reward and satisfaction. At the same time though, it is worth emphasizing that a large minority experience motherhood in essentially negative terms. Nearly a third of Boulton's sample neither enjoyed the daily routine of childcare nor gained much sense of meaning or purpose from their children. A further 30 per cent found only one of these aspects of the role rewarding (1983, p. 129). Significantly too, studies have shown that working-class women looking after pre-school children are particularly vulnerable to quite severe depression. In one survey, Brown, Ni Bhrol-chain and Harris (1975) found that over 40 per cent of working-class women with a child under six at home had suffered recent and chronic depression, though only 5 per cent of middle-class women in a similar situation had. While this class-based variation is difficult to explain, such levels of depression − quite separate from the so-called 'normal baby blues' that somewhere between half and three-quarters of mothers experi-ence after childbirth (Oakley, 1980) − give some indication of the toll that mothering young children can exact.

Returning to employment

From all this, it is evident that structurally full-time housewives/mothers are less socially integrated than most other workers. There is little opportunity or reason for interaction with others through the tasks they perform in their work. Any attempt to overcome the isolation and loneliness likely to result must be based on bonds they are able to construct in other spheres or solely on an informal basis rather than on relationships integral to their work situation. This point warrants repeated emphasis, given the centrality of domestic labour in most married women's social existence and those dominant masculine images which stress the freedom domestic work entails. The chief questions posed by this concern the ways in which housewives have attempted to compensate for their domestic isolation. One response to this situation − the large increase in wives' participation in the labour force − will be discussed now. Another possibility − the development of informal relationships with friends, relatives and neighbours − will be considered in the next chapter.

The dissatisfactions inherent in the full-time housewife/mother role are most apparent when the number who supplement it by taking up some form of employment are considered. Whatever that employment is, as well as an income, it provides many women with an activity that helps compensate for the monotony and boredom of domestic work. While some of the existing studies of women's work − like many husbands − underestimate the significance for the domestic economy of wives' ear-nings, they are correct in stressing that social contact is perceived by married women as a major benefit of their employment. This comes out clearly in many of the statements made by respondents in Cragg and Dawson's study of female unemployment. One said:

I miss the company — I never see a soul. I'm sick of housework. I'm all right if I've got something to do to keep me occupied. I'm all right at the weekend because I've got someone to talk to.

Another explained:

Obviously you think about the money first. But it isn't only the money. Because you had other things to talk about. When my husband comes home I've got nothing to say to him other than what the baby's done that day. Whereas when I was working you could talk about things that happened at work or things that someone at work had told you about.

A third said:

I'm totally bored. You know — I mean, fair enough, I can find things to do. There's always plenty to do in the house. But I like a natter and I like to mix. It's the company more than anything. Well, don't get me wrong. Now it's the money more than the company. Then it was the company more than the money . . . Just to mix you know. (Cragg and Dawson, 1984, pp. 24–6).

It is evident from these statements that in addition to providing an income, employment is valued for the contacts and interest it generates. It may be argued that given their relatively poor rates of pay, this is an understandable legitimation of the situation in which many employed wives find themselves. It is more important though to recognize that above anything else these perceptions of the social benefits of employment reflect the isolation characteristic of these workers' experience of full-time domestic work. That such feelings exist despite the inferior conditions of much female employment is a testimony to the drudgery that domestic work represents for many of them. To suggest that married women work for 'pin money' is to miss the point and seriously overestimate the financial and social alternatives open to many married women.

As was seen earlier, the number of employed married women has risen quite dramatically since the Second World War. Currently two-thirds of female employees are married, with women as a whole making up 40 per cent of the total labour force. Indeed, as Martin and Roberts (1984, p. 186) point out, marriage alone no longer really influences whether or not women are employed. What matters is the presence of children in the home and especially the age of the youngest child — in other words, the woman's family role. As is well known, the labour market is highly segregated, so that the majority of women work in predominantly 'female' occupations and industries, most of which involve an element of servicing others. For example, more than 90 per cent of all typists, secretaries, nurses and canteen assistants are female, as are more than three-quarters of all shop assistants, cleaners, kitchen hands and telephonists (Wainwright, 1978; see also Martin and Roberts, 1984).

This gender division in the occupational structure is one reason why female wage rates remain markedly below those of men. On average even full-time female employees earn somewhat less than two-thirds the amount full-time male employees of equivalent status earn, a gap which has not narrowed noticeably despite recent legislation. An additional factor in explaining the relatively low earnings of even full-time female employees is the limited promotional opportunities available to them. Not only do markedly few women reach jobs at the very top of the occupational hierarchy, but at every level from chargehand to director men are far more likely than women to be promoted to positions of authority and control. Even in those occupations with a high proportion of female workers, it is men who tend to get the more senior posts. As an illustration, while women make up 59 per cent of all full-time teachers, only 39 per cent of head teachers are female, the great majority of these being heads of primary schools (DES, 1982, pp. 26–7).

Table 3.6   Mean gross earnings in pounds, April 1983

| | Full-time men | | Full-time women | | Part-time women |
	weekly	hourly	weekly	hourly	hourly
Manual	143.6	3.26	87.9	2.24	1.99
Non-manual	194.9	5.03	115.1	3.10	2.55
All	167.5	3.99	108.8	2.88	2.27

Source: New Earnings Survey, 1983

As Table 3.6 indicates, women working part time (i.e. under 30 hours a week) are paid least well of all. This is particularly significant because, as we saw earlier in the chapter, the post-war increase in the proportion of married women employed has resulted very largely from the growth of part-time employment. Despite its low pay, this form of employment has attracted increasing numbers of married women because it is easier to combine with their domestic responsibilities. In Martin and Roberts's national study of women's employment patterns, 55 per cent of employed married women were working part time. Nearly two-thirds of these part-time workers worked between 16 and 30 hours a week, but over a third worked less than 16 hours per week, with the average for part-time workers as a whole being 18.5 hours (Martin and Roberts, 1984, pp. 17, 34). As well as tending to be paid at a lower rate than full-time workers, part-time workers are also likely to be disadvantaged in other ways. They are, for example, less likely to be covered by employment protection legislation, less likely to be given paid holidays, less likely to receive sick pay from their employers and less likely to belong to an occupational pension scheme. While these factors apply to all part-time workers, given the predominance of married women in part-time employment, it is clearly they who are most affected by them.

These then are some of the facts of married women's employment, but to what extent does such employment affect the domestic responsibilities and 'work situation' of mothers and housewives? The answer to this will become clearer in the next two chapters, but here we can note that while employment provides wives with some resources to counter the more blatant disadvantages discussed in earlier sections, the extent to which this happens is easily overestimated. Not only are the earnings of married women generally significantly smaller than their husbands' but equally the everyday expectations that inform much social life are premised on the assumption that wives rather than husbands will be responsible for the running of the home. A range of constraints, from the denial inherent in National Insurance and DHSS regulations that wives could be the main income earners to the pressure exerted by kin and peer groups, discourage alternative forms of domestic organization, even in those minority of cases where husbands and wives have access to equally well-paid jobs.

So, in general, husbands continue to be seen as the primary income earner, with wives being assigned principal responsibility for domestic tasks. As Pauline Hunt (1978) reports in her research, despite the increasing number of families whose life style depends on the earnings of wives, amongst many married couples the belief is that the family could, if necessary, survive without the wife's income but not without the husband's. Her money is used to buy luxuries — indeed luxuries may be defined as those objects and activities her work finances — but the real needs of the family are seen as met by the husband. If the situation is defined in this way with the wife's work and income being seen as somewhat peripheral to basic requirements, the logic is that the wife is choosing to work in a way the husband is not. He has to work or else the family could not survive. Consequently it would be unfair for her, the logic continues, to refuse to carry out her domestic duties solely because she is choosing to be employed — with, it might be added, the assistance and support of the remaining family members. So while their earnings allow wives some control over resources — they regard their earnings as more their own, just as they do their husband's more his — it does not necessarily reduce their domestic obligations. Because her wage is secondary, and usually significantly less than her husband's, — (in Martin and Roberts's study, only 7 per cent of wives earned the same or more than their husbands (1984, p. 99)) — the wife continues to be expected to be the main person responsible for domestic services. In addition, some of her earned income is probably required for the purchase of extra gadgetry, convenience food and other forms of help to free her from domestic tasks so that she can meet the demands of employment. The limited difference that wives' employment makes to domestic arrangements is shown by the hours they spend doing domestic work, and by the domestic division of labour at weekends. All studies show that the wife continues to bear the brunt of domestic responsiblities irrespective of her employment during the week (see Chapter 4).

Similarly while employment provides some direct compensation for the isolation of domestic work, it does so only within the context of that employment. In passing we can note that very little sociological research has been concerned specifically with female work relationships. While this is slowly being altered, most studies of work have either ignored women totally, have treated all workers as equivalent regardless of gender, or else have seen women workers as a social problem (Brown, 1976). Certainly, very little work has been done specifically on the social integration of married women in work, though this is slowly being rectified (see for example, McNally, 1979; Pollert, 1981; West, 1982; Gamarnikow, 1983; Coyle, 1984). Given that employed wives continue to be assigned the bulk of domestic responsibilities, it is not surprising that employment has only a limited impact on their social life. For most, the combination of employment and domestic commitment leaves them with just as little opportunity and often less time for social involvement as full-time housewives. Their husbands may help them somewhat more in domestic tasks than they would if they were not employed, but the emphasis is very much on 'help' rather than equal sharing (see Chapter 5). The cost of employment for many wives then is that the pressures of domestic work become greater, with standards needing to be cut somewhat, especially for non-essential tasks — rooms may be hoovered and cleaned less frequently or thoroughly, more items of clothing left unironed, and so on. Tasks like shopping and meal production may be 'rationalized' by having weekly or monthly shopping trips, using convenience food and cooking and freezing meals in bulk. Thus employment involves the need for a greater organizational capacity rather than a reduction of household responsibilities. Clearly one reason for married women's reduced participation in trade union and other work-based activities is their concomitant higher level of participation in domestic matters. Extra-work activities are a luxury that cannot be squeezed into their daily routine, however organized and rationalized they may become.

The point to emphasize here then is that while many married women are employed, the social consequences of such work in their lives are rather different from those of their husbands'. As with the latter, work gives these wives an identity and an interest, and a chance to become involved with others. On the other hand, this work forms only part of their identity. Their domestic work still looms large and takes up a major portion of their 'non-employed' time. So their work does not give them the freedom in non-work hours that most husbands expect of theirs, for their 'non-work' time is spent organizing domestic life. In consequence while work provides a source of social integration for employed wives, and one which is particularly important for them given the isolation of domestic work, the degree to which they can develop work-based relationships is circumscribed by their domestic role. At work they may be equivalent to other workers, but once work stops it is arguable that their existence becomes even more privatized than that of full-time housewives. The few opportunities available to full-time housewives for sociable interaction are even more difficult for those with outside employment to fit in because of the pressure to complete domestic tasks in reduced time, though to some extent this will depend on the stage they have reached in their family cycle and the hours for which they are employed.

Similar pressures are experienced by couples in what, following the Rapoports' initiative (1971, 1976) have become known as 'dual-career families', that is families in which both spouses work in highly paid occupations. Despite the advantages that can be purchased by their high income, research indicates such couples are forced to give low priority to ties of sociability. The scheduling of their work lives to fit in with domestic requirements leaves little time for pure enjoyment. As the Rapoports have illustrated, despite their extensive use of domestic appliances and machinery to reduce the time spent on routine tasks and despite the aid provided by paid domestic workers (nannies, au pairs and domestic helps), the families they studied had little time left for anything other than their work and their families. Other studies have reached similar conclusions. Now if this is so with couples who can afford to pay others for domestic services and to buy the most efficient labour-saving devices, it highlights the problems faced by less prosperous two-job families. In those where the wife assumes responsibility for domestic organization without the aid of paid assistance, her 'free-time' is likely to be quite severely curtailed. As with the families the Rapoports studied, her sociable interaction is likely to be limited and given low priority in comparison with employment and domestic work.

4

Home and Leisure

This chapter is concerned with family members' social involvement outside the home, and, conversely, the extent to which family life has become privatized. Conventionally, industrialization is said to have led to the breakdown of communal solidarity, replacing the small-scale, integrated rural communities of the past with more anonymous, disorganized urban centres. Yet there is evidence that in some instances urbanization actually fostered the growth of family and community solidarity, albeit of a different form to that found in rural areas. For example, to the evident surprise of those who then thought that urban relations were, in Wirth's (1938) famous phrase, indubitably 'impersonal, superficial, transitory and segmental', researchers like Mogey (1956), Dennis et al. (1956), Young and Willmott (1957), Kerr (1958) and Tunstall (1962) pointed out the existence of close-knit, supportive communities within working-class urban areas. Even though at the time the character of these areas was being undermined by new housing policies and greater affluence, their existence demonstrated that communal solidarity was not incompatible with urban social life.

Within these 'traditional working-class communities', as they have since become known, people were embedded in a set of social relationships that were both extensive and enduring. In the absence of much inward geographical mobility, relatively large numbers of people in the locality were known either personally or through intermediaries. Whether kin, workmates, neighbours, old school friends or what have you, people were integrated into the community through their involvement with a circle of familiars. As Klein (1965) discusses, marriage and kinship were particularly important in sustaining local solidarity because of the wide range of links, no matter how distant, they established between individuals and families in the area. These, like other contacts, allowed people to 'place' each other and so helped create the community feelings and sense of belonging for which the localities were famous. Equally though, the poverty of these areas and in particular the poor standard of housing encouraged social involvement between neighbours who often had to share basic amenities. The need to co-operate over the use of cooking or washing facilities, or over the cleaning of communal halls and toilets ensured a knowledge, often quite intimate, of those around you and created an inter-dependence that could not easily be ignored. Although not emphasising kinship or gender divisions sufficiently, David Lockwood captures the image we now have of these traditional communities rather well in the following passage:

> The existence of such closely knit cliques of friends, workmates, neighbours and relatives is the hallmark of the traditional working-class community. The values expressed through these social networks emphasize mutual aid in everyday life and the obligation to join in the gregarious pattern of leisure.. . . As a form of social life, this communal sociability has a ritualistic quality, creating a high moral density and reinforcing sentiments of belongingness to a work-dominated collectivity. (1966, p. 251)

But times have changed. No longer do these traditional communities with their friendly intimacy and support appear to exist. They have been replaced by the more anonymous, new peripheral estates which, despite the planners' intentions, have failed to generate an equivalent community involvement. In general, family life seems to have become more privatized and insulated since the war. Instead of the old networks of mutual support and interdependence, neighbourhoods now consist of separate and independent families who have relatively little to do with each other. Not depending on neighbours or being needed by them in any consistent fashion, families seem more 'atomized' and contained much more within the four walls of their home. Some neighbours may be known, as may the names of a few others, but missing is any sense of solidarity generated through networks of local social involvement. Each family goes on its own way, minding its own business, living in an area but not belonging to it or identifying with it in any meaningful fashion.

As with images of community breakdown in other eras (see Williams, 1975), these perceptions of the demise of urban communities and the privatization of family life are neither true nor false. Like all folk histories, they selectively emphasize some elements of the past at the expense of others and contrast the resultant image with a similarly distorted picture of the present so as to provide a framework for interpreting the changes that are occurring. None the less, disentangling some of the different strands of argument in this community breakdown/privatization thesis is a useful starting point for analysing the significance of informal and 'communal' ties in contemporary domestic life. In particular the 'inward' and 'outward' looking elements of this portrayal can be separated even though they often seem to complement each other, rather like centrifugal and centripetal forces in mechanics. The 'centrifugal', outward looking elements of the theories are those which emphasize the breakdown of community, kinship and other informal bonds and concentrate on the resultant isolation of individual households. The 'centripetal', inward looking elements tend to reverse the process and focus on those internal changes that have occurred in domestic life making familial relationships more demanding and consequently limiting the 'resources' available for developing relationships with non-family others. While these two elements are often presented as different sides of the same coin, they are not necessarily contingent on each other. Even if the domestic sphere has become a more central component of males' as well as females' lives, this does not necessarily entail non-domestic relationships becoming insignificant. These relationships may not be neighbourhood-based any more, for developments in transport have helped make geography less constraining, at least for some, but equally 'home-centredness', as I shall term it, does not of itself entail the demise of all external 'community' bonds. To see this, let us first examine the changes there have been in the ambience of the home and the meanings attached to it, and then later in the chapter consider the organization of non-domestic leisure opportunities and involvement in sociable relationships.

Home-centredness

Undoubtedly this century has seen major changes in the material quality of domestic life, changes which have been accompanied by shifts in people's conception of the home and the social relationships within it. Improvements in housing and living standards, together with changes in the social and economic dependencies of different family members have encouraged the generation of novel perspectives and expectations about appropriate family attitudes and behaviour. Specifying exactly how these factors have modified domestic and family life is not straightforward, but their general drift or force can be asserted with some confidence as the various changes have, in their different fashions, all encouraged a similar shift in the way domestic life is perceived and organized. Put at its simplest, this shift has been one that has encouraged an orientation best characterized as 'home-centred'.

The roots of this orientation lie in the changes created by industrializ-ation, especially the separation of commodity production from the home with the introduction of the factory system. Certainly ideologies emphasizing the contrast between domestic and other types of activity were well established, amongst some social strata at least, by the turn of the century. In 1901, for example, Ruskin wrote that the home 'is the place of peace; the shelter, not only from all injury, but from all terror, doubt and division . . . So far as the anxieties of the outer life penetrate into it . . . it ceases to be a home; it is then only a part of the outer world which you have roofed over and lighted fire in' (quoted in Zaretsky, 1976, p. 51). Yet it is in this century that the home and the varied activities occurring in it have come to be a major focus of interest for the family as a whole. Whatever the situation in the past, contemporary values emphasize the satisfactions and rewards to be gained from involvement in it and from family life generally. It is now quite acceptable, indeed expected, that people regard their home, and the relationships and activities it entails, as central to their definition of self and that the family provides a focus through which they interpret their experiences and justify their actions. It is in such ways, in terms of the orientations people hold and the normative assumptions they make, that home-centredness has become a major ele-ment in contemporary life styles.

Clearly though, this orientation has not had an equivalent impact on both genders, even though its ramifications have been experienced by both. While in a sense the increased significance of family- and home-based activities in men's consciousness has added a different dimension to their lives, for women it has arguably done the reverse and trapped them the more exclusively within the domestic world. Given that they have always had the major responsibility for domestic provision, in whatever histori-cally appropriate form, the emphasis on a home-centred orientation refer-red to here has merely reinforced the overriding significance of their servicing role. Although not without its contradictions, of which increas-ing employment rates are the most obvious, the result for many married women is the marked restriction of their lives discussed in the last chapter. These issues will be taken up again later.

Material changes

In the passage quoted above, Ruskin argues that a proper home is marked off and separated from 'the anxieties of the outer life'. This (male) view of the home as the antithesis of work, as a haven to which to return after the stresses and tensions of earning a living in the harsh world of industry and commerce, has if anything become more firmly established within our social imagery since the turn of the century. Indeed the home is now commonly accepted as providing personal fulfilment and satisfaction as well as the means of recuperating from the pressures of the working day. Material improvements in the standard and facilities of the home have been central to this perception of the value of home life. For the great majority the home now provides a physical ambience in which it is possible to relax; it is less crowded, cleaner, healthier and more luxurious than in the past. No longer is it necessary to go outside the home, to pubs or other public facilities, in order to sit in comfortable and warm surroundings. With greater affluence, these physical attractions have been brought inside the home.

This view of home life has been fostered by changes in housing structure including the process whereby large sections of the population who would once have lived within urban centres are being housed around the peripheries of towns and cities. Such a movement, only possible because of developments in transport, has, as a result of market economies as well as social planning, affected both privately owned and publicly rented housing. As the location of residential areas has become more removed from those of industry and business, it has encouraged a cognitive separation which reinforces the view that domestic activities are unconnected to other forms of action, in particular economically and industrially productive ones.

Table 4.1   Housing tenure in GB (percentage)

	Owner-occupation	Council	Privately rented	Other
1914	10	1	80	9
1945	26	12	54	8
1979	52	34	14	

Sources: Boddy, 1980; *Social Trends*, 1981

Radical increases in owner-occupation and council house tenancy have gone hand in hand with this 'suburban drift', as Table 4.1 shows. While the privately rented sector continues to perform an important function, its proportional size in the overall housing supply has declined dramatically. The reasons for these changes are complex, but include factors such as fiscal encouragement of home ownership through tax relief on mortgage interest, slum clearance programmes, rent controls, the expansion of building society activities, and the effective discouragement of new investment by private landlords. One of the most important outcomes has been the improvement of housing standards as the self-interest of home ownership and the financial gains to be made in periods of house price inflation, combined (until recently) with the imposition by central government of Parker Morris standards on local authority developments, have created standards that seem unlikely to have been matched if the privately rented sector had remained as significant as it was. In addition of course the provision of improvement grants by government has also helped to raise housing standards, even if the outcome has often been an unintentional change from privately rented to owner-occupied tenures (Mason, 1977).

The results of the improvements there have been in people's housing conditions are reflected in the official statistics. For example, housing densities have decreased quite markedly this century. In 1911 about a third of all households had a density of more than one person per room compared to around 5 per cent now (Halsey, 1972; Census, 1981). Even more dramatically, whereas in 1951 a fifth of all households were without exclusive use of a toilet and nearly two-fifths lacked a fixed bath, the figures for both are now close on 5 per cent.

Table 4.2   Household goods

Type of goods	Percentage of households possessing goods UK	
	1969	*1979*
Car	51.2	57.9
Central heating	25.1	55.0
Washing machine	62.7	76.6
Refrigerator	60.3	92.9
Television	91.2	95.8
Telephone	32.1	67.2

Source: Annual Abstract of Statistics, 1981

As well as improvements in basic amentities, there has been an equivalent increase in the material possessions found in the majority of homes. Although, of course, wide variations exist with many people still experiencing relative poverty, there has been an unquestionable rise in the general quality and quantity of domestic goods owned by most households. This is evident both in terms of the standard and number of commodities which are bought to improve the comfort and appearance of the home − carpets, furniture, decorative objects, etc. − and also of those bought to improve household efficiency, such as washing machines, fridges, freezers, and vacuum cleaners. An indication of this is given in Table 4.2 which, though only covering a ten-year period, points to the rapid growth in the proportion of households with consumer durables of a substantial kind. It is also worth noting the increasing expenditure on modifications and improvements to the fabric of the home. The amount of time and money spent on such things as decorating and refurbishing is well indicated by the rapid growth in do-it-yourself stores, evidently catering for a growing market, and by the continual development of equipment and materials which are suitable for use by individuals with relatively little skill or training.

All these changes have helped generate a home-centred orientation by making the home more comfortable and congenial. The development of home entertainment technology − radio, television, hi-fi, video, etc. − has also had some impact here by encouraging people to spend more time in the home. In particular, rather than destroying family solidarity as some critics claim, television helps integrate family members by involving them in similar experiences, by giving them topics − however mundane − to discuss, and by just producing a backcloth against which family interaction takes place. In many ways this last point is the crucial one as far as home-centredness is concerned, for what television effectively does, along with other forms of home entertainment, is provide a reason and a focus for family activity, thereby encouraging family members to be together, even if while they are together they are not doing anything particularly remarkable or creative.

These various developments in the material conditions of domestic life have helped change the way in which time spent in the home is perceived. Especially for males, the meaning of time spent there has been modified so that now the home tends to be seen as a centre for leisure and enjoyment as much as the location in which domestic activities, like eating and sleeping, necessary for the maintenance and well being of the individual are performed. This is not to say that all domestic life is now pleasurable or regarded as leisure, nor to suggest that the home is experienced in this way equally by all members of the family. Nor is it to imply that family life is free from tension, conflict or violence. Clearly none of these things is so. The point is rather that, in comparison with the past, the home has, for the majority of people, become a place for relaxation and engaging in various pastimes, a place in which it is reasonable to spend time for its own sake. This need not involve the pursuit of overtly constructive hobbies and activities to be found enjoyable or considered worthwhile. Simply being present in the domestic unit, doing nothing except those routine, unremarkable things most of us spend so much of our time doing, is valued and this in itself reflects the ethic of home-centredness.

Relational changes

Just as the home is perceived as an arena for relaxation as well as domestic service, so too relationships within it have come to be defined in a manner that is congruent with home-centredness. In particular, there has been increased emphasis placed on love and companionship within marriage. It is easy to misinterpret the tendencies there have been (see the next chapter), but the popularity of the claim that marriage is altering suggests that it at least fits some aspects of people's experiences. The usual explanation of this trend relates it to the changing economic functions of marriage. With the dominance of individual wage labour in industrial society, marital selection does not normally affect the material well-being of the wider kin group and so, in principal, can be left to the predilections of the potential spouses (Goode, 1963; Medick, 1976). While parents are still able, in Goode's words, to 'threaten, cajole, wheedle, bribe, and persuade their children to "go with the right people"' (1959, p. 45), these processes have led to the pre-eminence of an ideology which asserts that love is the only legitimate basis for marriage in contemporary society. Though love can be fashioned and moulded in various ways, ideas of personal attraction, compatibility of interests and the satisfaction that derive from being and doing things together are central to it. It is thus seen as a relationship from which personal fulfilment can be expected, a relationship which is rewarding in its psychological, sexual and social intimacy. While for many people these expectations are not matched by reality, they nevertheless fuel the belief that domestic life provides a major source of fulfilment and thus further legitimate a home-centred orientation.

Similarly changes in perceptions about normal parent – child relationships reinforce such an orientation, especially for fathers who have traditionally been involved little in childcare. As the discussion in Chapter 2 suggested, childhood has increasingly been recognized as a special stage of human development with its own peculiar requirements. This recognition has had repercussions for family life in that children occupy a position centre-stage, or very close to it, rather more than previously with family activities regularly being geared to their perceived needs. Thus encouraging children to enjoy a range of experiences and interests that are in the widest sense educationally valuable, and at the same time protecting them from the harsher realities of adult life is seen as a principal obligation of parents, if not quite the *raison d'être* of family life. As Harris (1977) has argued, families can be seen as 'child-producing' units, the final product of this domestic production being as much children *per se* as it is the adults they become. In other words, the aim is not just to socialize in the most appropriate fashion to produce fully competent and complete adults, but to create a childhood experience that is worthwhile for its own sake. Many of the satisfactions to be gained from family life are seen as emanating from an involvement in the (social) creation of children and a sharing with them of their gradually developing consciousnesses.

To the extent that that view of childhood represents a move towards home-centredness and a greater involvement in domestic life, it does so for mothers and fathers to differing degrees. Mothers have always been involved in childcare, though clearly their perceptions of childhood do not remain static but are modified by the changing position of children (and mothers) in the social structure. In this sense, it is fathers' interaction with their children that has altered the more radically. Whatever was the case previously, fathers now not only expect some involvement in their children's social development, but importantly recognize that such involvement generates its own rewards and satisfactions. As we saw in the last chapter, this does not mean that responsibility for childcare is shared equally. Women as mothers continue to have primary responsibility for their children, they are the ones who are most heavily involved in the routine and unexceptional activities of child-rearing. As numerous commentators have noted, men have become involved principally in the more interesting, constructive and rewarding tasks associated with childcare: with amusing and entertaining them for relatively short periods rather than with caring for their more basic physical needs on a daily basis. This latter burden continues to be borne predominantly by women. None the less the argument here is that the growth and socialization of children has increasingly come to be a major interest for fathers rather than simply a matter best left to females except when discipline is required. Indeed the moderation of disciplinary action against children by fathers especially − the replacement of the firm hand by a somewhat more tender, more appreciative and probably more caring approach − is itself a reflection of the changing perception of appropriate paternal involvement in child production. Such changes represent a further element in the evolving redefinition of the satisfactions to be derived from domestic life and consequently help generate a predominantly home-centred orientation.

Leisure and social integration

The proposition put forward so far in this chapter has been that home-centredness is a prominent orientation in contemporary life for men as well as women. The consistent use of the term 'orientation' here, however, is crucial for 'home-centred' seeks not so much to describe the activities and behaviour of family members — though these are of course important — as to convey the significance of contemporary family life in people's consciousness. It refers to a general conception of domestic matters, a conception that takes it for granted that family life is a central interest to its members, one at least as important as any other facet of their social life. The home is not simply the location for physical servicing but is an arena in which it is possible to relax and engage in a range of active or passive leisure pursuits with or without other members of the household.

Such an orientation in which home life is a legitimate focal concern for males as well as females, husbands as well as wives, is clearly going to have repercussions on the salience of other activities and relationships. If nothing else the more time spent at home or with the family the less time is available for other things. However a home-centred orientation, the recognition that activities and relationships based around the home are worthwhile in their own right, does not necessarily result in other relationships or pursuits being ruled out. The idea is not that an individual's world view is inevitably turned inwards, introvertedly focusing only on what goes on within his or her own domestic unit, but that this latter forms one central plank in the framework of their lives.

In some cases, of course, domestic activities may come to dominate all others, for husbands as well as wives, as they seem to do, for example, with Goldthorpe et al.'s privatized affluent workers (1969). But as these authors make clear, such a privatized life style — a home-centred orientation plus an absence of external sociable ties — is chosen by these workers rather than imposed on them. A central theme of the *Affluent Worker* research was that the respondents' existing attitude towards family life had led them to opt for a particular type of work — unpleasant but well paid — in order to provide a higher standard of living for their families. In turn the instrumental view of work they developed — the absence of any social involvement or moral attachment over and above the cash nexus — reinforced this prior commitment to family and domestic life and resulted in their life style being privatized.

In other cases, there is less reason to assume that a home-centred orientation in the sense outlined above is necessarily associated with an absence of sociable ties outside the home. Rather, the relation between such an orientation and the extent to which individuals are incorporated into socially integrative, non-domestic leisure time activities is an empirical rather than a logical matter, and must be analysed in these terms. In doing this, though, it is crucial to recognize that families are not single entities but social groups made up of individuals who as a result of their structural location within society have different interests and perceptions, different opportunities and obligations. In particular, of course, husbands and wives are likely to generate quite different configurations of domestic and non-domestic pursuits, a point that will be emphasized throughout the analysis.

Before doing this, however, it is worth briefly discussing the concept 'leisure'. In everyday parlance the essence of leisure is freedom, of periods in which individuals are in control of their own actions, doing as they like. This sense of autonomy and freedom is implicitly contrasted with the control and disciplined co-ordination of paid work. Work and leisure are conceptually antithetical, and with the development of industrial society are organizationally so too. As industrialization encouraged the compartmentalization and separation of employment, with its fixed hours and distinct settings, from other activities, so the boundary between paid work and leisure came to be more clearly drawn. Or at least it did for those whose major activity is this form of work − men especially. For wives, whose prime responsibility is domestic, the boundary is rather more blurred. In part this is because their work is not separated in time or space from the home, but it is also because the initial conception of leisure as freedom, with work as its polar opposite, is itself dubious. This becomes evident when activities which are socially necessary − and hence not freely chosen − yet not thought of as work are considered. The obvious examples are those which are done to maintain physical welfare, such as eating, sleeping, washing, etc., but there are other activities, like gardening, decorating and sewing, which though satisfying for some are perceived as duty and obligation by others. The organization and nature of housework makes it particularly difficult to categorize many of its constituent tasks within this common sense dichotomy, a fact which itself indicates the male bias in our normal definitions of leisure.

Importantly too, the idea of leisure as freedom underemphasizes the extent to which the leisure 'choices' open to people are themselves structured by social factors over which they have relatively little control. To begin with, access to different forms of leisure is socially circumscribed in that some forms are defined as suitable for one category of person − male, female, old, young, etc. − but not another. For example, competitive sports are more a male activity then a female one; popular dancing more for the young than the old, and so on. Equally, the resources, especially of time and money, that a person has available affects his/her leisure participation, and these are not distributed evenly either within or between families. Similarly, in terms of the extent to which leisure is socially integrating, an individual's (non-leisure) commitments will also shape the opportunities she/he has for becoming involved in leisure activites with others. For example, prior obligations may shape not just the amount of time that a person has free for leisure activity but also the pattern of that time and consequently the nature of the leisure pursuits that they can undertake. Thus many 'collective' leisure activities generate continuing obligations with the others involved − for instance, playing team sports may require attendance at coaching and training sessions as well as at matches; membership of voluntary associations may create demands for regular participation in meetings − which some people will find harder than others to fulfil.

Thus in looking at the socially integrative consequences of leisure, it is not enough to define leisure in ways such as 'relatively freely undertaken non-work activity' (Roberts, 1978, p. 3). Indeed examining leisure activities in terms of freedom and choice alone is a little like looking through a telescope the wrong way round. Instead the emphasis needs to be on the way that the overall configuration of an individual's existing obligations and commitments limit and constrain the freedom and opportunities she/he has to be involved in leisure activities with others. In this way it is possible to understand how leisure is structured and the role it plays in integrating people socially.

The freedom to participate

We saw in Chapter 3 that as well as incorporating the individual economically and politically, employment integrates people socially by providing the occasion and context for interacting with others. This, along with the absence of wages, is the major difference between domestic work and paid work, for housework is essentially isolating. With each household being serviced by its own resident worker, domestic work necessitates relatively little involvement with others. Indeed it actually provides few opportunities for meeting other people or developing relationships. In this sense there is no collective division of labour, no co-operation *per se*; nor are there communal mealbreaks or other organized interludes built into the work that encourage sociability. In such respects, the work experiences of most wives are quite different from those of their husbands. Even though relatively few work-based relationships are extended into leisure contexts, being involved in them at work provides husbands with an integrative factor largely missing from much of their wives' work.

Yet while it might be expected that leisure involvement could provide some compensation for this relative absence of work-based social relations, in practice the leisure opportunities available to women actually exacerbate the situation. Only recently however has this been recognized in the literature. For many years leisure specialists have constructed their theories around the idea that class was the single most important variable in leisure patterns, with the middle class generally being the more active and more likely to spend their spare time constructively, in ways that are appreciated by the country's leisure lobby. Yet if class is a key factor in structuring leisure activities, it is now recognized as not so crucial as gender. As Roberts writes: 'In general leisure time is not evenly distributed between husbands and wives. Women are very much the second-class citizens. Inequalities in the distribution of leisure time within families make the contrasts that can be drawn between social classes pale to insignificance' (1978, p. 96). However it is not just leisure time which is distributed unequally, so too are leisure facilities. There are comparatively few activities which are as open to women as they are to men. Leisure in our society tends to be directed far more towards men or family groups, including couples, than unaccompanied women. This reflects women's domestic responsibilities, and the unequal division of resources and rewards between the genders.

Such differences are apparent in the range of voluntary associations and organizations that exist. As many community studies have shown, the middle class tend to join voluntary associations of all sorts rather more than the working class. Similarly in associations with mixed class membership, positions of authority and control in them normally tend to be held disproportionately by the professional and managerial strata (see, for example, Stacey et al., 1975). Yet while the middle-class bias of voluntary associations is real enough, it is more than matched by their male bias. The majority — be they political parties, sports clubs, social clubs, trade unions, welfare associations or what have you — are run by, and largely for, men. The number of such organizations which are female oriented is remarkably small, and many of those which are, like the Women's Institute and Young Wives Clubs, tend to build upon, and thereby reinforce rather than counter, the domestic identity of their members. Equally where associations are formally open to both genders, they are frequently controlled by men. Women rarely obtain powerful positions within them, except when they are allowed to run separate female sections. Indeed in a good few voluntary associations, female participation seems to be encouraged partly so that refreshments and/or clerical services can be provided while the men proceed with the business in hand, be it cricket, religion or politics.

Indicative of the gender imbalance of voluntary associations is the relative absence of female sports. There is far greater opportunity for male sporting endeavour than there is for female, both because the number of sports contested is smaller and because the number of participants in those there are is less. Socialization encourages girls and women to see themselves as weaker and less competitive than men, and consequently less suitable for physical exertion. As in other spheres, the resultant image that competitive sports are not quite natural for women is consequently reinforced in practice. Gymnastics − a combination of dance and sport − is one of the very few sports organized on a mass level for young girls, and this only since Olga Korbut's (literally) inspirational performance in the Munich Olympics. Yet as in another main female sport − swimming − retirement is early. Compare this with the sporting opportunities open to young, and not so young, males.

Similarly much socially oriented commercial leisure provision is biased more towards males than females. This is not so in a formal sense, but the social conventions applying in places like pubs, social clubs, and even dance halls are such as to discourage genuinely equal female participation. So while women are not usually barred from such places, they are none the less sometimes made to feel uncomfortable in them and as a consequence are often somewhat reluctant to enter them alone. Given the importance of alcohol in social life, the gender conventions of pub drinking illustrate most aptly the restricted opportunities for social involvement these informal types of leisure provision offer women. Aside from the implicitly male character of the pastimes, like darts and pool, that are catered for, male control of pub life is most evident in the way unaccompanied females are often treated. As Whitehead's (1976) study of a Herefordshire pub highlights, the glances and stares, the private joking, the innuendo and bantering developing into teasing and horseplay, all serve to make women feel uneasy and out of place. Such forms of control are the more effective because they are wrapped up in what purports to be joking and good-natured humour. If women aren't prepared to enter into the spirit of such things, the argument goes, they shouldn't come in − which of course they don't, thereby legitimating the whole process. The result is that most women prefer not to take the chance of these situations arising so that public drinking remains something of a male or, at best, 'couple' preserve, offering women only limited opportunities for social integration in their own right.

So too other public leisure facilities tend to be defined in male or couple terms. There are some exceptions of course. Female participation rates in evening classes tend to be higher than male rates (*Statistics of Education*, vol. 3, 1981), not so much, one suspects, because women are more committed to educational or cultural activities than men, but because of the relative absence of alternative leisure pursuits. Bingo too is a predominantly, though not exclusively, female pastime, one of the few to combine quick-wittedness and suspense with sociability. Yet its popularity is based less on the excitement of waiting for a particular number to come up or the chance of winning the resultant prize than on the fact that it is one of the few forms of public entertainment that working-class women can go to alone without worrying about the consequences. Not only are they unlikely to be teased (or worse) there, but, as importantly, it is a pastime husbands are prepared to sanction as posing no threat (Hobson, 1981; Dixey and Talbot, 1982).

This point is important generally for male control of female leisure does not only occur outside the home. It is also reflected in the different-ial knowledge of each other's activities to which spouses traditionally have a right and the different demands they can make of each other. Whereas husbands often feel it is quite reasonable for them to be indepen-dent and do as they please without their wife knowing every detail, this rarely applies the other way round. Whether it be from a subtle and apparently liberal desire to protect their wives, or for more restrictive reasons, few wives go out alone without their husband's full knowledge. This particular double standard is facilitated by normal childcare arrange-ments. Whereas husbands can often assume wives will babysit whilst they are out, wives, being responsible for such matters, normally have to ask husbands if they will do it or make alternative arrangements.

One additional factor here is the effective male domination of private transport. Willmott has argued that car ownership has now become 'at least as important an independent influence as class upon people's leisure and possibly more so' (quoted in Pearson, 1978, p. 38). Car ownership is of course unequally distributed, but so too is the ability to drive. Males under 50 are almost twice as likely to hold full licences as women under 50, and men over 50 are nearly three times as likely to have them as women of that age (*Social Trends*, 1981). Given also that husbands are often thought to have greater rights to the (so-called) family car than wives, it follows that married women's freedom of movement is on average more curtailed than their husbands'. Husbands encourage such patterns more or less subtly by, for example, demanding the car for work or discouraging their wives from learning to drive − ('I don't mind you learning but you're not going to ruin my gear-box while you're doing it' or 'It's no good me teaching you, you never take any notice of what I say', etc.) − thereby protecting their own more privileged position.

The result of all these processes is that the leisure experiences of husbands and wives, and men and women generally, are quite different (Griffin, 1981). In Deem's (1982) terms, the 'space' that a person has for leisure is very much structured by gender. This idea of 'space' is a useful one because its references are both physical and temporal. That is, it involves space in terms of the time that people can set aside for leisure out of their daily routine, as well as in the more obvious sense of their access to leisure facilities. In both these respects men are advantaged in comparison to women. In this, leisure patterns are directly related to, and built upon, the dominant division of paid and domestic work in our society.

Being employment, men's work is normally bounded in time and space, materially rewarded and socially integrative. As a consequence leisure activities can be clearly demarcated from work ones. Having done their work and earned their money, men can claim a right to some relaxation and enjoyment, and have created the necessary leisure facilities and institutions to do this. Of course not all their non-work time is used for such purposes, but the pattern and rhythm of their lives does at least allow them to construct space for leisure. The particular ways this space is used, the activities and pursuits involved, will vary depending on a range of factors, including the individual's class position and the finances he has available. Yet the point remains. As with work, so too leisure provides a forum for men to meet and engage with others.

For women generally, and married ones especially, the position is rather different. The nature of domestic work — the absence of fixed hours or tasks, the lack of a separate location, its 'never-endingness', its 'bittiness', and so on — means that the rhythm of the wife's day is very different from that of her husband. Whether or not she is employed, she generally lacks the 'space' for leisure that the organization of his work affords him. But even if, amongst all her different tasks and duties, she can create the space within her day for leisure, the opportunities for using it are lacking. Not only is domestic work isolating, occurring within the private household and necessitating little co-operation with others, but as importantly, the demands of men generally, and husbands specifically, have meant that few female-oriented leisure organizations have developed which might compensate for this. Again there are differences here between women with different class and family cycle positions, but generally in comparison to their husbands wives have less opportunity to integrate themselves into community life. As Roberts argues:

> Married women, especially working-class wives, recorded exceptionally low rates of participation across nearly every form of out-of-home recreation, and in their homes they did little that could be described as leisure except watch television. When the women went outside their homes for recreation it was nearly always as a couple or as a family group; rarely alone or with friends. (1978, p. 97)

Nowhere is the unequal distribution of leisure space more evident than at weekends. For most men, the weekend is a period of relaxation in which different sporting and leisure activities can be enjoyed, a period that is to some extent organized to suit their particular moods and interests. Of course, as the earlier part of this chapter suggested, much of the time may be spent with the family in a domestic context, and in tasks which are a necessary part of domestic life. None the less the nature of these tasks and the meaning they have for the husband are markedly different from the nature and meaning of his wife's weekend activities. His activities within the home are usually quite different from his employment, and they tend to be less regular and less mundane tasks than his wife performs. They tend in other words to be activities which are to some degree chosen, creative and relaxing, if only because they are a contrast to work.

His wife's weekend is normally structured rather differently. It is considered by her family and herself less as leisure time for her to use in sporting or other active pursuits and more as a continuation of her workday routine. She consequently spends much of it providing domestic services, especially meals, for her family. If she is a full-time housewife it may be a more pleasant part of the week because, with her family at home she at least has company and is a little less involved in cleaning and washing which can wait until the weekend is over. But if she is employed as well, the weekend is often the period of most intense domestic activity. It must be used to organize the week ahead and catch up on tasks such as cleaning and changing the beds for which there has been little time in the week. Either way, her weekend usually differs from her husband's in the manner in which her time and activities are structured.

In summary the main point being made in this section is that the freedom to participate in leisure activites and become incorporated with others is quite different for husbands and wives. The full-time housewife and mother especially can be thought of as doubly trapped in her home by her work and by the lack of appropriate leisure provision and opportunity. She comes, therefore, to be quite dependent on her husband for social involve‐ ment outside the home as well as inside it. As a result, married women tend to rely rather more than their husbands do on joint or 'couple' participation in leisure activities. As in the discussion of public drinking earlier, their husbands' participation is less frequently conditional on their wives' involvement. Similarly their structural dependence on husbands goes some way towards explaining why many wives are prepared to take on the more menial tasks required in male-dominated leisure activities. While, for example, making tea with other wives for cricketing husbands is not particularly exhilarating, it is often a pleasanter way of spending a weekend day than yet again being cooped up at home with young children.

Employed wives are somewhat less dependent on their husbands for social involvement as their employment itself brings them into contact with others. Given that a good deal of their remaining time is spent catching up on domestic tasks, the absence of female leisure provision may be of less direct concern to them than to the full-time housewife. In such respects the notion that employment acts almost like a hobby, providing married women with an 'interest' outside the home, is not quite as absurd as it would otherwise be, notwithstanding the inherent monotony of much female employment.

Sociable relations

From all this, it is clear that the extent to which husbands and wives are socially integrated through their involvement in the institutions and organizations of work and leisure differs systematically. But what about those informal ties of friendship and kinship that exist irrespective of involvement in social organizations? To what extent can these relationships compensate for lack of involvement elsewhere? A preliminary point to recognize is that though kinship does not depend on institutional membership, the issue is not quite so clear-cut with friendship. Even if those ties which are primarily based upon common membership of some organization can be distinguished from those which are not, many of the latter are none the less created and serviced through mutual involvement in formal or semi-formal organizations of one sort or another. Consequently while it is important to analyse ties of kinship and friendship in examining social involvement, it needs to be remembered that the ease with which such ties can be generated itself depends in some measure on the sorts of factor considered in the last section.

The implications of this for married women's social involvement are evident. Not being party to voluntary associations and their like to the extent their husbands are, their patterns of sociability are necessarily more dependent on 'free-floating', non-institutional ties. Yet here, of course, is the catch: the pool of others available for this is smaller precisely because they are less involved in the settings and contexts by means of which most such bonds are initially generated − that is, formal and semi-formal organizations of one type or another. As a result, the degree to which close bonds can be developed with those who are met becomes of major consequence to many wives. As kin ties are to some extent 'given', the ability to convert at least some casual relationships into more intimate ties of friendship is particularly important, especially for wives who have been geographically mobile and so cannot simply rely on the networks of friendships they developed during childhood and adolescence.

Yet despite their significance, especially for full-time housewives, the processes involved in generating friendships, without much 'institutional' support and back-up, has received little attention in the literature. How contacts made in the neighbourhood, outside the school gates or in the park, through baby-sitting circles, husbands and children, at evening classes or other voluntary associations catering for women, or wherever, are turned into friendships is not seen as a problem. However, as we saw in Chapter 3, a great many women experience it as one, particularly during the child-rearing phase of the family cycle or if their husband's career demands mobility. (One study which provides an exception to this generalization is Edgell's (1980) account of 'spiralist' family life. See also Finch, 1983.) The different 'solutions' adopted to this problem are shaped by social class variations in friendship patterns generally, and by the use made of the home especially.

Class differences

Despite the common view that working-class life tends to be the more intimate and friendly, research has demonstrated that it is the middle class who maintain the greater number of friendships. In study after study, middle-class respondents have listed more friends than their working-class equivalents, with the latter indeed often not able to muster the small number — usually only three, four or five — of 'best friends' normally asked about. The commonest reason given for this class difference is that the middle class, largely because of the inherent mobility of their career patterns, have developed appropriate social skills for generating and sustaining friendships, whereas the working class have not. The middle class know how 'to put down roots quickly wherever they live' (Willmott and Young, 1971, p. 92), such arguments go, whilst the working class lack 'the social skills involved in making new acquaintanceships and transforming these acquaintanceships into friendships' (Gavron, 1966, p. 98). Whilst this explanation of class differences in friendship is useful in its tacit recognition that friendships are socially organized, it is deficient in implying that 'friendship' is the only form that such relationships can take and that the working class are simply unable 'to indicate and preserve [the] delicate social distances [necessary] if the chances of making friends are not to be impaired by a wrong move in the initial stages' (Klein, 1965, p. 352).

A more appropriate explanation of these class differences concerns the way in which non-kin relationships are developed and organized, and in particular the part the home plays in this. When middle-class people meet someone they like and decide to get to know them better, they are likely to do so by inviting them back to their homes and involving them in areas of activity that are not part of the original context in which they met.

Whatever that context might be — be it work, a sports club, the neighbourhood or what have you — the relationship is developed into one of
friendship by broadening its basis, thereby making it more than just a
colleague, team-mate, or neighbour relationship. This process of
extending the boundaries of more important relationships means that the
relationships themselves, rather than the specific contexts of interaction in
which they originate, are defined as central, which is itself one of the prime
criteria of friendship. The use of the home to entertain friends is particularly significant in sustaining this in two respects. Firstly, it clearly
serves to 'decontextualize' the relationship and differentiate it from others
which arise simply because both sides happen to be doing the same thing at
the same time. Secondly, it symbolizes the closeness of the tie by bringing
the friend into the private domain, by showing him or her the 'real self' of
the other as they are when they are being themselves, relaxing away from
the glare of outsiders. This too is an important element of friendship, as
only the trusted few are allowed 'back-stage' to see the individual as she/he
really is (Goffman, 1959; Suttles, 1970).

The working class on the other hand tend to limit their relationships
rather more and do not allow them to develop in the same way. Even important informal relationships tend to be restricted to the contexts in which
they first arose with little effort being made to enlarge them or alter their
character by incorporating them into other activities. Rather, they are
normally defined quite narrowly, deliberately being compartmentalized
and contained within specific contexts, such as work, the pub, or the
neighbourhood. As with the middle class, the use made of the home is a
significant element in this, but in the opposite way. Generally in working-
class life, contrary to popular wisdom, the home tends to be defined as a
private arena reserved principally for family members. Normally non-kin
are not entertained in it, unless through some exceptional circumstance
they have come to be regarded as almost 'honorary' family members. In
this sense, the working-class home can be viewed as something of a refuge
from the outside world, a protective retreat into which unrelated others are
not often invited. Certainly using the home as a means of actually
developing relationships and getting to know acquaintances better is
foreign to traditional working-class ways. Because the use made of the
home is restricted in this way, the specific contextual boundaries drawn
around most non-kin relationships are more easily maintained (Allan,
1979, especially Chapters 5 and 6).

The reasons why working-class sociability is shaped in this fashion are
probably various. To begin with, entertaining in the home can be quite
expensive, as it generates circles of obligation which can be hard to meet
on a low budget. To put this the other way round, not entertaining in the

home allows a greater control over the resources invested in a relationship. Indeed, more generally, containing relationships in specific contexts and not broadening their basis serves to limit the demands that can be made of them. In this way, their being tightly structured allows greater control over them. This can be important when, as in much working-class life, resources are scarce. But equally as Oxley (1974) has shown in his interesting study of 'mateship' in Australia, limiting the settings and activities defined as relevant to a relationship tends to emphasize the equality of the participants by making any distinctions of, say, wealth, status or life-style irrelevant to their interaction. All that counts is what occurs in the immediate setting, as the relationship is framed so as to exclude any other issues. In this way too, then, restricting the scope of relationships helps protect the social standing of individuals with relatively few resources.

Gender differences

For most men, there is little problem in forming social relationships. Apart from their work incorporating them socially, the opportunities available to them to participate in voluntary or commercial leisure organizations enables them to meet others and develop informal ties. The result may not always be especially deep friendships of the form philosophers seem to favour, but they are significant in incorporating males into the social fabric. As noted there are significant class differences in this. The fact that some, though not all, middle-class contacts are entertained in the home means, for example, that middle-class wives become involved in some of their husband's friendships, so that the unit of friendship becomes the two couples. Working-class men rarely bring their contacts into the home, so their wives are less likely to become involved in the relationship. Equally this leads to working-class men claiming few 'friends' as such. Their emphasis on the context of interaction rather than its abstract content makes the label 'friend' seem inappropriate as a description. But this absence of acknowledged friendship does not mean that working-class men are socially isolated, rather it means their social contacts are referred to in other terms, 'mates' being the most common (see Allan 1979, for a discussion of this). Given all the above, there is little evidence to suggest that men of any class lead privatized social lives; in both work and leisure they have the opportunities to integrate themselves with others.

For women generally, and wives in particular, the situation is less clear-cut. The constraints on their activities outside the home and consequently on the opportunities open to them to meet and develop relationships with non-kin are greater. As we have seen, their involvement in leisure is often limited and sometimes dependent on the presence of a male partner. However the extent of these disadvantages are also affected by class, with middle-class females generally being in a slightly better position than working-class ones to fight back in some way. Certainly, like their husbands, they claim more friends and are probably involved in more non-kin sociability than their working-class equivalents. Their use of the home to entertain and meet with others, especially as full-time housewives, compensates to some degree for the privatization their domestic role entails. It not only allows a middle-class wife to be more intimate with those she does know, but also means she is able to arrange specific episodes of sociability in her own or others' houses rather than being dependent on more haphazard 'public' meetings. This also means she can get to know people through her friends and thus increase her own social circle. In a similar way, the fact that her husband uses the home for entertaining means that she can meet people through him.

The existence of non-kin friendships tends to reduce the centrality of kinship in middle-class life, but it would be wrong to think that kin are of no significance, especially for middle-class women. As well as being turned to in times of crisis, mothers are regularly involved in their daughter's social and domestic routines, though not necessarily on a daily basis. Their experience is not the only resource available to their daughters, but none the less it is one. Equally where they live sufficiently close to allow such contact, quite frequent meetings normally occur which are valued by both sides. In many instances they allow young mothers a rare chance to relax from their childcare responsibilities, though their mother's help in this normally also means being more receptive to critical advice. Often, though, middle-class career patterns result in the long-range geographical separation of the generations, so that mothers are not at hand to relieve their daughters from domestic pressure. While the telephone and extended visits help maintain contact, they are less effective in countering routine domestic isolation.

The social isolation of working-class women can be much greater than is usual amongst the middle class, especially where there is separation from primary kin. For full-time housewives, childcare responsibilities and the absence of opportunities for interaction outside the home combine strongly here with the limitations just discussed governing the way in which the home is used. The tendency to think that the home is for family rather than non-kin, means that working-class wives have rather few opportunities to develop non-kin relationships. People may be met at the shops, the park or the school, but in the absence of a context in which to develop the relationship – even if its boundaries would still remain tightly defined – it is unlikely to become a particularly deep one. Interaction may certainly be looked forward to and play some part in incorporating the housewife into a wider circle, but this is more a reflection of the absence of other social involvement than a true indication of the strength of the casual relationships that occur.

It is from this structural position that working-class wives' greater dependence on their female primary kin needs to be interpreted. Since the 'rediscovery' of kinship by writers like Mogey (1956), Firth (1956) and Young and Willmott (1957) in Britain and Sussman (1959) in the United States, the predominant importance of kinship in working-class female life has been firmly established. Mothers and sisters appear regularly as significant figures provided they are reasonably accessible, with mothers-in-law and sisters-in-law occasionally also playing their part. These are the people who can be relied upon and who will not let you down. They not only provide help and aid when it is needed, but are also central in these wives' social networks, helping to combat the isolation many experience. More than anyone else they provide the practical and emotional support needed for coping with the routine demands of running a home, though often the form of support given is shaped by external factors, in particular long- or short-range geographical mobility and the stages the individuals have reached in their family cycles (Rosser and Harris, 1965; Allan, 1979).

In such respects, the importance of primary kin ties should not be underestimated. Kinship does form the basis of the nearest thing to a trade union these housewives possess. It serves to protect them and counter the contingencies of their work. On the other hand, it should also be recognized that kinship is significant in the social life of working class housewives partly because there are so few alternatives. The nature and organization of their work precludes other bonds of solidarity, leaving kinship to fill the resulting void. Clearly there are costs as well as benefits to this. In particular it could be argued that such a degree of involvement with primary kin tends to reinforce traditional images of female domestic responsibility, thereby helping to perpetuate the situation it is supposedly relieving. The housewife is a little less likely to question her domestic subservience because of her social dependence on people whose own existence would be devalued if they were to encourage her to be more adventurous in her life-style. Other factors are of course crucial here too, in particular the economic constraints that make her financially dependent on her husband, but mothers especially may play a key though subtle role in persuading their daughters to accept their domestic experiences stoically. What was right for them is right for their daughters as domestic work is by nature female. And who else would care for the children? While such processes should not be emphasized unduly, as elsewhere, patterns of social organization can be seen to generate responses which reinforce the original patterns and make change the more difficult to achieve.

'Community loss'

One final issue to return to in this chapter concerns the significance of locality in contemporary social life. At the beginning of the chapter, reference was made to those views that suggest there has been a decline in community and neighbourhood ties, a decline which of itself represents a form of privatization. As will be clear from the arguments already expressed, this is a questionable idea. Undoubtedly the global process we term 'industrialization' has decreased our dependence on immediate neighbours. With urbanization, the range of people available to provide services for us is nowhere near as restricted as it was previously. To put this another way, the networks we are involved in are far less close-knit than they would have been in earlier eras, when people were forced by the absence of alternatives to rely on relatively few others who were all known to each other. Developments in communication and transport technologies have thus radically affected the extent to which we are dependent on local ties for our everyday needs. So in this sense, there clearly has been an overall decline in the significance in social life of the local community.

However the extent to which this loss of 'community' involvement represents a necessary move towards privatization is a different matter. Precisely because of improvements in transport and communications, social relationships of all sorts can be maintained irrespective of locality. Geography is less constraining both in the sense that contact can be maintained with kin and friends living long distances away and, more importantly, in that ties with others living in the same urban area but not the immediate locality can be serviced quite readily. The individual's (and family's) social network then is likely to include some people from the immediate neighbourhood but others who live at various distances away. The neighbourhood is clearly not a cohesive unit – and probably never was – but individuals are not necessarily privatized as a consequence.

Clearly though, the extent to which individuals are able to service non-local relationships and consequently the extent to which they are dependent on local ties will vary. In part it will depend on their access to transport, but also, more generally, on the amount of 'space' they can construct in their lives for non-local interaction. In line with the earlier arguments of the chapter, we would normally expect adult males and the middle class to be less reliant on local ties, with housewives, especially working-class ones, being more so. Equally the elderly and the young — children and adolescents — are likely to depend more on the immediate area for much of their social life. Consequently here, as earlier, the issue that matters is the degree to which these groups have access to organizations and institutions whereby they can generate ties in the locality. The young have the advantage of neighbourhood-based schools where they can meet and come to know their peers. Apart from their own social clubs, the elderly have less of an institutional base through which to develop relationships, in part because the social process of ageing tends to involve some degree of institutional disengagement. As a result of the absence of such a base, together with the shrinkage of their social networks through their peers' infirmity or death, many elderly come to rely quite heavily on their immediate kin, especially their descendants. If these kin do not live locally themselves, the elderly can become very isolated and have extremely privatized existences, though again this is likely to be more true of working-class than middle-class elderly.

In summary, the issue of 'community solidarity' is a far from simple one. At times local populations do mobilize themselves into a more or less cohesive unit, for example when their environment is threatened by plans for a new road or other major development. Normally, though, 'communities' do not exist as single entities. The degree to which people are enmeshed in them varies, in part as a result of the differential opportunities open to them to sustain sociable ties elsewhere. Certainly of itself a lack of local involvement does not necessarily mean that individuals or families are privatized. On the other hand some groups in the population are quite heavily dependent on local ties, at least for their day-to-day, non-domestic social contacts. For such people, generating neighbourhood relations is not always an easy matter as the opportunities to become involved with others living in the locality do not arise in any systematic or institutionalized way. In other words the structural conditions that might, and traditionally did, encourage some degree of local integration — the population's social and economic interdependence — do not operate sufficiently widely to tie people together.

5

Marriage: an Unequal Relationship

A popular theme in contemporary life is that marriage is becoming a far more equal relationship than it has been in the past. In Young and Willmott's (1973) terminology, it is now seen as a more symmetrical arrangement in which tasks and activities are shared equitably, thereby allowing each spouse similar opportunities for individual satisfaction and fulfilment. Some, like Shorter (1975) and Stone (1979), see this process as having quite a long history, starting in the seventeenth and eighteenth centuries with the development of new ideologies which stressed personal freedom above communal obligation. Others take evidence of more recent social change, both inside and outside the home, to provide support for their ideas. The emphasis on personal attraction and romantic love as the basis of marriage, the growth of home-centredness, the ready availability of divorce for terminating unhappy marriages, the increased number of married women working, the formal encouragement by various governments of equal opportunities for both genders, the increasing awareness of the women's movement as a political lobby — all these and similar changes have encouraged the perception that women's position in the family and society at large is altering. No longer are they simply second-class citizens whose lot, as a consequence of their economic dependence, is to service their husbands and accept his authority, however unjust. Instead women are now seen as having the opportunity to shape their own lives and, not being so caught up in a web of male dominance, the power to control and counter any unreasonable demands their husbands may make of them. Marriage is thought of much more as a genuine partnership, with neither side dominating the other, each instead achieving his or her goals with the other's co-operation.

Such an ideology of marriage is a popular one, but there is very little evidence to suggest that it is in any real sense true. Despite the changes that are occurring, some of which are happening far more slowly than others, marriage remains an essentially unequal relationship, still structured around principles of male advantage. This chapter is concerned with exploring this and assessing the degree of symmetry or otherwise in marriage. Quite clearly, the extent to which marriages are seen as equal depends on the way in which equality is defined and measured. Generally, it is the case that those studies which have seen marriage as changing towards equality have tended to examine the relationship from a somewhat narrow perspective. In particular, they have tended to ignore the societal context in which marital relationships are played out, concentrating instead on the statements husbands or, more usually, wives make about their marriages. Such data are, of course, important but they are not all there is to evaluating the contemporary character of this social relationship. Equally important are the differential constraints and opportunities present in the wider society that, while often taken for granted as normal or even natural, shape domestic organization including the marital bond.

In this chapter three main approaches to the analysis of marital equality will be discussed. Each of these three approaches focuses on a different aspect of the conjugal relationship, but this does not mean they are unrelated or have nothing to contribute to each other. On the contrary, the aim in discussing them is to build up an overall picture of the extent of marital equality and the structural conditions which mould it. The three perspectives focus on (1) decision-making; (2) the distribution of domestic activities; and (3) the structure of dependence. Each will be considered in turn.

Decision-making approaches

The pioneering and most influential study of marital power was published by Robert Blood and Donald Wolfe under the title *Husbands and Wives: The Dynamics of Married Living* (1960). Blood and Wolfe's strategy was to isolate eight areas in which decisions have to be made by families, and then to ask their respondents — over 900 married women from Buffalo in the United States — whether it was their husbands or they who had the final say over these decisions. The areas they asked about decision-making ranged from the husband's choice of work to which doctor to go to when someone was sick, and included such things as what house or apartment to live in, where to go on holiday, and whether the wife should be employed. Each answer was assigned a score, and these scores summed to give a measure of family power. When they analysed their results, Blood and Wolfe found, as would be expected, that husbands tended to be more powerful than their wives in that they were the ones to make most of the decisions. The extent to which this was the case, though, depended on the relative social standing of the spouses. For example, the higher the husband's occupational status, the more power he had; conversely if a wife was employed, her husband's power was somewhat lessened. Equally, the greater the difference between spouses in such measures as education, organizational membership and church attendance, the greater the power of the spouse with the higher score. Blood and Wolfe attempted to explain these findings by a 'theory of resources' which argues that the spouse who brings the more resources to the marriage will be the more powerful.

Many similar studies have been carried out in numerous countries throughout the world by social scientists interested in marital power. Some directly replicate Blood and Wolfe's schedule, others modify the questions in accordance with local circumstances (for a summary see Safilios-Rothschild, 1970; Cromwell and Olsen, 1975). While the results of these studies are not altogether in accordance with each other, this approach to marital power is certainly helpful in pinpointing many of the problems and difficulties entailed in assessing the degree of equality between spouses. It is these issues that will be discussed here as they make the results of such surveys as Blood and Wolfe's questionable.

An initial point to make concerns the validity of the answers received in the type of survey normally used in these investigations. An immediate problem is that the responses given to questions about decision-making within the family have been shown to vary substantially depending on whether the husband or the wife is asked the questions (see Safilios-Rothschild, 1969). Yet very few studies ask both spouses their views on power-holding within their relationship, most, like Blood and Wolfe, conveniently supposing that married reality is a shared reality. However as there does tend to be variation between the answers spouses give, on what grounds do we select the correct version? How are we to decide between them? Indeed how can we know whether either spouse's answer reflects the true position, the more so as there is no correlation between the results obtained from decision-making studies of family power and those obtained by other techniques such as laboratory experiments. It is after all arguable that the process of decision-making is not one about which the individuals are fully conscious. Decisions get made but not necessarily in a straightforward fashion. Where discussion and negotiation occur over some period, as they are quite likely to over decisions of consequence, the relative impact of each person's views, their salience for the final outcome, may be forgotten or never fully appreciated. Where there is outright disagreement with one side's views prevailing over the other's, then the decision-making process may be recalled accurately. (Even here difficulties arise though. Say, for example, husband and wife were in favour of buying two different cars. If one side eventually says to the other: 'OK, let's buy the model you want,' who is making the decision and who is the more powerful?) However in those numerous other decisions where the conflict is less overt or where the outcome is a consequence of quite long-term negotiation and consultation, is it reasonable to suppose that either individual will be in a position to answer the simplistic question 'Who decided?' in an interview?

A further difficulty in measuring marital power by concentrating on decision-making lies in the inevitable arbitrariness of the decisons asked about. Clearly there is a limit to the number of questions that can be asked in any survey, so how are the areas of decision making to be selected? How wide or how narrow a range should there be? Blood and Wolfe, and most of their followers, include a wide range of issues. In some, decisions are made frequently; in others, quite rarely — in some cases only once or twice in a lifetime. Similarly not all the decisions asked about are as important in their consequences as one another, and indeed how important any one is thought to be may well vary between different couples and between spouses. So whilst this varied and catholic approach may be praised precisely because it does take in such a range of decision-making, it raises problems of validity. Is it really sensible to consider decisions about whether the wife is employed as equivalent to ones about which doctor should be consulted when someone is ill? If not, what weight should be attached to each decision in creating a cumulative measure of family power? Either way it would seem that the thing termed 'family power structure' changes depending on the questions asked and the weight assigned to them.

In one of the most significant pieces of British research into marital power, Edgell (1980) shows how some of these problems can be broached. As well as complementing the decision-making approach with other forms of analysis, Edgell restricted his sample to 38 professional couples. This allowed him to delve into the decision-making process more fully than is normal and consequently counter some of the problems raised above. Not only did he interview both husband and wife about their decision-making on a wide range of issues, but he also related their responses to the frequency with which the decisions had to be made and, most importantly, to his respondents' own assessment of the importance of the decisions. His data show very clearly that the husbands in the families he studied had far more impact on decisions the couple perceived to be important than their wives did. As Table 5.1 shows the latter controlled areas like food purchases, children's clothing and household decoration, none of which was normally regarded as particularly important, whereas husbands had far more say in 'big' decisions that involved more expense or disruption, like moving house and overall financial control. Wives were normally consulted over any of these major decisions but in the end it was usually the husband who decided. Three quotations from husbands in Edgell's study illustrate the not so delicate balance between consultation and control. One husband said: 'I never decide anything without consulting her, ever. But I usually decide.' Another commented: 'I would not decide without consulting my wife, but maintain chairman's prerogative of the casting vote.' A third said: 'By and large I decide nearly everything. Everything that matters I decide. I do consult my wife and she always agrees with me' (Edgell, 1980, p. 67).

Table 5.1   The importance, frequency and pattern of decision-making in different areas of family life

Decision area	Perceived importance	Frequency	Decision-maker (majority pattern)
Moving	Very important	Infrequent	Husband
Finance	Very imporant	Infrequent	Husband
Car	Important	Infrequent	Husband
House	Very important	Infrequent	Husband and wife
Children's education	Very important	Infrequent	Husband and wife
Holidays	Important	Infrequent	Husband and wife
Weekends	Not important	Frequent	Husband and wife
Other leisure activities	Not important	Frequent	Husband and wife
Furniture	Not important	Infrequent	Husband and wife
Interior decorations	Not important	Infrequent	Wife
Food and other domestic spending	Not important	Frequent	Wife
Children's clothes	Not important	Frequent	Wife

Source: Edgell, 1980, p. 58

This domination of crucial decisions is particularly significant because Edgell's professional respondents are drawn from precisely that group that more optimistic writers — and especially Young and Willmott (1973) — claim are at the forefront of the drive to equality in marriage. The inequalities and male domination Edgell highlights make such a view highly suspect, an argument that will be returned to later in the chapter.

So far the decision-making perspective has been criticized primarily on methodological grounds. What has been questioned is the validity of the data used, especially when they are gathered by means of large-scale surveys involving one-off interviews with one spouse. The approach is also open to theoretical criticisms similar to those developed against studies of community power that, following Dahl (1961), also dwell exclusively on decision-making. The most telling critiques have tended to be of a Marxist ilk. Essentially they argue that power is about interests rather than decisions. What matters is not who makes particular decisions but who benefits most from those decisions. Indeed by allowing subordinates to make some decisions, the powerful may protect their position by giving those they control a spurious sense of participation in an apparently democratic set-up. What counts here of course, as Lukes (1974) amongst others has pointed out, is not solely the control of decisions that are made but also, more importantly, the control of which issues are seen as contentious and therefore come to have decisions made about them. In other words, the powerful have their interests protected by these interests being built into the standard assumptions and expectations that are the bedrock of our routine social organization. So, for example, in the work place, those who control and gain most from capitalism can afford to allow trade unions to negotiate about wages and conditions so long as the framework of such negotiations remains unquestionably capitalist. Consequently in examining power one should not look at decision-making but instead should try to estimate the extent to which different groups' interests are furthered by the operation of the system as it stands.

These criticisms apply equally to decision-making approaches in the study of marital power. They make it very difficult to tell when power is being exercised directly as against when it is merely being delegated. Is the person making a decision doing so because she/he has particular power over the area concerned or because, on the contrary, she/he is being allowed to do so by the more powerful who cement their own position further by creating an image of democracy and consultation? Now, in political analysis the focus is usually on the consequences for decision-making of class domination or 'hegemony' – the manner in which the ruling group is able to maintain its legitimacy by so dominating the political agenda that the basis of their power remains essentially unquestioned. In analysing power in families we are more interested in what Bell and Newby (1976) term 'male hegemony': the taken-for-granted assumptions which emphasize the predominance of the male over the female in almost every sphere of domestic and social life. Yet approaches like Blood and Wolfe's imply that the distribution of power within marriage is simply the result of a struggle fought out between the spouses individually, and thus ignores the fact that the female is chronically disadvantaged from the start by the socially constructed framework of values and norms which constrain her options in work, leisure and domestic life. As a consequence it can be argued along with Gillespie (1972, p. 127), that wives' chances of winning any competition with their husbands for ascendancy in 'power, personal autonomy, and self-realization' are rather slim.

To summarize then, criticisms of the decision-making approach are useful for sensitizing us to the dangers of assuming that power can be understood and measured in a straightforward manner. The idea that power has, as it were, a 'deep structure' and that some issues are so embedded in social practices that they are rarely questioned and therefore do not have decisions made about them needs to be confronted, though, by itself, the decision-making approach is ill-equipped to do so. It is too simplistic in concentrating uncritically on what people say about marital decision-making without examining the organization of the wider social formations which shape the decision-making process. The alternative position, that the analyst is able to specify people's real interest objectively without reference to their own perceptions, is also problematic, principally for precluding the possibility of falsification. In this view, even if people are satisfied with their lot, this proves only that the powerful have managed to hide their true interests from them. But unlike the decision-making approach it at least recognizes the complexity inherent in the concept of power, and that questions of equality cannot be determined without reference to the wider structural features that govern the opportunities and options open to people.

Domestic division of labour

The decision-making approach has many conceptual and methodological problems. The second approach to examining the equalities or otherwise of marriage is rather more straightforward and possibly for this reason has been used more extensively in British empirical studies. This approach focuses on the distribution of activities between the couple rather than on the control of decisions they make. It is concerned with the mundane, day-to-day organization of tasks and with evaluating whether the distribution of responsibilities between husband and wife is equitable. While it is somewhat simpler than the first approach, this second one none the less contains a number of methodological difficulties. However, as we shall see, the major problem associated with it is the conceptual one of specifying exactly what an equal division of labour entails, especially where the two sides are involved in different types of task which cannot be contrasted readily on any unilineal scale. These issues will be discussed more fully after some of the empirical studies have been examined.

To begin with, we can consider the distribution of domestic labour, especially housework and childcare tasks, within the home. A pattern of clear inequality emerges from the various research reports, with wives spending far more of their time cooking, cleaning, dusting, washing, ironing and looking after the needs of children than their husbands do. Indeed husbands appear to need to contribute very little to such activities to get the reputation of being 'very good' within the home. A little bit of help can reap rich rewards not only from their wives but also from kin and other intimates of the family. As discussed in Chapter 3, the dominant assumption is that the onus for domestic work falls on the wife, not just for those 50 per cent of married women who are not employed outside the home but also for those who are. Whilst these latter can more legitimately demand some assistance from their husbands and children, the amount they get is generally limited with housework continuing to be defined as primarily their responsibility. Nowhere is this better indicated than in the common belief held by many married women that they would not be able to cope with even a part-time job without the goodwill and active support of their families.

Table 5.2   Husband's participation in housework and childcare

| | (a) Housework | | | (b) Childcare | | |
	High	Medium	Low	High	Medium	Low
Middle class	4	9	7	8	4	8
Working class	2	1	17	2	8	10
Total	6	10	24	10	12	18

Source: Oakley, 1974, p. 137

A measure of the contribution made by husbands to the running of the home is provided by Oakley (1974) in her study of 40 housewives/ mothers, six of whom were employed outside the home. She classified the relative involvement of husbands in both housework and childcare as either 'high', 'medium' or 'low', giving examples to illustrate her categories. Jeremy Abbott, for instance, regularly cooked meals, hoovered, washed up and cleaned windows and consequently scored 'high' for housework. In contrast Robert Bevan, despite being 'high' on the childcare score, was 'low' for housework as, according to his wife, he never even washed up, doing 'just little things' like occasionally clearing the table after a meal or making a pot of tea (Oakley, 1974, pp. 138–40). Oakley's results are summarized in Table 5.2. As can be seen, only 6 of the 40 husbands were ranked high for their participation in housework, whereas 24 — including 17 of the 20 working-class husbands — were, like Mr Bevan, ranked 'low'. In other words, the 'low' level of participation is the majority pattern, with a full 60 per cent of husbands being found in it.

As might be expected, there was greater participation in childcare, though again nearly half the husbands scored 'low'. In other words despite enjoying playing with their children and in some cases being thought of as 'good fathers' by their wives, 45 per cent of these husbands refused to take responsibility for looking after their child for any length of time. In total, half the working-class husbands were ranked 'low' for participation in both childcare and housework, though generally there was only a slight correlation between the two spheres, a significant point in itself. Oakley reaches three broad conclusions: (a) there are class differences in the extent of husbands' participation in domestic and childcare tasks, with fewer middle-class husbands receiving 'low' scores; (b) husbands tend to be rather more involved in childcare activities than in housework ones; and most importantly, (c) 'only a minority of husbands give the kind of help that assertions of equality in modern marriage imply' (1974, p. 138).

Table 5.3   The degree of conjugal role segregation in domestic and childcare tasks

	In domestic tasks					
	Segregated		*Intermediate*		*Joint*	
In childcare tasks	*No.*	*(%)*	*No.*	*(%)*	*No.*	*(%)*
Segregated	3	(8)	3	(8)	0	(0)
Intermediate	5	(13)	10	(26.3)	0	(0)
Joint	10	(26.3)	7	(18.3)	0	(0)

Source: Edgell, 1980, p. 36

The last two conclusions are fully supported by Stephen Edgell (1980) in the study referred to earlier. Edgell analyses his data somewhat differently from Oakley, using an amended form of Bott's (1971) concept of conjugal role relationship. He placed his respondents into one of three categories — joint, intermediate and segregated — treating childcare and domestic work separately. 'Joint' describes those couples where the majority of activities were genuinely shared; 'segregated' those where the dominant pattern was for tasks never to be shared. Those couples where there was sharing to a limited extent were classified as 'intermediate'. In using this scheme Edgell is at pains to point out that a high degree of role segregation does not simply mean that husband and wife do different domestic or childcare tasks, but rather that the husband does very few of them, leaving them to his wife. His results are summarized in Table 5.3.

As can be seen from this table, whereas nearly half the husbands are actively involved in childcare, none at all is characterized as being equally involved in housework. Indeed 21 of the 38 are minimally involved in either housework or childcare or both. In line with Oakley, Edgell concludes: 'high levels of husband participation in [domestic tasks] are conspicuously absent' (1980, p. 35).

This finding clearly runs counter to the thrust of Young and Willmott's argument that contemporary marriage is becoming symmetrical, with husbands doing many jobs in the home 'which are not at all traditional men's ones' (1973, p. 94). In contrast to these other studies, they report, for instance, that a full 85 per cent of husbands offer their wives help in domestic tasks. Yet on examination, the disagreement seems to be less about the actual facts of domestic labour than about the meaning and interpretation of these facts. Thus, their estimate of the proportion of husbands helping their wives with domestic chores was arrived at by asking respondents a single question: 'Do you/does your husband help at least once a week with any household jobs like washing up, making beds, (helping with the children), ironing, cooking or cleaning?' (1973, p. 331, q. 92). Given that this was the only question asked on the topic, that childcare and housework tasks are lumped together, and that the criterion of helpfulness is doing one activity only once a week, it is not surprising that a high proportion of husbands were found to 'help' their wives. Indeed it seems far more remarkable, given Young and Willmott's thesis, that a full 15 per cent of the husbands give their wife no help and that a further 13 per cent only help by washing up (1973, p. 95).

Allowing for the limited information asked for, it would seem that Young and Willmott's data are roughly similar to Edgell's and Oakley's. For example, 8 per cent of the husbands in Edgell's sample scored low on both housework and childcare, compared to 14 per cent of professional and managerial respondents in Young and Willmott's sample who gave their wives no assistance. Similarly 29 per cent of Edgell's husbands were assigned to the lowest category for participation in housework and/or childcare, compared with 30 per cent of Young and Willmott's professional/managerial husbands who, at most, did the washing up (1973, p. 95). Young and Willmott's results are also interesting in that they indicate, albeit in a limited form, the consequence of wives' employment on husbands' participation in domestic and childcare taks. Again though, a major problem lies in the shallowness of the data obtained. As Table 5.4 shows, the tendency is for husbands to be more actively involved in household tasks when their wives are employed outside the home. Note though that over a fifth of husbands help at most by washing up even though their wives are working full-time, while nearly a tenth of such husbands offer no help at all. One could argue that these are the most remarkable of all Young and Willmott's findings.

Table 5.4   Husband's help in the home

Reported help by husband at least once a week	Not employed	Employed part time	Employed full time
No help	22%	17%	9%
Washing up only	14%	15%	12%
Other	64%	68%	79%
Number	539	320	293

Source: Young and Willmott, 1973, p. 115

Overall the research evidence does suggest that housework tasks and, to a lesser extent, childcare ones are not distributed evenly between husband and wife. If there has been a change in the domestic division of labour over the last generation or so, as many contend, it has not been particularly radical. The help the majority of husbands give their wives around the home appears to be limited and occasional. Few marriages could in this sense be called genuinely symmetrical. The very fact that the issue here is the extent to which husbands help their wives demonstrates how the routine assumption so firmly grounded in contemporary society is that domestic labour is primarily the responsibility of wives (and normally wives' primary responsibility).

This in itself has led some to argue that contemporary marriage is unequal: that the symmetry so regularly commented on is more mythical than real. However such arguments are incomplete, for the premise they are based on is that equality in marriage is governed solely by the sharing (or otherwise) of activities like washing, ironing, cooking and childcare. It would seem more reasonable to recognize that this is not only a relatively narrow conception of domestic labour, which should also include gardening, decorating, home repair, car maintenance, etc., but, further, that the labour necessary for maintaining the household also normally includes wage labour of one form or another. In other words, in assessing whether marital relationships are equal, one must examine all the necessary work both husband and wife do in maintaining the home. So, however unlikely, it is logically possible that the division of labour between spouses could be highly segregated − each having their own tasks which they do without help, comment or encouragement from the other − and yet be entirely equitable – each side putting as much effort as the other into their respective tasks and thus contributing equally to the total running of the home.

One of the few studies to take such a view at all seriously is Young and Willmott's *The Symmetrical Family* (1973). In this they compute the average time husbands and wives spend on tasks necessary for the running of the home. The information for this was obtained by asking respondents to their main survey who were married and aged between 30 and 49 to keep a time-budget diary for one weekday and one weekend. The broad results for the 411 respondents who completed the diaries are given in Table 5.5.

Table 5.5   Average weekly hours spent in paid work and household tasks

	Men	Women working full time	Women working part time	Women not in paid work
Paid work and travel to work	49.5	40.2	26.3	—
Household tasks	9.9	23.1	35.3	45.5
Total	59.4	63.3	61.6	45.5
No. of people	188	46	55	61

Source: Young and Willmott, 1973, p. 113

What is remarkable about these figures is the relative equality in the time spent by the two sexes in tasks which contribute to the domestic economy in its widest sense. While full-time housewives appear to spend the least time involved in such tasks, men and women who are in any way involved in paid employment differ from one another by little more than half an hour per day.

Such evidence as this is, however, inevitably open to a range of interpretations and criticisms. Just how accurate it is as a description of the way people spend their time can be questioned, as can the extent to which it is a good indicator of marital equality. To begin with, there are the methodological problems of collecting data in this way. As Richard Mills points out in his appendix to Young and Willmott's book, a major problem with self-recorded time-budget diaries is that respondents 'edit' entries so that few provide information that covers the full time period requested. The entries rarely add up to the 24 hours of the day. Given this, it is reasonable to assume that in the main those tasks/activities that are omitted or ignored by the respondents are those that they regard as too mundane or insignificant to warrant entering into the diary. This is especially likely to be the case when respondents fill in the diary at the end of a time block, for example when they are sitting down with little else to do, rather than regularly each half hour. As a result it is quite feasible that women particularly underestimate the amount of time they spend doing routine housework tasks. As discussed in Chapter 3, female domestic activities tend to be both mundane and fragmented, so it is unlikely they would all be recorded accurately in this type of exercise. Men's work, on the other hand, tends to be more systematic and within the home often involves projects with a longer time span − e.g. fixing the car, mowing the lawn − that are less likely to be omitted or thought too insignificant to record.

Thus female domestic activities seem more likely than male ones to be underrepresented in the diaries kept. Certainly Young and Willmott's figures are strikingly dissimilar from those reported earlier from other studies of housewives. It will be remembered, for example, that the average weekly working hours of Oakley's housewife respondents was 77 hours. The difference may also reflect the different stages in the family cycle from which the two samples of respondents were chosen. Oakley's consisted of mothers between the ages of 20 and 30, Young and Willmott's, on the other hand, consisted of people aged between 30 and 49. There were consequently likely to be relatively few women in Young and Willmott's sample with young children to care for, and indeed some who would have been at the post-parenting stage with their children having left home. Consequently the amount of domestic labour required, the amount of cooking and food preparation, cleaning, washing and ironing, etc., is likely to be somewhat less for the population sampled by Young and Willmott than for Oakley's. Clearly there is no point in debating which of these stages more accurately reflects wives' and mothers' 'true' situation, but it is worth recognizing that Young and Willmott's data explicitly exclude the age range when women are most likely to be involved in full-time childcare. The picture that emerges from it is consequently not wholly representative of women's domestic experiences.

By definition, time-budget diaries are based on activities. As a result they do not provide a very good indication of the distribution or extent of responsibilities within the home. Yet who takes responsibility for a range of necessary tasks, even if those tasks are not in fact undertaken in any given period, is a matter of some consequence, especially with regard to childcare. Who is it who needs to plan and organize the running of the household? Who is it who has to ensure that someone is caring for the children? Who is it who takes responsibility, and consequently needs to be on hand should things go wrong − such as children being sick or in need of comfort? The suggestion here is that housewives are in a similar position to junior hospital doctors. They are 'on call' for long periods of time, but often not required to be active for portions of this time. Just as any time-budget diaries that concentrated on active medical care would under-estimate the work load of these doctors, so too it can be argued that they are likely to misrepresent the real involvement of many women within the home. Young and Willmott do not consider this point and so do not even provide information about the spread or configuration of domestic and other work tasks. While this would give only a rough and ready check, one suspects it would at least highlight some major differences in the rhythm of the working day. Specifically, whereas paid employment, and travel to it, is normally undertaken in solid blocks each day, domestic work is inevitably far more disjointed. Consequently even if husbands and wives spend similar amounts of time working either inside or outside the home, the nature of female domestic tasks is likely to result in their having less freedom to use their apparently free time as they please. Hannah Mitchell's description of 'the tyranny of meals', the need to prepare, cook and clear away two or three meals each and every day, comes to mind here (Land, 1978, p. 277). As with the other points mentioned, the result is that Young and Willmott's time-budget data need to be interpreted with some care. On all these grounds, the data are likely to imply a greater equality than actually exists in the time spent by husbands and wives contributing to the running of the household.

So far the criticisms discussed in this section have focused more on the validity of the data used in 'time distribution' studies than on that of the approach's underlying assumptions. More radical criticisms can be made which dispute the idea that the amount of time worked is itself a useful criterion for assessing marital equality. Here the argument is that as well as examining how many hours each party devotes to domestic or paid tasks, the nature of those tasks also needs considering. Thus simply because employers work the same hours as employees, their relationship is not as a consequence equal. What matters is the structure of their relationship and the character of their respective tasks within the division of labour they operate. So similarly, husband and wife relationships cannot be judged simply by the hours each puts in. Some tasks are, after all, more enjoyable, some more rewarding than others. As discussed in Chapter 3, much female domestic work is monotonous and mundane, providing few intrinsic satisfactions and, as it is unpaid, even fewer extrinsic ones.

Thus within the home, women's work is largely uninspiring and repeti-tive, providing little self-enhancement or esteem. Many of its tasks are undone almost as soon as they are completed, so that they can never be regarded as genuinely finished. As we have said, men's work within the home frequently involves more or less long-term projects which not only have a definite end but are also sufficiently novel to warrant encourage-ment and appreciation. So, for example, however much they are seen as chores, decorating or 'do-it-yourself' improvements are clearly more rewarding and provide a greater sense of achievement than hoovering or preparing yet another evening meal. Even those more repetitive forms of domestic work that fall into the traditional male orbit, such as gardening or car maintenance, are undone less quickly than much routine housework. Weeds grow less quickly than dust settles, and even young children trample on flower beds less consistently than they dirty fresh clothes or generate chaos in tidied rooms.

Perhaps most importantly of all, the types of indicator of marital equality discussed in this section ignore the hierarchical connotations of the normal division of labour within the home. Even if equal time is spent on required paid and unpaid work, the contribution made by wives tends to involve an element of servicing other household members far more than does that of husbands. Female domestic tasks involve cooking for, washing for, ironing for, making beds for, putting clothes away for other members of the family. Male work involves the performance of tasks but rarely with the same emphasis on doing them for others in any direct way. Where work is done for others, the other is often the wife, but in the very different senses of either giving her a gift or favour − as in putting up shelves for her − or helping her in her own servicing responsibilities − helping her wash up or put the children to bed − rather than serving her directly (Bell and Newby, 1976). Like other status reversals, those occasions, almost ritualistic in character, when husbands provide breakfast in bed for their wives serve to reinforce this rather than contradict it (see Turner, 1974). This element of personal servicing by wives of their husbands' and children's needs signifies their subordinate position for in content it differs little from the work of domestic servants apart from being unpaid and protected by no formal employment contract. In general, this too − housework as unpaid non-employment − augments the subservient role of wives within marriage as the work provides neither extrinsic compensation nor a respected social status. Being unpaid, it gets treated as worthless and of no value. It is to these issues that we turn in the next section, which will build upon some of the arguments made earlier.

The structure of dependence

Arguments like these highlight the limitations of studies which attempt to assess marital equality simply by contrasting the effort each spouse puts into the domestic economy. Whilst providing a useful starting point, such an approach needs to be complemented by an examination of the structural basis of contemporary marriage. This means analysing the economic and social dependencies that occur within most marital relationships. Some of the issues raised in the previous two chapters are clearly pertinent to this and provide a convenient starting point.

As we have seen, some 50 per cent of married women are now employed compared to 10 per cent 50 years ago. This is quite a remarkable change in a relatively short time. Equally remarkable, though, from a somewhat different stance, is its converse: the fact that a full 40 per cent of married women under 60 are not employed outside the home. As shown in Table 3.5, leaving aside those over retirement age, women with dependent children are particularly likely to be 'economically inactive'. To put this another way, given current child-bearing patterns, being solely a housewife and mother is a normal stage in the 'career' of a wife, though most occupy it for a shorter period now than in the past.

During this stage of her life cycle, a wife is self-evidently economically dependent on her husband. Notwithstanding her part in transforming the wage into the household's living standards, domestic labour appears to be non-economic, adding nothing to family income. Instead this income is seen as consequent solely on the husband's effort in his work. It follows implicitly that his work is the more crucial, and hers the more dependent. Only by his efforts can the wife fulfil her role for without his earnings she would have to rely on state benefits to survive. He, on the other hand, could always purchase the services she provides through the market. (Such a view is maintained even though an unknown number of wives may be better off financially without their husbands. This applies not only to those families which could receive more in supplementary benefits than they obtain by working, but also to those whose family income is higher but where its division within the family leave wives and children in poverty (J. Pahl, 1980).)

As a result of these processes most full-time housewives accept that they are in an economically dependent position and often feel that they have little right to money to spend on themselves. As we saw in Chapter 3, this is so even when they appear on the surface to have full control of domestic spending, for, no matter how household income is organized, the money available to the housewife is normally for the family rather than her own personal consumption. It is rightly labelled 'housekeeping' rather than 'income', for it is not in any real sense payment for her effort for her to spend as she chooses. Her unpaid task is to manage that money so as to provide the best possible standard of living for her family. Because the money for doing this is usually quite limited, she will often attempt to stretch the housekeeping that bit further in ways that implicitly undermine her own worth. She may for example try to shop around for bargains to an extent that is only rational if her time has no value in itself. Alternatively she may 'make do' on her own requirements to a degree she would think unfair to impose on other family members (P. Hunt, 1978). In this context, the stereotype of housewives being extravagant is, like that of their spending their time gossiping, so far removed from reality that its continued existence can only be understood as a device that in its way helps husbands to maintain their dominant position by undermining the value of their wives' contribution to the management of resources.

From this one would expect the situation to be rather different when wives return to the labour force and earn an income of their own. To a limited degree this is so. Their financial dependence on their husbands is reduced in that they at least have some right to control the expenditure of their earnings and to use a portion of it for their own personal requirements. However, to accept this fully and argue that dual employment results in structural equality would be far from true. In large measure this is because the employment opportunities open to women generally, and married women in particular, continue to reflect and reinforce the conventional division of labour within the home. That is, rather than providing some counter to prevailing conceptions of domestic organization, married women's employment is superimposed upon the framework established in the formative, child-bearing and early child-rearing years of the marriage.

As emphasized in Chapter 3, with women's pay being approximately two-thirds of men's, even those wives employed full time earn on average significantly less than their husbands. In addition, though, many wives are only employed part time, so their weekly earnings are a lot lower than their husbands'. This means that a wife's earnings are seen as secondary to her husband's. His income is the one used to purchase domestic commodities essential for the family's well-being — rent/mortgage, food, power, etc. Her income improves the family's living standards, but does so by providing less essential goods and services, little luxuries that the family could, in the end, manage without. However arbitrary this division of income in fact is, it is maintained in principle, not least by wives who want to assert their control over the little they do earn. As a result though, the wife's financial contribution is effectively devalued and in practice her employment does not allow her the independence or freedom her husband's allows him.

Within this set-up, then, she remains dependent on her husband for the necessities of life. Equally though, because her earnings are secondary and less crucial than her husband's, the wife's prime obligation remains that of caring and providing for the domestic needs of the family. Her going out to work is seen as something of an optional extra, so normally provides little justification for neglecting these other, more important duties. The 'Catch 22s' of this situation are widely recognized. Take, for example, the need to spend some of her earnings on items that ease her domestic burden, or her desire, born out of guilt, to compensate her family for the disturbance her going out to work causes by buying them special treats. Both these can be seen as prima-facie evidence that the wife's income is not essential and consequently reinforce the evident truth that her employment outside the home is secondary to both that of the principal wage earner and her own responsibilities within the home.

Finch (1983) demonstrates another facet of the secondary nature of wives' employment in showing how wives are regularly incorporated into their husband's work in ways that few husbands are in their wife's. For example, as mentioned in Chapter 3, a wife's activities — her domestic routines, her opportunities for leisure, and even the pattern of her own employment — are frequently shaped by the demands and circumstances of her husband's employment. So too wives often take an active part in supporting their husband's work. Aside from the servicing tasks commonly associated with the housewife role, this support can range from, say, entertaining clients and colleagues to taking messages and acting as unpaid secretary. A minority of wives find themselves incorporated into their husband's work even more fully. For instance, some of those married to GPs or clergymen, or with husbands in the police or armed services, find their own social identity merges in with their husband's occupational role to a degree that limits their own activities and relationships. Others, whose husbands' work requires geographical mobility, may have to sacrifice their own employment and their existing network of friends for the sake of their husbands' careers. As Edgell (1980) and Finch (1983) argue, such processes as these indicate the higher priority given to husbands' jobs. The point to emphasize is that these things rarely apply the other way round. Few husbands organize their lives around their wives' employment to the same extent or ever provide the same sort of support. So in this respect too a wife's employment is generally treated as secondary and as less significant than her husband's.

In summary, it is evident that even when wives are employed, the structure of the marital relationship is normally not altered very markedly. As a result of occupational discrimination, the primary responsibilities within marriage continue to be governed by gender, and this in turn, of course, helps justify the continuation of occupational inequalities. The self-perpetuating and circular ideologies that arise out of this situation mean that wives remain financially dependent on their husbands even when they are themselves employed, and lack the economic freedom that his work gives him. This structurally inferior economic position of wives fosters many of the other inequalities that are apparent in the organization of contemporary marriages, so that one suspects that significant change could only occur if the economic opportunities open to wives first altered radically.

However, important though earning power is in sustaining these definitions of marriage, it is by no means the only factor shaping the inequality of conjugal relationships. Also of consequence are those patterns of everyday life which encourage the social dependence of wives on their husbands. As discussed in the last chapter, rather than simply being the result of decisions individual couples negotiate, the different opportunities husbands and wives have for social integration are shaped by convention and practices which exist independently of any particular marriage. These conventions and practices are part and parcel of the framework from which individual marriages are constructed.

The greater social dependence of wives on their husbands is encouraged by many of the factors discussed in the last two chapters. The social isolation inherent in housework; the daily and weekly spread of its workload, the limited opportunities to meet others because of its individual and privatized organization, the relative absence of 'free' time, not least when domestic responsibilities are combined with paid work; the sparsity of female-oriented leisure provision; all these and other features of women's experience as housewives and carers tend to leave wives more reliant on their husbands for social involvement than the latter are on them. This reliance is, of course, not total, as some informal relationships with kin, neighbours and other friends can be established and maintained independently of husbands. But without husbands' involvement the scope and extent of these 'independent' relationships tends to be restricted. As we have seen, wives tend to be encapsulated in the private domestic sphere far more than their husbands; the physical and symbolic boundaries of their lives tend to be drawn much closer to home. It is in this sense that the scope of these 'independent' relationships is likely to be limited. By and large, their active content is routinely dominated by domestic and family issues, as is well illustrated, for instance, by kin relationships whose focus is often on the mundane events affecting family members.

The social dependence of wives is particularly evident in non-domestic settings. For many wives, simply meeting people outside the home and taking part in activities which broaden their horizons by providing an alternative focus to the domestic concerns of the day can be problematic if they are not accompanied by their husbands. As a result of the male bias of pubs and social clubs, the relative absence of sports clubs, voluntary associations and other leisure provision catering specifically for the needs of women, the widespread fear of being attacked or embarrassed if out alone, and so on, developing interests and participating socially outside the home is that much more difficult for women lacking the 'patronage' of a male partner. Husbands, on the other hand, are much less likely to require their wife's presence; they do not need to be 'sponsored' in this way to engage in the majority of social activities. Without reiterating the arguments of the last chapter any more, it is in this sense that wives can be said to be more socially dependent on their husbands than their husbands are on them. This imbalance of social opportunities and the resultant need for wives to be accompanied by their husbands thus re-inforces the economic inequalities built into most marriages.

Of course this greater dependency of female on male partners does not occur only within marriage. It is part of the general structure of gender relations, and as such is reflected in the common modes of thought and language which often portray the female as something helpless and impotent (e.g. 'chick', 'doll', 'baby'). More interestingly, the organization and vocabulary of dating make the figuration of male dominance and female dependence quite evident. The male is traditionally the one who takes the initiative, chatting up the female and asking her out. She has to rely on more subtle guiles to show her interest. Once on the date, his dominance in looking after her is routine. He takes her out, rather than the other way round; he picks her up — possibly in more than one sense — and drives her home; he opens doors and orders meals; he arranges where to go and pays the bill; and so forth. The whole scenario is based on his active to her passive, his control to her deference.

More generally such patterns result from the routine inculcation of gender identity through differential socialization. From an early age (indeed often before they know what their age is), children are conscious of their gender and begin to construct a world in which gender divisions are central. Long before they leave primary school, and sometimes despite attempts to instill non-sexist ideologies in them, children become conscious that the genders occupy different positions within the social structure and that they can expect their lives to unfurl in a dissimilar fashion. That ultimately they do, however, is not simply a result of these different childhood experiences and expectations alone, but is rather the consequence of the intricate meshing of these assumptions with the reality of the social structures the genders face as adults. In other words, if socialization leads to an acceptance of particular ideologies, including sexist ones which specify more or less broadly that men and women fulfil different roles, these ideologies remain tenable, and thus essentially unquestioned, only because they match the external realities men and women, husbands and wives, face in coming to decisions — or rather non-decisions — about the roles they should fulfil. Clearly here the economic and occupational issues discussed earlier are part of this reality.

Important here too is the informal social pressure that friends, kin and other members of the peer group bring to bear, not just through their attitudes but also by their actions. Everyone else's acceptance of standard marital roles and organization serves to reaffirm habitually that such practices are indeed normal, even natural and hence inevitable. The very 'routineness' of conventional gender roles, especially those of husband and wife, makes it harder to adopt any others. Most people do not really try to. For those that do, 'normality' is asserted, and their deviance highlighted, in the comments, advice and questions of those they know. For example, reference is made to the 'innate' role of fathers as providers; the welfare of young children is discussed with working wives; husbands have their legs pulled for being under their wife's thumb; and so on. Such informal sanctions encourage the traditional division and inequalities, however dressed up, of marriage.

Female dependence within marriage is also encouraged by the assumptions that the state makes in many of its dealings with the family. While Britain has never had a co-ordinated set of family policies, its social legislation often presupposes, and thereby reinforces, particular forms of family life. As we saw in Chapter 2, the state's organization of schooling, health care and provision for the elderly is at least partially premised on the idea that in the majority of families somebody will be available to act as carer for other family members as necessary. While in principle the person who acts as carer in a family can be of either gender, in practice, for all the reasons discussed above, it is almost invariably a female, usually the wife/mother, who fulfils this role.

As will be discussed more fully in Chapter 9, the state does little to discourage or question conventional marital roles. Rather, as Hilary Land (1978; 1979; 1980; 1983) has shown in a stimulating series of papers, its relevant legislation is routinely framed in accordance with them. In particular the state's overriding acceptance that wives should be dependent on their husbands is revealed most clearly in the legislation designed to regulate family income. Many of the rules and procedures applying to this are explicitly formulated upon the assumption that a wife's primary responsibility is to act as housekeeper/carer to her husband and children, while his is to provide the family's income. Probably the best known instance is the ubiquitous 'cohabitation rule' which disqualifies any woman who is cohabiting with a male for five or more nights from receiving supplementary benefit in her own right. Similar principles underlie other aspects of supplementary benefit provision, and are also evident in the national insurance and income tax regulations. For example, while a married man can claim benefit for his wife simply because she is not employed, a married woman, even though paying a full contribution, can only claim benefit for her husband if he is actually incapable of paid employment. In other words, a wife is acceptable as a housekeeper/carer but for national insurance purposes a husband is not. Through mechanisms like these the state sanctions and encourages the conventional division of marital responsibilities. The rules and principles its agencies apply are usually quite compatible with the traditional views about husbands' and wives' roles within marriage, and so help sustain them by making them seem all the more natural and reasonable.

Conclusion

The argument of this section has been that marriage is not a relationship constructed solely by the two individuals most closely involved. It is a relationship that is shaped and constrained by the social structures that confront the couple throughout their married life. Their definition of their marriage; their view of the appropriate behaviour for each to adopt; the possibilities that they see open to them; these determine the organization of their marital relationship. However they are not based simply on individual preference but rather on preferences which are socially constructed and reflected in prevailing cultural assumptions and ideologies. Thus marriage is a structurally unequal relationship not simply because husbands dominate their wives, nor because wives' main responsibility is to service their husbands and families for no material reward. Marriage is essentially asymmetrical because it is a relationship constructed, played out and modified against a back-cloth of social inequality. Much of this inequality is economic but these economic inequalities are supported and fostered by a wide range of socially accepted norms and conventions which help assert that the married women's primary responsibility is to care for her family and home. The imbalance of opportunity open to males and females, husbands and wives, in our society both reflects and encourages a division of labour and responsibility within marriage that ensures the marital relationship continues, with whatever minor modifications may occur, to be asymmetrical. As we shall see in the next chapter, these same inequalities continue to shape women's lives when marriage ends.

6

Divorce and Single-Parent Families

The previous chapters have been concerned with the social organization of domestic life and the relationship between this and other spheres of activity. The argument has been that, despite appearances, the family is not independent of other social and economic arrangements, but that on the contrary its organization, and the activities its members perform, are structured and constrained quite markedly by the requirements of external agencies. In this, the gender-based division of labour in and outside the home is particularly important for it results in the tendency for married women's social lives to be centred quite firmly around family and home with relatively few opportunities for wider social involvement. Yet throughout the discussion of these issues the focus has been on what are often referred to as 'normal' families, families consisting of husband and wife, with or without dependent children. As a consequence rather little has been said about other family forms. This chapter seeks to redress the balance somewhat by examining the social and economic circumstances of single-parent families together with recent trends in divorce. It is this latter that will be considered first.

Divorce

As discussed in Chapter 3, there have been two major shifts in marriage patterns over the course of this century. Firstly, the proportion of people marrying has increased so that currently some 90 per cent of the population has married by their mid-forties. Secondly, people have tended to marry younger than previously, with, for example, the average age at marriage now being some two to three years younger than it was in the 1930s. These changes in marriage patterns, which indicate the increased social significance of marriage as a routine life event, have gone hand in hand with even greater changes in patterns of divorce, changes which themselves signify shifting marital standards. Thus, as shown in Table 6.1, the number of decrees absolute granted has increased substantially over the last 50 years. The increase has been most rapid since the passing of the 1969 Divorce Reform Act, though in reality this Act reflected rather than created these changes as the numbers involved were already growing rapidly by the time it was passed. The number of divorces occurring each year shows no signs of peaking, and more than matches the increased rates of marriage. As Table 6.1 also shows, the rate of divorce per 1000 married population has almost tripled since 1969, and has increased by some 2.5 points since 1971 when the new legislation became effective.

Table 6.1   Decrees absolute in England and Wales

	1931	*1951*	*1969*	*1972*	*1979*	*1982*
Decrees absolute	3,668	28,265	51,310	119,025	143,667	146,698
Rate per 1000 married population	0.4	2.6	4.1	9.5	11.6	12.1

Source: Social Trends, 1970; *Annual Abstract of Statistics*, 1981; OPCS Monitor FM 2 83/4

It is apparent too that people are tending to divorce at an earlier stage in their marriage. For example 10 per cent of the 1951 marriage cohort had divorced in 1975, approximately 25 years after their marriage. Yet a higher proportion, some 15 per cent, of those marrying in 1961 had already been divorced in 1975, i.e. after only 15 years of marriage (Leete 1979, p. 82). This trend of increasing numbers divorcing in successive marriage cohorts is likely to continue, so that estimates now suggest that something like a third of all marriages currently entered into will end in divorce (Haskey, 1982). Particularly at risk are those marriages contracted at an early age, as Leete's analysis reveals. Whereas the divorce rate per 1000 brides aged 20–24 who had completed five years of marriage was 23 in 1976, and only 18 per 1000 for those aged 25–29, it was 46 per 1000 for those who were married as teenagers (Leete 1979, p. 72).

It was sometimes argued that the increase in the divorce rate that occurred in the years immediately following the implementation of the Divorce Reform Act in 1971 was in large part a consequence of the 'backlog' of broken marriages in which the innocent party refused to sanction divorce. The new law, with its 'five year' clause enabling either spouse to sue for divorce irrespective of the other's wishes after five years of separation, led many legally intact but socially moribund marriages to be dissolved. Once this backlog had been processed by the courts, the argument went, the divorce rate would find its true, somewhat lower, level. While this argument correctly recognized that a significant number of empty marriages were waiting to be terminated, it underestimated the degree to which the new law itself reflected a gradually changing orientation towards marriage and divorce.

This continuing change in orientation towards divorce – and therefore towards marriage – has been characterized by Farber (1973) as a shift from a 'natural-family' paradigm or model to a 'legal-family' paradigm. In the 'natural-family' paradigm the elementary family group is taken to be a natural and universal unit. Marriage itself, within this framework, is governed by quite rigid rules, normally backed by legal and religious codes, of what is right and proper, appropriate and inappropriate, in the relationship between the spouses. Their obligations and responsibilities towards one another are laid down by custom and social convention rather than being individually negotiable. Marriage is a social fact, in the Durkheimian sense, external and constraining, of concern to the whole community and not just the individual couple.

Such a model of marriage is likely to predominate when the performance of the marital pair might have repercussions for the economic security of some wider kin group, a quite common feature of non-industrial economies. With industrialization and in particular the ascendancy of wage labour, the collective need for a fixed marital contract recedes. Instead marriage comes to be seen as more of a private, though legally recognized, arrangement between the two individuals most closely involved. Its rules are not fixed by convention, in any absolute fashion, but worked out by the couple, in theory without too much regard for the preferences of others. Equally, not being fixed, the marriage 'rules' can be changed and renegotiated as and when the conditions of domestic life alter. Under this second, legal-family paradigm, the purpose of marriage is not to sustain social order but to satisfy the idiosyncratic, and changing, personal needs of the couple.

Now just as the natural-family and legal-family paradigms involve different conceptions of marriage, so too they imply different criteria for divorce. Under the natural-family paradigm, divorce is discouraged as a threat to the natural social fabric. Where it is permitted, it is on the grounds that one partner's behaviour violates the externally specified rules of the marriage contract, as, for example, in the case of adultery, cruelty or desertion. Under the legal-family paradigm, divorce does not depend on miscreant behaviour but on the breakdown of the relationship as a source of fulfilment. Particular actions, like adultery, may be taken as an indication of such a breakdown, but of themselves are less important than the failure of the couple to sustain their personal commitment to one another. Thus, when the former paradigm is dominant, the divorce procedure is concerned with allocating and demonstrating blame and is consequently adversary in style. When the latter dominates, divorce, like marriage, is seen as a private arrangement, with the court's role being that of facilitating the legal separation and protecting the interests of all parties without need for recrimination. So the 1969 Divorce Reform Act in Britain can, from this perspective, be seen as part of the transition from a natural-family paradigm to a legal-family one. As such, it is not the cause of the increase in divorce rates, but a reflection of a change in contemporary conceptions of marriage. At the same time, though, it legitimates and hence reinforces this transition. It helps generate an acceptance that divorce is an appropriate solution to marital difficulties, even some that under the natural-family paradigm might be experienced as relatively short term.

Causes of divorce

In looking at the causes of divorce, it is necessary to separate two different levels of explanation: the structural and the individual. At the structural level, the concern is not with what happens to particular individuals or marriages but with the different conditions and circumstances in the society that either facilitate or discourage divorce as a solution to marital difficulties. Its focus is on the social and economic conditions that pattern the scale of divorce occurring at any time. Conversely, at the individual level, the concern is with explaining what happens in particular marriages. It asks questions about the factors that cause some marriages to last while others end up in the divorce courts. What is it that makes this marriage more vulnerable than that; this one more stable than another? Though the two levels of explanation are in the end related, they need to be analysed separately.

Some of the structural changes that have led to a higher divorce rate were raised in the previous section. Before discussing these more fully, a preliminary 'methodological' point is worth making. Divorce statistics measure divorce − a legal phenomenon − not the end of a marriage − a social one. A rise in the divorce rate in consequence need not necessarily mean that more marriages are being terminated. It could merely mean that the ending of a marriage is for some reason now more likely to be sanctioned and recorded legally than was previously the case. While no one would seriously suggest that recent increases in British divorce rates can be explained solely or even predominantly in such terms, in making historical (and cross-cultural) comparisons it needs to be recognized that divorce statistics are not a true reflection of the incidence of marital break-up (Chester, 1972; Brannen and Collard, 1982). Indeed only now that divorce is more easily available is there likely to be a high correspondence between the two.

As was already mentioned in discussing Farber's work, a major factor likely to affect the level of divorce in a society is the commitment that others outside the marriage have to its continuation. If marriage is defined as private, of concern principally to the married couple and having little external impact, divorce is likely to be more readily available. To quite a large degree, this is the case in Britain and other industrial societies where, above all else, marriage is seen to be about love and personal compatibility. The expectation is that marriage will be a — if not the — principal arena in which individuals find their personal fulfilment and emotional satisfaction. The growth of ideologies of companionship and equality within marriage both reflect and encourage this. Yet because marriage is defined in this fashion, because it is seen as an intense, personal and private relationship, the more likely it is to 'fail'. In a sense, it is caught here in something of a pincer movement. On the one side, the more that is expected of marriage and the heavier the burden of hopes and emotions it has to carry, the less likely it is to be found satisfactory. On the other side, again because marriage is essentially concerned with personal happiness and fulfilment, the 'support' it receives from outside diminishes. There is less pressure for a couple to stay together because their break-up has little impact outside the domestic sphere and causes fewer ripples than it would in a society where kinship is more central to the wider social organization. 'Since', as Goode has it, 'the only common enterprise is now the family itself, when this fails to yield the expected personal satisfactions, it cannot be surprising that the likelihood of divorce is greater than a century ago' (1971, p. 310).

A further important 'structural' factor related to the increasing divorce rate is the changed social position of married women in our society. Though, as earlier chapters have argued, men's and women's lives continue to be structured unequally, the social and economic opportunities now open to married women are certainly greater than they were earlier this century. To this extent marriage 'traps' women rather less than it once did. In particular, the opportunities there are for employment or, failing this, the availability of supplementary benefit makes separation and divorce a more realistic option than previously. For most women, the financial returns from either source are relatively low, as will be discussed more fully below, but they none the less mean that married women are no longer so tightly bound to their husbands by financial dependence. Given that wives are more likely than their husbands to be dissatisfied with their marriages (Bernard, 1976; Thornes and Collard, 1979), the existence of these alternative means of support for themselves (and their children) have made divorce more feasible and consequently increased its incidence (Cherlin, 1981).

One further factor affecting the level of divorce is the legitimacy accorded it in a society. In Britain, as divorce has become more common, so too its social and moral significance has diminished quite markedly. Whereas little more than a generation ago, there was a strong stigma attached to divorce, even for the apparently innocent party, this is now far less the case. People who have been through a divorce may still feel a sense of shame and failure, but the societal reaction is nowhere near as strong as it once was. As more and more people have some experience of divorce, either at first hand or through someone close to them being divorced, the less opprobrium it carries. In this way, divorce has become a more normal and less remarkable life event — one to regret rather than condemn. As a result, there is now less pressure put on couples who are having marital problems to stay together. This may be the initial advice, especially if there are children, but as the arguments and conflict become more prolonged, the pressure from relatives, friends and others to persevere in the marriage is likely to decline. They are likely to see divorce as a reasonable solution if the marriage is in sufficient trouble rather than something to be resisted at any cost (Goode, 1971). The point here, of course, is that what is defined as 'sufficient trouble' to warrant divorce itself changes as divorce becomes more common. Though divorce is still traumatic and not entered into lightly, what was once held to be tolerable within a marriage may now be seen as sufficient reason for divorce.

The way in which divorce is thought to affect children provides an interesting indication of our social imagery of divorce. Until the 1960s there was no doubt that divorce damaged children. Parents were encouraged to stay together no matter what their own circumstances for the children's sake. Since then, though, different ideologies have come into play. While divorce is still seen as harmful to children, popular wisdom accepts that living with parents who are in continual conflict with each other can be even more damaging. Far better, it is now believed, for the parents to separate so that the child can be provided with a less tempestuous and more emotionally stable home life. This changed imagery could well reflect reality — as the stigma attached to divorce reduces, so the difficulties the child faces and the anxieties generated may also decline. Equally, though, it can be seen as part of the process by which our culture has accommodated and legitimized divorce as a solution to marital discord.

While these structural factors help to account for the increased incidence of divorce, they cannot explain divorce at the individual level. In trying to understand divorce, we also need to look at questions like: Why is it that some marriages end in divorce while others do not? What is it that makes a particular marriage endure? Can factors that lead to marriages being 'high-risk' be identified? Unfortunately, the answer to these questions is that we, in fact, know rather little about the actual processes that lead to marital breakdown, notwithstanding the evident social, economic and personal importance of them. As Thornes and Collard comment at the end of their analysis of *Who Divorces?*:

> Research into the causes of marital dissolution, both in this country and in the USA, has so far not enabled the firm identification of any one, or even several, dominant variables. It therefore seems probable that the variables which characterize those who divorce will not only be both numerous and subtle in their interaction with one another but also likely to be indicative of a wide variety of different pathways to divorce. (1979, p. 132).

Indeed, in the main, those factors which have been identified as being correlated with high incidence of divorce take us little further than common sense would suggest. For example, couples who have only had a short courtship are more likely to divorce, as are couples with dissimilar backgrounds in terms of, say, class, religion or age. However, the single factor that is most frequently discussed in analysing marital breakdown is age at marriage. Teenage marriages are far more likely to end in divorce than those occurring later, as was discussed earlier in the chapter. The reasons for this are complex, as Ineichen (1977) demonstates in his analysis of the 'vortex of disadvantage' such couples face. To begin with, the courtship stage tends to be rather shorter for those marrying young than for other couples, so that they have less time to accommodate to each other and develop their relationship. In addition though, these couples also tend to be the most materially disadvantaged and are likely to have children early in their marriage. In Ineichen's own survey of 179 marriages in Bristol, the husbands of teenage brides were far more likely to be in manual employment than the husbands of older brides, with over a third of them being semi- or unskilled. These young couples were also found to suffer the worst housing conditions, with more than half the teenage wives having to start married life sharing a home with relatives. The personal strains that such difficulties create are, for these couples, likely to be exacerbated by their need to adjust to one another and by their likelihood of having a child early in the marriage. Nationally, Leete's analysis (1979) shows that some 20 per cent of all teenage brides are pregnant including 33 per cent of brides under 18. In Ineichen's research, nearly half the teenage brides were pregnant or had already had a child after eighteen months of marriage compared to a quarter of the older brides. So even discounting the possibility of poor marital selection and the increased likelihood of incompatibilities arising as the spouses mature and develop personally, it is not surprising that a high proportion of teenage marriages break down. In effect, the youngest, least experienced couples are materially the most constrained in respect of both housing and income, and have the least chance of organizing and constructing their marital relationship privately.

One-parent families

A major consequence of the increased divorce rate of the last 20 or so years has been the growing number of one-parent families, many of whom are socially and economically disadvantaged. At the present time, with about a quarter of all marriages ending in divorce, two-thirds of all divorces involve couples with children under 16 and roughly a quarter involves couples with children under five (Leete, 1979). Of course not all single-parent families result from divorce or marital separation. Many are created through widowhood and unmarried parenthood. Estimates of the numbers of different forms of one-parent families are given in Tables 6.2 and 6.3.

From these tables it can be seen that the total number of single-parent families has increased by some 50 per cent over the last decade, mainly as a result of marital disruption, though the number of unmarried mothers caring for their children has doubled in this time. While these figures are the official estimates, others suggest the numbers may be even higher. The National Council for One-Parent Families, for example, believes that there are now some 1 million single-parent families with 1.6 million children in them. Either way, there is general agreement that the numbers are

Table 6.2   One-parent families with dependent children

	1971	*1979*
Female-headed		
Divorced	120,000	310,000
Separated	170,000	200,000
Unmarried	90,000	140,000
Widowed	120,000	110,000
Male headed	70,000	100,000
Total number of one-parent families	570,000	860,000
Number of dependent children in one-parent families	1,000,000	1,400,000

Source: Popay, Rimmer and Rossiter, 1983

Table 6.3   Families with dependent children (percentage)

	1971–3	1975–7	1980–2
Lone mother			
Divorced	1.9	3.2	4.4
Separated	2.1	2.1	2.3
Unmarried	1.2	1.5	2.3
Widowed	1.8	2.0	1.7
Lone father	1.2	1.3	1.4
Single parent	8.3	10.1	12.1
Married couple	91.8	89.8	87.9

Source: OPCS Monitor, GHS 83/2

increasing and that roughly one child in eight lives in a one-parent family (Popay, Rimmer and Rossiter, 1983).

The circumstances and experiences of these one-parent families are by no means uniform. The economic and social situation of unmarried mothers is, for example, likely to be different from that of most widows and different again from those of the divorced and separated. Equally those single-parent families in which there are young children will have different problems to face than those in which the children are adolescent. None the less there are a number of regularities evident in the situation of most one-parent families. For instance, from Tables 6.2 and 6.3 it can be seen that nearly 90 per cent of these families are female-headed and that their number is increasing at a greater rate than are motherless families. As a result, many of these families are disadvantaged by the structurally based gender inequalities discussed earlier, especially those associated with the labour market. Equally, some research suggests that single-parent families come disproportionately from lower class backgrounds. In the National Child Development Study, for example, children whose fathers were in professional or managerial occupations were far less likely to be part of a single-parent family than children with fathers in semi- or unskilled work. Only one in 18 children from social classes I and II did not live with both their natural parents compared to one in seven children from social class V (see the discussion in Popay, Rimmer and Rossiter, 1983, pp. 12–13).

A point to emphasize about the statistics in Tables 6.2 and 6.3 — and others like them — is that they are cross-sectional and static. What they do is present a 'snapshot' of the situation at a given point in time. They give no idea of the movement there is in and out of the one-parent category, nor of their 'life-span'. Indeed, considering recent concern for this family form, we have rather little knowledge of the dynamics of single-parent families.

Of the evidence available, that of the General Household Survey is amongst the most informative. In 1979 it found that apart from those currently living in single-parent families, some 3 per cent of children under five were living in families 'reconstituted' to the two-parent form through remarriage or cohabitation, as were 6 per cent of five- to nine-year-olds and 8 per cent of 10- to 15-year-olds. (Popay, Rimmer and Rossiter, 1983). Certainly data such as this suggest that rather more than the one child in eight implied by the 'static' data will live in a one-parent family for at least some portion of their lives. Altogether, a significant minority of children will experience this family form at one time or another for shorter or longer periods.

Material circumstances of single-parent families

As mentioned earlier, there are quite important differences in the circumstances of the different types of one-parent family. Yet it is now well recognized that a great many one-parent families endure material disadvantages of a substantial form. In 1974, the Finer Report, the outcome of a Royal Commission into the conditions of single-parent families, estimated that approximately half of all fatherless families relied on supplementary benefit for their income. A further 45 per cent of the remainder had net income either at or below supplementary benefit level or else were only marginally above it. In other words, some 70 per cent of fatherless families were living at or very close to the official poverty line. There is little evidence that this has changed a great deal over the last ten years. Mother-headed families continue to be amongst the most materially disadvantaged groups in our society. The Study Commission on the Family has recently published one of the fullest discussions since Finer of the financial conditions under which one-parent families currently live (Popay, Rimmer and Rossiter, 1983). In this, it is shown that in 1979 some 50 per cent of female-headed single-parent families still relied primarily on state benefits for their income, compared to 5 per cent of two-parent families.

This heavy reliance on state benefits is a consequence of a number of factors. In particular, the structural inequalities of the labour market combine with the workings of the supplementary benefit system to act as disincentive for lone mothers to seek employment, the more so given the difficulty many experience in finding adequate childcare facilities at a price they can afford. Clearly social class is an important variable here. Those women with high educational achievement and occupational qualifications are more likely to be able both to earn sufficiently high salaries to maintain a more adequate standard of living and to develop their careers so as to achieve a level of social integration and personal fulfilment. However such women are in a minority, not least amongst those separated and divorced women who gave up education and employment to marry young and have children. Such women are disadvantaged twice over in the labour market, both as women and through having been married. As we have seen, the female sector of the labour market is consistently less well paid than the male sector. In addition though, the time spent servicing others' domestic needs often reduces wives' occupational potential and bargaining position. Their level of training, work experience, expertise, skill, seniority, and so on are all generally lower than they would otherwise have been had they not had household responsibilities tying them down (Delphy, 1984). On top of this, there is some evidence that lone mothers are concentrated disproportionately at the bottom end of the earnings league, being particularly likely to be employed in low-paying industries like the food, textile and distributive ones (Popay, Rimmer and Rossiter, 1983, pp. 50-l).

As a consequence of such factors, it can be recognized that employment offers many lone mothers only a very partial solution to their difficulties. In the end, the earnings they can achieve are too low to provide adequately for their families, so that even when employed many still rely on state benefit. In particular, the proportion of families claiming Family Income Supplement that are single-parent families is surprisingly high, even allowing for the fact that full-time work is defined for these families as 24 hours per week instead of 30. Popay, Rimmer and Rossiter (1983, p. 55) report that in December 1981 63,250 of the 131,510 families receiving FIS were single-parent families. Thus single-parent families made up virtually half the total claiming this benefit, and, as significantly, this represents a sixth of all those single-parent families dependent primarily on earnings for their income. Overall, evidence like this suggests that many employed single-parents, especially lone mothers, remain very close to the official poverty line, just as they did when the Finer Report was published in 1974. Once travelling and child-minding costs are taken into account, the benefits of employment are for many social rather than economic.

The low marginal returns of employment for many lone mothers are exacerbated by the regulations governing the provison of state benefits. Given the low pay of the female labour market and the costs associated with going to work, the claw-back element of the supplementary benefit system, whereby benefit is reduced as earnings rise, operates as a disincentive to employment. This was especially the case up to 1980 when the maximum permitted earnings were only £6, with benefit being reduced pound for pound for any income above this. Since then a new 'tapered' system has been applied to lone parents with benefits being reduced by only 50p for every pound earned between £4 and £20. While more generous than the previous one, the new system still effectively imposes a very high rate of taxation on earnings. Consequently many lone mothers find the marginal financial returns of employment are too low to make it worthwhile, irrespective of the opportunities it provides for much needed social involvement. This applies especially to part-time employment, a form in which lone mothers are notably underrepresented with only 25 per cent of them so employed compared with 36 per cent of all mothers (Popay, Rimmer and Rossiter, 1983 p. 49).

As would be expected, many one-parent families experience other forms of material disadvantage in addition to financial hardship. Housing was identified by the Finer Committee as one of the major problems many face and the evidence suggests that it remains so, though the degree of disadvantage here is less easy to measure than for income. To begin with, single-parent families are only half as likely as other families with dependent children to live in owner-occupied housing. Equally, they are twice as likely to be in council accommodation (Popay, Rimmer and Rossiter, 1983, p. 61) In addition, nearly a quarter of all single-parent families share housing with parents or friends compared with only 5 per cent of two-parent families (*General Household Survey*, 1980, Table 2.16). While sharing a home can alleviate problems of isolation and child-minding, it can also result in overcrowding and strain. Importantly too, single-parent families as a group tend to move home more often and have less security of tenure than other households, as is indicated by statistics on homelessness. In 1979, one-parent families comprised more than a third of all officially homeless households and over 50 per cent of those with children (*Social Trends*, 1981).

All in all, it can be seen from these data that single-parent families tend to be materially disadvantaged in comparison to two-parent families. Of course, there are important differences between one-parent families, as already noted. In particular lone fathers tend to be better off than lone mothers, and, within this latter category, widows better off than the divorced, separated and unmarried. But given that these last three types make up some 75 per cent of all single-parent families, it is clear that poverty is quite a common experience for lone mothers. As Chester notes, 'economic deprivation is normal for female-headed one-parent families and clearly this undermines the viability of [this] family form' (1977, p. 156). Indeed, given our knowledge of the effects of poverty and poor housing on family life − the increased health risks, the educational and cultural deprivation, the stress of constantly struggling to make ends meet, the lack of resources to participate in those social activities the rest of the population take for granted, and so on (Townsend, 1979) – it can be recognized that the economic hardships one-parent families face may in the long run be more damaging to their well-being than the absence of the additional parent/spouse in itself.

Children and divorce

About 60 per cent of divorces are between couples who have dependent children. In 1981, this involved some 160,000 children, as detailed in Table 6.4. To put this in broader perspective, the parents of something like a fifth of all children born this year will divorce before the children leave school (Haskey, 1983). Given this, it is quite important to ask what consequences parental separation is likely to have for the psychological development and personal well-being of those children involved.

Table 6.4   Ages of children of divorcing parents, 1981

Child's age	0–4	5–10	11–15
Number of children involved	40,281	67,582	51,540

Source: OPCS, Monitor FM 2 83/1

In short, the answer is that we do not really know, though the evidence there is suggests its impact is probably less than is often supposed. The major problem here is that surprisingly little research has been done on this topic especially in this country. A number of American studies have been published but many are beset with methodological and conceptual diffi-culties. A significant proportion, for example, start off linking divorce with pathological behaviour by taking as their sample children in trouble with the school or police, or who are in some way emotionally disturbed. They cannot in consequence tell us anything about the impact of family disruption on the majority of children who are not in this kind of difficulty (Levitin, 1979). Alternatively, some studies have asked parents and teachers about the behaviour and orientation of children who have experi-enced divorce and then contrasted this with data on children from intact families. The problem with this approach is that everyday assumptions about the impact of divorce on children are likely to bias what is perceived and reported, so that, in the absence of more objective measures, the findings are likely to indicate as much about these folk theories as they are about the reality of divorce (Bernard and Nesbitt, 1981).

A further difficulty is that a number of studies analyse divorce from a legal rather than social perspective, treating it as a once and for all event rather than as a process. Yet it is clearly experienced, both by children and parents, as a process, and one which is often quite drawn out. This is an obvious but none the less important point. In assessing the impact of divorce on children, the focus needs to be on the sequence of events that lead up to and follow on from the decision of the couple to separate rather than on the formal termination of the marriage in court (Hetherington, 1979). Unfortunately, as Richards (1982, p. 152) notes, while it 'seems very likely that the ''natural history'' of a separation may have a great deal to do with the way in which children react . . . this is a point that research has hardly touched on so far.'

The importance of conceptualizing divorce as a process is illustrated in the longitudinal study carried out by Wallerstein and Kelly in California (1979, 1980). One of their major themes is the importance of separating the short-term effects of divorce and separation from the longer-term ones. In the short term nearly all children experience divorce as a crisis period in their lives, as of course do their parents. How this crisis is manifested depends on the age of the child, but feelings of sadness, grief, anger and resentment are common. As might be expected many feel an increased vulnerability and uncertainty, worrying about their own and their parents' future. A prominent fear in younger children is of abandonment, while older ones may have a sense of being alone, based not only on the 'loss' of a parent but also on their perception of now being different from their friends. Wallerstein and Kelly characterize these responses collectively as a form of 'reactive depression' (1979, p. 469), and certainly all the available evidence suggests that this first stage is an extremely difficult one for children to cope with.

The crisis that occurs in the child's life at this stage is not just a consequence of the psychological turmoil that separation from a parent entails. While this is, of course, a major factor, it is exacerbated by the social and economic changes that so regularly accompany the formation of one-parent households. As we have seen, this is likely to involve a lower standard of living for the whole family including the children because of the reduced income available. It also frequently entails a move to a new home, the consequences of which may be particularly disruptive for children if it means their going to a new school and the loss of their previous friends in the neighbourhood. As Richards (1982) notes, children find such changes difficult to cope with at the best of times but their effects can be far more unsettling when they follow parental separation. In addition to these factors, many parents are themselves under a great deal of stress at the time of their separation and so are less able to provide the consistency of emotional support their children need to get them through this crisis period. Indeed in some cases, children are under the additional pressure of wanting, perhaps impotently, to help a parent handle their own evident anxiety and trauma.

While separation and divorce disrupts children's psychological and social well-being in the short run, it is far from clear what the long-term consequences are. Reliable research on this topic is so meagre that it is hard to draw any firm conclusions, especially as the little evidence there is is American rather than British. In one of the few longitudinal studies, Wallerstein and Kelly (1979; 1980) found that five years after their parents' divorce roughly a third of their sample of 131 children were doing very well on the various measures that were used to assess their adjustment. A further third had resumed what the authors term 'appropriate developmental progress' (1979, p. 471), but continued to have some periods of resentment and unhappiness. The remaining third were judged to be suffering from moderate to severe depression which was manifested in such things as delinquency, poor learning, drug abuse or apathy. While this implies divorce can have unfortunate long-term consequences for a large minority of children, the issue is confused by the fact that the sample was constructed from those children sent for counselling services and is thus very likely to be biased towards children initially experiencing most difficulty. In this light the fact that so many of the children were functioning adequately may be taken to suggest that the traumas of divorce are not as all pervasive or long lasting as common wisdom sometimes implies.

This conclusion is supported by other research like that by Kulka and Weingarten (1979) who examined the current circumstances of children whose parents divorced in 1957. They found relatively little evidence of any long-term consequences of divorce in their sample, arguing that such experiences have at most a minor effect on adult adjustment. Some other studies have reported differences between children from disrupted and intact families, with the former experiencing more problems in later life. However these differences tend to be fairly small, to conceal important variations within the intact and the disrupted groups, and often to disappear once other factors, especially economic ones, are taken into account (Richards, 1982). In Bane's words: 'Studies that adequately control for economic status challenge the popular homily that divorce is disastrous for children' (1976, p. 111).

The whole issue of the long-term consequences of marital disruption for children is indeed a murky one. Far more research is needed, particularly on the pre- and post-divorce situation of children and their families, before any firm conclusions can be drawn. It would seem though that divorce need not be as troubling in the long run as is sometimes thought, but that none the less it leaves its mark on some children. As Sprey (1971) argues, somewhat blandly, children's reactions to divorce are shaped by a complex set of factors — as indeed all child development is. To go back to the point made earlier, separation and divorce must be seen as a social process not as a single event, and their consequences interpreted in this light. In other words, what matters for children's welfare is not just the fact of divorce but the way in which the parental separation is organized and managed. Just as earlier research suggested that bad marriages were more injurious to children than divorce (Nye, 1957; Burchinal, 1964), so too the evidence now implies that much depends on the nature of the parental discord prior to the separation and on the quality of the relationship the child is able to maintain with each parent afterwards. Certainly, there is little evidence to support the view that a 'clean break' with the departing parent makes it easier for the child to cope in the future (Richards, 1982). Much more research is needed, though, on the long-term consequences of marital disruption on children. Only then can the differential impact of material, social, psychological and organizational factors be separated and an adequate knowledge of the most appropriate ways to support the increasing number of children caught up in marital separation and divorce be found.

Divorce, social isolation and remarriage

Earlier in the chapter the economic circumstances of one-parent families, especially female-headed ones, were discussed. In this section the focus will be on the social consequences of divorce and separation, principally again for lone mothers. As discussed in Chapter 4, females, especially those with domestic and childcare responsibilities, tend to have less opportunity for social involvement than males. Given that the majority of formal or semi-formal social activity is male-dominated or couple-oriented, single women, not least those past the first flush of youth, are quite likely to find it difficult to generate social relationships through such participation. As before, the consequence is that while informal relations of friendship and kinship are particularly significant in integrating these women socially, their opportunities for creating and servicing such rela-tionships are limited.

This is particularly unfortunate for many separated women as they often experience difficulty in maintaining the sociable relationships they have developed and built up whilst they were married. Many find that their social networks slowly modify and change, gradually coming to be dominated by others in a similar position to themselves, in a manner that demonstrates that the presence of a partner is far more relevant for social involvement than it appears to be on the surface. Slowly, as the separation becomes more long standing, as the initial concern wears thin, those married individuals and couples who used to be part of one's sociable network drift away. They tend to be seen a little less frequently; involvement with them diminishes. More than anything, this is illustrative of the principle of 'homophily' central to most forms of friendship. The emphasis on reciprocity and equality of exchange in these relationships firmly encourages the tendency for those involved to be of more or less similar status. This applies not only with respect to age, gender and class position, but also marital status. An interesting demonstration of this was provided by Zena Blau (1961). In her study of the widowed she found that the most lonely elderly were those who were out of phase with their contemporaries: those widowed at an age when others are still married, and those still married when their contemporaries are widowed. Tensions similar to those Blau describes arise in the friendship networks of the recently separated. Whether as a result of friends' split loyalties; the problems of 'pairing' the single at social events like dinner parties; the difficulty of servicing a couple tie by oneself and of maintaining equality and reciprocity in, for example, buying rounds of drinks; the hassles associated with the sexual advances which the husbands of apparently happily married friends make; all these and other seemingly minor tensions gradually create distance between those who were previously friends, and encourage their replacement by non-married others. While this leaves a relatively small 'hole' to fill for the still-married others, it can present major difficulties for the recently separated with their lack of resources, minority position and the difficulties they face in generating new relationships at a time when their confidence is undermined by feelings of personal inadequacy and failure following marital breakdown. The whole process was nicely summed up in the words of a recently divorced woman talking about her previous friends: 'I've crossed all those people off my visiting list. The trouble is they don't seem to have noticed!'

In theory various solutions to these problems of social isolation are possible, but most of them are not very practical for many unattached women. Greater career and occupational involvement provides an avenue for some, though for the majority domestic commitments and lack of qualifications combine with the inequalities of the occupational marketplace to make it more of a cul-de-sac. Even when single mothers are employed, the opportunites this provides for social involvement are limited by their own domestic responsibilities and, as importantly, by those of their fellow workers. As we have seen, the time most female employees have to develop sociable relationships with work-mates outside work is restricted by their need to be home for children, to provide meals and to catch up on domestic chores. Equally, taking up new hobbies and developing new interests so as to meet people is hardly a realistic strategy for the majority of separated women, given their lack of resources and confidence and the relative absence of suitable organized provision.

A rather different response has been the growth of clubs specifically catering for the separated and divorced. Admirable though the idea is of creating a forum in which mutual problems can be aired and support given, as Hart's (1976) research suggests, these clubs are more likely to act as marriage markets than to facilitate the development of many more wide-ranging social relationships. In routine social life, sociable relationships are developed through participation in various activities — work, hobbies, sports or whatever — that have a rationale over and above sociability *per se*. Instead, sociability is seen as almost incidental to the activity and hence natural rather than contrived. In contrast, contact clubs of whatever form are quite clearly contrived. Their explicit purpose is sociability; they have no other function. As such, they fit rather uneasily into our standard picture of normal patterns of social involvement. They carry a certain stigma and are seen, often by members as well as outsiders, as reflecting poorly on the social competence of those who need to go to them. As Hart (1976) showed, they consequently tend to defeat their own purpose by indicating the inadequacy of those who belong — hardly an auspicious framework for developing worthwhile relationships.

Thus our society has not only failed to develop adequate ways for providing emotional and material support for those coping with the often traumatic process of separation and divorce, but, as importantly, has failed to institutionalize mechanisms for integrating the divorced and separated into the mainstream of routine adult social life. They remain somewhat apart, despite their numbers, having an ambiguous and slightly stigmatized identity (Goode, 1965). Not surprisingly, then, the most common 'solution' for the divorced is to leave this status behind and re-enter the world of the married. As Chester argues, 'the absence of structured provision for the consequences of broken marriage . . . [presses single-parents] towards remarriage as the only normatively sanctioned and institutionally provided avenue of relief for their manifold (and at least partially socially induced) problems' (1977, p. 159). While accurate statistics on life-time remarriage rates are unavailable, current estimates are that upwards of two-thirds of divorcees adopt this 'solution' and eventually remarry, with the likelihood being greater the younger the person was at the time of the divorce (Kiernan, 1983). In the fullest British study to date, Leete and Anthony (1979) found that roughly half their sample of 1000 couples who divorced in 1973 had already remarried by the end of 1977, the majority within a year of their divorce.

In comparison to the status of divorcee, the attractions of marriage, or of a less formal, long-term stable union are evident, especially for females. As well as easing domestic and childcare difficulties and providing greater financial security, having a regular partner and being, once again, part of a couple encourages the development of fuller social networks and often leads to the individual being more fully integrated into social life. In addition, despite myths of permissiveness, the inconvenience of organizing sexual relations outside a stable union should not be underestimated, especially when children are present to reduce the privacy available. It is issues like this which led Delphy (1984) to argue that divorce should be seen as much as a continuation of marriage as a break with it. Her point is that while individual marriages may end, the institution of marriage continues to constrain and draw women back into it even after they have divorced. Of particular importance in this process are financial considerations, especially the way that marriage fosters women's dependence on a husband figure − if not this one, then some other one − by leaving wives chronically disadvantaged in the labour market. As she writes:

> When women marry or have a child they often stop working or indeed studying.. . . Ten years after the wedding day, marriage is even more necessary than before because of the dual process whereby women lose ground or at best remain at the same place in the labour market, while married men make great progress in their work as they are not hampered by household obligations.. . . Thus it can be said that, from the woman's standpoint, marriage creates the conditions for its own continuation and encourages entry into a second marriage if a particular union comes to an end. (Delphy, 1984, pp. 97–8)

Given all this, it is not really surprising that, as Hart has shown, many of the divorced and separated hold remarriage to be the ideal, the desired solution to the difficulties they face. The circularity of this is clear: in the absence of alternative 'solutions', the more desirable remarriage becomes; yet the more remarriage is seen as 'the only viable solution in a couple-oriented society' (Hart, 1976, p. 219), the less chance there is of developing alternative forms or mechanisms of social incorporation. From this perspective, the high rate of remarriage is less an indicator of satisfaction with the marital state, and more the operation of coercive, though perhaps latent, social pressure. As Chester notes, the crucial issue is 'the considerably lesser eligibility of available alternatives' (1977,

p. 159). It is this rather than romantic notions of marital fulfilment — though these are present often enough — that lead people back into marriage.

Reconstituted families

As the number of divorces and remarriages increases, so too does the number of families in which there are step-children and step-parents. These 'reconstituted' families take many different forms, depending on whether one or both of the new spouses bring children to the marriage, whether all their children reside in the new household, whether any new children are born in the marriage, and so on. The nature and quality of the relationships created by reconstituted families are obviously even more diverse. Yet while reconstituted families are undoubtedly increasing in number — at least in comparison to the recent past — as with so many issues related to divorce, our knowledge of their circumstances is very limited. Indeed it is remarkable how little interest has been shown in step-families not just by social scientists but by society in general. Adoption and fostering are covered by a range of regulations and laws, but step-families are left very much to their own devices (Robinson, 1980). One consequence is that we do not really know how many of these families there are or how many children are involved in step-relationships. The census, for example, makes no attempt to distinguish between natural and step-children. However what evidence there is suggests that about one in 14 children currently lives with step-parents. For instance, according to Burgoyne and Clark (1982, p. 290), unpublished data from the Family Formation Survey indicate that some 7 per cent of all children under 17 were step-children, while in the 1982 General Household Survey 6 per cent of children aged up to 16 lived with their natural mother and a step-father. Information is entirely lacking on the number of children involved in non-residential step-relationships.

By definition reconstituted families are different from those created by first marriages, however much those in the new marriage cling to the nuclear family ideal (Burgoyne and Clark, 1982). Those forming these families bring with them a history, a set of relationships, antagonisms and loyalties, that inevitably influence the pattern of their family life (Burgoyne and Clark, 1984). Whether they wish it or not, their relationships will be more complex than in first-time families. Walker and Messinger (1979) express a similar theme in arguing that the 'boundaries' around reconstituted families are different from those in other families. The very notion of 'family' implies a common identity and shared responsibilities between members. Each family is marked off and separated from other similar units, within limits making its own decisions and following its own schedules. In reconstituted families, this autonomy and independence is less clear-cut, especially where there is continuing contact with the non-custodial parent. In Walker and Messinger's (1979) terms, the boundaries of the family become 'more permeable' with remarriage. The new family cannot develop in isolation but needs to co-ordinate and accommodate its actions with those of the previously existing families. As an illustration, Walker and Messinger use the example of family rituals, like Christmas and children's birthdays, which normally serve to express family solidarity. For reconstituted families, these occasions can be much more problematic. Rather than symbolizing the unity of the family, they can highlight the different allegiances of its members. For instance, the involvement of the non-custodial parent in birthday and Christmas celebrations may be recognized by all as important for the child, but at the same time represent something of an intrusion for the new spouse and a reminder that their family life is 'imperfect' according to the conventional ideal.

A major problem for reconstituted families is the absence of socially recognized and approved roles for step-parents and step-children to follow. Earlier in the chapter, it was pointed out that our society has so far failed to generate effective mechanisms for integrating the divorced and separated into main-stream adult life. In a similar fashion, standard rules and guidelines governing step-relationships have not been established. In this sense, as Cherlin (1978) argues, remarriage is incompletely institutionalized in social life despite its high incidence. As he writes:

> because of their complex structure, families of remarriages after divorce that include children from previous marriages must solve problems unknown to other types of families. For many of these problems, such as proper kinship terms, authority to discipline stepchildren, and legal relationships, no institutionalized solutions have emerged. As a result, there is more opportunity for disagreements and divisions among family members and more strain in many remarriages after divorce. (1978, p. 636. Also see Maddox, 1975)

Cherlin is here recognizing the role ambiguity and conflict inherent in step-relationships. This ambiguity stems from the step-parent being at one and the same time both a parent and yet not a parent. The issue of just 'how much to be a parent' is, as Fast and Cain (1966) note, the central unresolved question. Importantly, the ambiguity in the relationship lies not only in the step-parent's own uncertainty about the degree to which she/he can and should intervene in different aspects of the step-child's life, nor in the step-child's reaction to such intervention, though these are both important. It also stems from the contradictory expectation that others — the spouse/parent, the non-custodial parent, relatives, friends, neighbours, etc. — have of the tie. As Giles-Sims argues:

> In some cases stepparents may be sanctioned for trying to become more like a parent . . . and in other cases they may be sanctioned for remaining in the stepparental role, which carries the weight of negative stereotypes and creates suspicion about degree of interest in and commitment to the children involved. This situation may place stepparents in a classical double bind situation, receiving pressure to become more like a parent at one level of communication and being told through other communicative means to remain at a distance. (1984, p. 119).

There is no simple solution to this double bind for it is unlikely that step-parenthood could ever be fully institutionalized in the sense of there being more or less precise guidelines governing appropriate behaviour. As Fast and Cain (1966, p. 485) emphasize, 'organizational disturbance in step-families is inevitable'; the contradictions and ambiguities in the relationship are structural and so will not easily disappear. On the one hand, the step-parent cannot simply fall into the parental role. The love and trust that develops between parent and child is not substitutable, especially when the child still has loyalties to the non-custodial parent. On the other hand, the step-parent is involved in the day-to-day life of the child, helping order all those routine events and happenings which are normally the province of parents. Within this context each side has to accommodate the other, a process which is bound to create some tension and conflict. Indeed it is not always recognized that this is a two-way process. As Walczak and Burns (1984) point out, children have to make allowances and adjust to the intrusion of a step-parent into their world as much as the step-parent has to fit into the patterns established in the existing family.

The ease or otherwise of this process of adjustment will depend on a range of factors — the age of the children, their relationship with the non-custodial parent, the compatibility of the step-parent and child, the length of time the relationship has had to develop, etc. The response to and of the step-parent also depends on the role that step-parent has in the new family. Because of the standard division of labour, the problems step-mothers and step-fathers face tend to be rather different. Generally step-fathers are likely to be less involved than step-mothers in their step-children's lives. As Ferri (1984) notes, some step-fathers will see their main contribution to the family in terms of the financial and emotional support they provide for the mother, though often the issue of discipline — traditionally the responsibility of fathers — can cause problems. Because of the parent/non-parent ambiguity, step-fathers may expect — and be expected — to exercise authority and control over children, yet not be sure how far they can take this. Tension is especially likely to arise if they do not share the same standards or methods of dealing with discipline previously established in the family (Burgoyne and Clark, 1984). The mother/wife may also feel ambivalent over this subject — wanting the step-father to be integrated fully into the family and accept responsibility, yet also feeling a desire to protect her children from someone who does not really understand them in the way they need to be understood. Equally the child may accept some direction from the step-father, but still question his right to impose his will. 'I don't have to do what you say. You can't make me. You're not my father.'

For step-mothers, the problems are rather different because of their greater involvement in the day-to-day life of the children. This obviously applies most to the minority of reconstituted families where fathers have custody of the children, but also to a lesser extent in families where children spend weekends or holidays with their father. Because of the conventional division of responsibilities within families, step-mothers are likely both to spend more time with their step-children than step-fathers and to be responsible for issues — the varied tasks of mothering and household organization — which impinge more directly on them. As a result, the adjustment each side has to make to the other's fads and foibles, likes and dislikes, is the greater and so consequently is the potential for minor niggles and disagreements to arise. Indeed, a danger in the relationship, especially with older children, is that small irritations — over, say, leaving clothes lying around or not being in on time for meals — get built up into major issues. Part of the problem here is that the somewhat tenuous solidarity between step-mother and child inhibits the 'natural' expression of anger and frustration. Whereas natural mothers can nag and argue with their children without undermining the relationship, step-mothers are generally wary of letting their feelings show too overtly for fear that it will disrupt the carefully constructed harmony of the new family. Yet, somewhat paradoxically, being 'on guard' like this can be more damaging to the relationship as resentment and irritation build up without being satisfactorily expressed or resolved. Though step-fathers experience something of these pressures, they usually do so less than step-mothers because they are not so involved in the routine supervision of the child.

A final point to make in this section is that it is not just the step-parent role — the pattern of behaviour expected in the relationship — which is ambiguous. Ambiguity and contradiction are often also present in the feelings step-parents and children have towards one another. Whereas the love and solidarity between parents and children is in a sense unconditional, this is rarely true of step-relationships. Here loyalty is much less well grounded, being firstly mediated through the relationship each has with the real parent/spouse and secondly constrained by the ties there are to the other real parent. The tensions this can create in step-children are now well recognized. Walker and Messinger recount the story of 'the little girl who stood helping her father's new mate do the dishes, saying, apparently quite happily, "I hate you, I hate you." ' They go on to point out how other children 'seemingly test the new adult by permitting occasional moments of sharing or closeness only to be followed by immediate rejection' (1979, p. 190). Such events appear to be experienced at some time or another by most step-parents.

In their turn, step-parents often have similarly ambiguous emotions towards their step-children, feeling both a sense of commitment and imposition, a desire to be loved yet a resentment at having to put up with them. Such feelings are hardly surprising given all the dilemmas and contradictions discussed above. At the heart of the problem lies the different significance of children to parents and step-parents. Whereas children are taken, ideally, to bind their parents together and symbolize their unity, step-children in effect do the opposite. Rather than being a joint 'creation', socially as well as biologically, step-children represent an unshared past and a somewhat divided present. Consequently, even while fully understanding and supporting the parent's love and commitment to the child(ren), step-parents none the less often feel some resentment at the way they intervene and disrupt their own relationship with the parent. At the one level, the solidarity between parent and children, the alliances they form and the loyalty they have, can be accepted as entirely natural and right. At another though, like the children's rejection of them, it signifies the boundaries there are within the family and the 'outsider' status the step-parent has. Under these circumstances it is understandable that ambiguous feelings develop, though as before their negative aspects cannot easily be expressed, partly because they appear on the surface so petty and unreasonable and partly because there is no solution anyway. If, as often happens, the step-parent's irritation is vented on the parent, the latter may try to appease matters by 'stepping in' more between the step-parent and the children and shielding them from each other. This, though, is often counterproductive as it reinforces the boundaries within the family that lie at the root of the problem. Undoubtedly it takes a good deal of tolerance and understanding on all sides to cope with these various issues and resolve them satisfactorily. Indeed, against this background, we can begin to appreciate why divorce rates appear to be higher amongst second marriages than first ones. The problems that the remarried couple with children face are much more complex than those encountered in first marriages.

7

The Elderly, the Family and Community Care

An area of family and community life that is currently giving rise to social concern is the care the elderly receive. Our attention is regularly drawn to those elderly who, alone and isolated, are unable to cope properly by themselves. According to some, the major problem is that families can no longer be relied upon to provide the elderly with care and security in the way that was common in the past. In this view, the traditional extended family has given way to the smaller nuclear form in which there is little scope for the elderly whose needs are not compatible with the comparatively selfish life-styles of today's society. Without any useful role to fulfil and accorded little respect, the elderly represent a social and economic burden that families are all to ready to ignore or leave to others. Yet at the same time, as part of the general privatization of family life, community solidarity has also broken down so that there are few people prepared to offer the elderly alternative forms of care or provide for their needs. Consequently the state, and to a lesser extent voluntary organizations, have had to act in lieu; to step in and take over responsibilities that in a more moral society the family and local community would automatically assume.

While views such as these are regularly confirmed by media and other representations, at best they are distortions of reality and at worst completely misleading. In particular there is surprisingly little evidence to support the view that families are failing to care for the elderly. The numerous studies that there have been of the elderly attest to the routine, active support and assistance their families give the elderly and demonstrate that on the whole the isolated old tend to be those without direct descendants to care for them. In this chapter the nature of family provision for the elderly will be examined. The potential there is within the wider community for generating forms of 'community care' for the elderly (and other dependent groups) will also be assessed. Before doing this, there are two aspects of the above portrayal that warrant critical comment.

Firstly, despite their reference to the past, such views are historically naïve. They fail to appreciate the degree to which care for the elderly is, in a real sense, a new problem. While a few individuals in the past lived to an old age, the great majority did not. So whereas in contemporary times, a person can expect to live long enough to see their great-grandchildren, in pre-industrial England the majority of the population could expect to die soon after their grandchildren were born. As Stone (1979) shows for example, life expectancy at birth was only 32 in 1640, compared to 70 now. The same feature is shown quite graphically in Table 7.1. Particularly noticeable here is this century's increase in the number of people aged 75 + and 85 + in the population. Over the course of this century, these will have grown respectively two and four times as fast as the 65 + population, which itself has increased more than five times as fast as the general population.

Table 7.1   Age structure of population (England and Wales)

	Thousands				Percentage increase
	1901	*1951*	*1981*	*2001*[a]	*1901 – 2001*
Total population	32,528	43,815	49,219	51,270	58
65 and over	1,529	4,840	7,413	7,287	377
75 and over	396	1,581	2,856	3,314	737
85 and over	50	201	514	778	1,456

[a] projected

Source: Rossiter and Wicks, 1982

Secondly, the above views are deficient in implicitly treating the elderly as a single category, that is, as a specific group of people who all face similar difficulties and consequently need equivalent support. The image they conjure up is of the infirm old who are socially dependent and unable to cope with the routine of daily life on their own. A proportion of the elderly clearly are in this position, but a majority at any time are equally clearly not. If the elderly are defined as the 65 +, many obviously remain quite capable of living independent lives and would feel affronted if anyone were to suggest otherwise by implying they now need family assistance. Indeed, contrary to the popular image, this in itself can be a problem for families. Finding ways of providing a degree of support without threatening the elderly's self-image can be quite tricky. As with other age groups, independence is highly valued as a symbol of competence and is not given up very readily. The important issue here though is that the needs of different sections of the elderly are not the same. The healthy and mobile 65 + do not require the help which the infirm 80 + do; the widowed may need support of a rather different character from the still-married; and so on. In assessing the role that families — or for that matter the state — play in providing care for the elderly, such differences need to be borne sharply in mind.

This can be put in another way. Rather than being expressed by the somewhat static formula of 'the family' and 'the elderly', the issue here is better conceptualized as a question concerning the nature of the relationship between two or more generations during different phases of their family and life cycles. Perceiving the relationship in this way as more of a process — like ageing itself — helps avoid the pitfalls of stereotyping the elderly and encourages a more adequate appreciation of their involvement with their families. The point here is that the older generation do not suddenly emerge as a problem that families have to deal with once they reach the age of 65, 80 or whatever, but rather that with time there are gradual shifts in the exchange basis of their continuing relationships. In other words, the character of the generational relationship is slowly modified as the requirements of each side alter with their changing circumstances.

Here it is worth emphasizing the fact that while the majority of people do not normally live in three-generational households, most are involved quite actively in three-generational family relationships, demography permitting. The various kinship studies there have been, whether of working-class or middle-class families, in urban or rural settings, all demonstrate that the solidarity of the parent—child tie continues after the second generation becomes adult, leaves home and has its own families. These relationships only very rarely break down completely, though there may, at times, be some degree of friction (Allan, 1979). The early studies of established 'traditional' working-class localities highlighted the crucial role of mothers especially in helping their adult daughters cope with the routine pressures and demands of their daily life (e.g. Young and Willmott, 1957; Rosser and Harris, 1965). Later studies of middle-class kinship similarly emphasized the continuing support the parental generation gives, though the form this support takes is affected by their rather different economic and geographical circumstances (Bell 1968; Firth, Hubert and Forge, 1970). Barker's (1972) work is particularly interesting in this respect for, along with Bell's (1968) study, it shows how parental support of the younger generation in the early stages of their marriage permits the older generation to continue being involved in the lives of their apparently independent children. The role of grandchildren is especially significant in cementing the relationship between the first and second generations. As Rosser and Harris's perceptive respondent Griffith Hughes noted: 'Grandchildren? Well, yes, there of course is the real tie'

(1965, p. 8). Firstly, grandchildren provide a focus for grandparental —parental contact and involvement. And secondly, they mould this relationship by incorporating the generations in a system of exchange, involving gifts and services, which, being directed at and hence mediated through the still-dependent grandchildren, provides material advantage for the second generation without threatening their independence (Bell, 1968).

It is against this nexus of existing solidarity that relationships between the elderly and their families develop. On reaching retirement age the majority of the elderly will not need any additional support or care, although their family ties may become more central to their identity than they were previously. To the extent that increased age involves some degree of 'disengagement' (Cumming and Henry, 1961) from activities previously undertaken, then those activities and relationships that remain are likely to become more significant. Of course, the degree to which increased age does entail such disengagement will depend on the patterns developed by each individual over the previous years. Some have a range of interests and non-occupational pursuits that take up their time and are most effective in integrating them socially. Equally some, because of temperament or habit, are quite adept at developing new relationships to replace any they are no longer involved in. Others are far less active and less capable of creating new relationships and so suffer greater isolation. In either case, as the process evolves, the elderly tend to rely more heavily on their children and grandchildren for social involvement than previously. Slowly the latter become more important figures in the elderly's social landscape than they are in their children's or grandchildren's. Their children's circumstances are unlikely to have altered much while, if anything, their grandchildren will themselves be becoming more independent as they approach adulthood and consequently need their grandparent's attention rather less. So gradually a social imbalance is created between the generations as the elderly's alternative modes of social involvement become more limited.

This structural imbalance in the exchange basis of the relationship between the two generations is an incipient process, often developing gradually over a number of years. While its primary cause lies in the disengagement of the elderly from various social activities and their difficulty in finding compensating alternatives, its form is a measure of the long-term solidarity that routinely exists between the generations. It is a reflection of the moral commitment − diffuse but enduring, as Schneider (1968) depicts it − that our kinship system engenders. The constant cultural representations about its demise and the lack of solidarity between the generations should be seen as a mechanism that helps ensure its continuation by furbishing a level of guilt and potential stigma should there be a failure. Yet at the same time the contradiction is that the younger generation should be motivated by genuine concern and caring rather than by duty or moral pressure *per se*. Otherwise the relationship's imbalance and the elderly's social dependence becomes too overt to be acceptable to them. The support needs to be given in a manner that allows the elderly's appearance of social competence to be sustained.

At particular stages the elderly's social dependence on the next generation becomes more marked, for example with widowhood or increased infirmity when the elderly's life style can alter radically and their needs become quite different. Indeed, generally with age the increasing frailty of the elderly requires a rather different form of support from the younger generation. Its 'tending' element (Parker, 1981) — the provision of more personal services, like help with shopping, cleaning, cooking, personal hygience, and so on — is likely to increase and result in additional burdens being placed on the second generation with repercussions for their own life style. The ability of the second generation to respond to the changing needs of their parents in old age will obviously depend on their own personal circumstances — their geographical location, their other domestic and familial obligations, their occupational commitments, their own age and state of health. What is noticeable is the extent to which families are prepared and able to mould their own lives to meet the needs of the elderly. In this respect 'the family', as Litwak argues, is a remarkably flexible and adaptive agency, capable of meeting the changing particularistic needs of its defined members — which for this purpose includes parents as well as children.

Many studies have pointed to the significant role that families play in caring for the elderly. While only a minority of the elderly routinely require help from others at any one time, where help is needed much of it is provided by family members, either inside or outside the household. In many cases the person providing support will be the spouse. However as the support and care that is required gradually becomes more extensive with increasing age, the more likely it is to be provided by other relatives, principally daughters or daughters-in-law. Study after study attests to the crucial role such relatives play in sustaining the elderly and providing those who require it with assistance in such tasks as preparing food, shopping, laundering and toileting (Hunt, 1978; Equal Opportunities Commission, 1982; Nissel and Bonnerjea, 1982; for a summary see Rossiter and Wicks, 1982).

Two points about this family care are worth stressing. Firstly the real costs of providing care can be very high. In a sense with increasing frailty, the problems faced by the elderly become less the social ones of disengagement and isolation — though these remain — and more health care and medical ones. The consequence is that the support they require fits in less easily with all the other activities family members normally expect to engage in. Gradually, the tending they need becomes far more demanding and time-consuming. In effect, it is the equivalent of a full-time job, though it differs from employment in precisely the same ways that being a full-time housewife/mother does, being privatized, unpaid, fragmented and without fixed hours. In particular, as the studies by Nissel and Bonnerjea (1982) and the Equal Opportunities Commission (1982) show clearly, caring for the elderly can be physically wearing and emotionally draining. For example, lifting and carrying the elderly and dealing with the washing and laundering that results from incontinence is hard work, especially for those who are themselves no longer young. In many instances, this is made worse by the tiredness and strain induced by being on constant call and having sleep regularly disrupted, with few opportunities to relax and recharge batteries through leisure activities. Further, caring for an elderly person, especially in the same household, can often generate a good deal of friction and emotional tension in relationships with other family members, particularly spouses.

The second point to stress is that, while here we are talking of family support, and while caring for the elderly can make demands on all family members, the brunt of the burden is undoubtedly borne by women. Just as the bulk of housework and childcare is undertaken by mothers, so too by far the largest portion of the routine tending for the elderly is provided by daughters, and occasionally daughters-in-law. Their domestic responsibilities are 'naturally' extended to incorporate the care and support the elderly require. Not only are women seen as more suited for and skilled in these matters, but additionally, as Ungerson (1983) has pointed out, many of the more intimate tasks of tending, especially those to do with personal hygiene, have taboos attached to them that lead to their being defined as essentially women's work. A striking illustration of the consequences of these factors is provided by Nissel and Bonnerjea (1982) who calculated that on average husbands in their study spent some eight minutes per day actually caring for an elderly dependent relative compared to the two to three hours spent by their wives. While this point has been made before, it warrants repeating: any discussion of 'family support' for the elderly — or any other dependent group — is as misleading as it is helpful. The support at a daily level is almost wholly given by women and is defined as a development of their routine domestic role. This responsibility for providing care for the infirm elderly has major repercussions on their own social activities at a stage in their life cycle when they might be looking forward to greater freedom as other claims on their time decline.

Community care

While most people would recognize the desirability and morality of the elderly being cared for by their own families, the cost of this caring for individual family members should not be forgotten. At the same time it has become clear that the traditional form of state provision for the elderly in large scale 'asylum' type institutions is both socially undesirable and expensive. In particular the 'totality' of these institutions — the extent to which they exercise control over every facet of a resident's life — is now recognized as encouraging a level of dependence which is socially and economically counterproductive (see Goffman (1964) for the classic analysis of these issues). As a result, more flexible policies designed to enable the elderly — and other dependent groups such as the mentally ill and the physically and mentally handicapped — to be cared for within communities have emerged. Yet the fine sentiments many of these policy initiatives embody have not been acted on with sufficient determination. In particular, while most formulations emphasize the need to spread the responsibility for caring more widely throughout the community, in practice relatively little has been done to achieve this. As we shall see, one of the central problems that remains is graphically expressed by the catch phrase 'Who cares for the carers?' Yet without realistic measures to ensure this, the whole notion of 'community care' is a nonsense.

Indeed the notion is in any case a highly ambiguous one, an ambiguity which mirrors that of 'community' itself. This ambiguity lies in the idea of community as territory or locality, on the one hand, and as integration or involvement on the other. If the emphasis is on locality, then community care might be taken to imply 'care in the community' in the sense of the institutional and residential units — homes, hospitals or what have you — being geographically located within normal residential areas rather than set apart from them like the traditional asylums. Clearly though, without some greater involvement with the 'host' community, such a form of care provision hardly warrants the label 'community care'. Greater involvement may be generated if, as is usually the case, the units located within ordinary residential areas are smaller in size and scale than asylum-type institutions. This may encourage access by those living nearby, though often local residents object to having such units in their particular neighbourhood, especially if they are for the handicapped or mentally ill. More importantly, small-scale units are likely to reduce the totality of the institution for its residents. Rather than having all their needs organized and met by the institution and its employees, they would have more opportunity to make use of the services and amenities provided in the immediate area, and hence become more involved in local relationships. For example, they might use local shops, leisure facilities, medical and social service personnel, and so on rather than rely on those provided by and located within the institution.

This model of care in the community may, in policy terms, be a realistic one to aim for, and from the residents' viewpoint has the advantage of discouraging dependence and institutionalization. Yet it is clearly more suitable to some groups than others as it assumes a level of mobility that is not found amongst all those in need of care. It may thus be more appropriate for, say, the mentally ill or even the mentally and physically handicapped than for the more infirm elderly currently receiving institutional care. More importantly in the context of the present discussion, it still represents a quite limited conception of community care. For most people, the notion signifies a more active role for other members of the community than is involved here, with the 'integrative' aspect of community being emphasized as much as its 'territorial' one. From this perspective, in other words, community care means not just care in the community but also care by the community (Bayley, 1973). Thus, as well as the provision of professional, specialized services within the locality, the informal resources of the community − that is, the help and support that can be offered by friends, neighbours, volunteers and so on − should be drawn upon so as to create a more socially integrative form of care provision that will help regenerate community solidarity as well as benefiting those in need.

To clarify the issues involved here it is appropriate to reconsider Litwak's formulation of the relationship between formal and informal care provision which was discussed in Chapter 2. As will be recalled, Litwak's argument is that formal organizations and bureaucracies, being universalistic and achievement-oriented, are able to provide those services which are systematic and regular. What such organizations cannot do so readily is react to irregular and idiosyncratic needs. For these some form of primary group or network, able to act particularistically, is required. As we have seen, this primary network is normally based around family relationships, though in practice is better characterized as the 'modified elementary family' rather than the 'modified extended family' Litwak suggests.

Within this framework the implications of community care can be seen to be twofold. Firstly there is the idea just discussed that the professional, specialized and often bureaucratically organized services required by those needing extensive care should be locally based. As well as discouraging any tendency for the segregation of those in need from others in the locality, this is likely to make such service provision less rigid and more responsive to the special requirements of the area. Secondly, there is the idea that the primary network of others who support the bureaucratic organizations by providing them with particularistic back-up can itself be extended. Rather than consisting only of immediate family members, it could theoretically be broadened to include a range of friends, neighbours and others who all provide informal care and support as it is required.

Before discussing whether in practice this second theme, which lies at the heart of much of the community care debate, is feasible, and consequently whether social policies could be satisfactorily organized around such an extension of the primary caring network, the crucial distinction which is contained in Litwak's analysis needs underlining. His contrast is not between professional or paid support, on the one hand, and voluntary or unpaid support on the other. His distinction is between support which because it is required in a routine and regular fashion is conducive to bureaucratic organization and formal provision, and support which is by its nature required more haphazardly and idiosyncratically and hence cannot so readily be provided formally. The distinction, in other words, is one or organization not of pay or even expertise or specialization, though these enter into it.

This point is important for in practice the care and support required by many of the elderly (and others) for whom community care is seen as appropriate is most decidedly routine and regular. It is needed constantly and not just on occasion or haphazardly. Indeed it is the long-term burden of constantly providing support for those with chronic needs that is so difficult for families to carry. Thus, for such people at least, the support they and their carers receive from the 'community' needs to be regular and reliable. In consequence, there is no intrinsic reason, apart from cost, why this support is best provided by the voluntary or informal sectors. On the contrary, because their need is for systematic support, basing policy upon the assistance informal contacts like friends, neighbours and other community members can provide may be singularly inappropriate.

Community care and informal relationships

In any case the potential for informal contacts to provide assistance of the necessary form is easily exaggerated. The idea that with a little encouragement networks of friends, neighbours and others within a locality could be orchestrated to provide effective support for those in need is not as self-evident as some proponents of community care assume (see, for example, the Government White Paper *Growing Older* (DHSS, 1981) or the Barclay Report (1982) on the future of social work). In part, what lies behind the belief that they could be is the lingering appeal of the communal solidarity found in the type of traditional working-class localities studied in the immediate post-war period (Mogey, 1956; Young and Willmott, 1957; Dennis, Henriques and Slaughter, 1956; Hoggart, 1957; Jackson, 1968). In these close-knit communities the elderly were rarely isolated or left to cope on their own, as there would always be someone on hand to check that they were all right and to provide help whenever it was needed. (This, at least, is the image. Townsend's (1957) study of the old in Bethnal Green suggests it was less likely to be true for those without close kin in the locality.) Either way, the view that equivalent forms of communal solidarity could be recreated under contemporary urban conditions − even if they may need more formal co-ordination and encouragement than in the past − seems questionable. As mentioned in Chapter 4, the social and economic conditions that led to the development of extensive local networks in these areas have disappeared. Essentially what held these communities together was poverty − insecure and generally low wages, poor housing, shared amenities, and the like. Interdependence was generated by the lack of resources and the need to co-operate over the use of domestic facilities of one sort or another. To quote Philip Abrams, in such localities

> three circumstances impel the growth of neighbourhood care: *extreme social homogeneity* because in every respect everyone is in the same awful boat; *permanence* because there is no prospect of anyone around you getting into any other boat; and *threat* because the waves and winds could overturn and drown the whole lot of you two minutes from now, tomorrow, next week, anytime. (1980, pp. 14−15; emphases in original)

As Abrams goes on to discuss, such constraints within the locality invariably foster a mutual dependence, one which is generally based upon a necessary yet none the less calculative reciprocity (see also Abrams, 1977, pp. 129–35).

But 30 years on, such conditions no longer flourish. Poverty certainly still exists, but its form is different. Most of the slum areas studied, and others like them, have been cleared and their populations rehoused. No longer are facilities and amenities shared; no longer are people so dependent on their neighbours; no longer are they trapped by their locality in quite the way they were. Of course there are exceptions. The poor, the handicapped, the infirm elderly are especially likely to be constrained by geography. Equally, as was discussed in Chapter 3, many housewives and mothers of young children are effectively tied to their homes and localities, but the conditions they now operate under are distinct from those of their parents and grandparents. The point is that with changing material circumstances — increased living standards, improved housing, greater mobility, the greater employment of married women, etc. — the basis of the solidarities described in the traditional studies have withered, and cannot in consequence be easily resurrected.

Equally, though, the view that non-kin normally played a significant part in informal caring in the traditional urban communities can be questioned. Certainly there is comparatively little evidence in the monographs themselves that they did. As mentioned in Chapter 4, on close reading it is clear that people were differentiated from one another on the basis of whether they were kin (Allan, 1979). Whereas there was intimacy between family members — interpreted quite broadly — there was far less between non-kin. Even though the latter may happen to know a good deal about you through local gossip, they tended to be defined as people to chat to and be friendly with rather than as people with whom to share feelings, concerns and problems. In other words, they were generally 'familiars' rather than 'intimates' in that relationships with them tended to be 'public', mainly occurring in non-domestic, open settings: the street, the pub, at work, in the stairwells or at the shops. Only rarely and on special occasions did non-kin venture into each other's homes. Given this demarcation between kin and non-kin, it seems unlikely that non-kin were routinely involved in informal caring. As a result of the way the relationships were organized, such caring was inevitably seen as being predominantly a kinship obligation. Consequently it would be mistaken to think that, even if traditional solidarities could somehow be recreated, the job of caring for the elderly or helping families with this care would necessarily be shared more widely. The more general point here concerns the need to consider the organization and 'content' of different categories of relationship in creating appropriate strategies for fostering informal care, for only then can their relative potential for providing particular forms of informal support be gauged. As will become apparent, studies which have examined the normative patterning and exchange content of informal relationships, in particular kin, friend and neighbour ones, suggest that it is most unlikely that they can all be successfully incorporated into a system of informal caring.

One of the most important sets of relationships from the community care perspective is that of neighbouring. Being so readily on hand, incorporating neighbours into the informal network of carers for the elderly is an evident strategy. Yet if we exclude those kin who happen to live nearby, then the dominant form of neighbour relationship in contemporary society is not one which includes an element of caring. Indeed it can be better characterized by the concept of 'friendly distance'. That is, most people aim, without always succeeding, to maintain friendly, cordial relations with those they live near to but do not seek to become highly involved with them. Most neighbours value their privacy and do not want their neighbours interfering in their lives or forever being on top of them. What is called for is a reciprocal respect for each other's personal space and the exercise of control over behaviour likely to cause disturbance (Abrams, 1977; 1980).

Within this pattern, the contingencies of everyday living often result in more active co-operation between particular neighbours with each helping the other out in small ways — taking in parcels, letting in repair men, keeping an eye on the house and feeding the cat while one is on holiday, and so on. As these services are relatively minor, they are easily reciprocated and do not normally escalate to involve either side in extensive inconvenience. Nor do they necessarily lead to a high degree of social involvement, though this is more likely amongst some groups such as full-time housewives who, as we have seen, are often otherwise isolated. More generally, the essence of good neighbouring lies in maintaining the tension between co-operation and privacy, helpfulness and non-interference, between friendliness and distance.

It follows that the predominant organization of neighbour relationships is not particularly suited for the sort of caring the broader community care models imply. Consistent caring is not an obvious extension of neighbour relations but a break from their routine patterning. It would create a greater dependence, a reduction in privacy, and, of course, the possibility of public recognition of one's private troubles. While many people profess in the abstract to be willing to provide some care for neighbours, in practice such caring is rarely forthcoming. In any case not everyone would be willing to receive it unless there was a more secure basis of solidarity than neighbouring alone. Yet if there is an exception here it is the provision of practical services for the elderly who have nobody else available. Because of the legitimacy accorded their incapacity, doing such things as cutting lawns, replacing light bulbs, helping out with the shopping, and so on is feasible without the need for reciprocity (Rossiter and Wicks, 1982). It is unlikely though that such practical assistance could be readily extended into the realm of regular 'tending'. The more personal form of caring this entails is problematic because it involves a degree of intrusion into personal life that lies well outside the normal rules of neighbouring. To the extent such aid is given, it is likely to occur between people who are more than just neighbours, for the neighbour bond *per se* is usually defined in too limited a fashion.

But if the majority of neighbour relationships offer little potential for significant long-term care of the elderly — or other groups — the same is true of friendships, a second category that appears intuitively to be a potential source of informal caring. While part of friendship is caring about each other to a greater or lesser degree, caring for one another is not an element inherent in the routine organization of friendship. As discussed in Chapter 4, the specific way in which non-kin relationships are constructed — the 'rules' that are applied to them — is shaped partly by class, with differences in the way the home is used being particularly important. Irrespective, though, of the structuring of the relationship, a principal element in all forms of friendship is the degree of equality between those involved. There is, in other words, a direct equivalence built into the exchange basis of these relationships, with neither side giving or receiving a disproportionate amount. This is seen quite clearly in the rituals that attend friendship — the reciprocity of rounds of drinks bought or meals provided or visits made. However it is also apparent in the more or less equivalent social position of the majority of friends. As mentioned earlier, friends are normally roughly the same age, the same status, at the same stage of the family cycle, and so on. In part, this is the result of their choosing as friends those with similar interests, but equally it reflects the principle that friends contribute — and therefore are in a position to contribute — equivalent financial and emotional resources to the relationship. It is in the nature of friendships as routinely organized that if ever this balance is threatened the relationship is likely to become more distant. This happens at a direct level when the equivalency of exchange breaks down, but also, more interestingly, it often happens when one side changes status, e.g. if they get a rapid promotion, or get married or divorced.

Because of such factors, the majority of routine friendships are not particularly well suited for providing the sort of caring community care entails, notwithstanding the friendship ideals that might make one think they would be. While friends are likely to be concerned for each other's welfare, transforming this into long-term active 'tending' is a different matter. There are two processes involved here. Firstly, the majority of friendships are defined as being about sociability rather than caring as such. Most are a forum for enjoyment rather than assistance and so cannot easily be turned into the kind of relationship in which caring is defined as paramount. They are more likely to become slowly inactive. Some, of course, will not. Those that people refer to as 'real' or 'true' friendships are more likely to provide the basis for caring — indeed often it seems ordinary friendships are transformed into 'real' ones through the friend remaining particularly loyal in times of need (see Allan, 1979) — but they are very much in a minority. Most friendships cannot carry this sort of 'load'. A second, though related, point is that the basis of equivalency — so important in friendship — breaks down when one side is unilaterally in need of and receiving care from the other. Even though the giver may not tire of providing care — though again this is quite a normal reaction — the receiver is likely to feel some reluctance about continually accepting aid without any means of reciprocating. In other words, the inherent imbalance such caring generates is ultimately likely to undermine the relationship's basis. So, as with neighbouring, the organization of friendship is not really compatible with the requirement of the tending role — be it for the elderly or for others. Friends often help each other out in the short run, but they cannot be expected to be involved very highly in the provision of long-term care of a unilateral kind.

Similar processes apply when the friends involved are those of the primary carer rather than the people receiving care. This was illustrated, for example, in Wilkin's study of the mentally handicapped. A number of the mothers of mentally handicapped children whom he interviewed found they lost friends when their handicapped child was born, partly as a result of their own sensitivity about the problems they posed for their friends (Wilkin, 1979, p. 143). While the specific problems faced by those caring for the elderly are different, similar considerations are none the less likely to apply. Together with the time and effort extensive tending entails, concern over the exchange basis of their relationships is likely to result in the social networks of most main carers being quite limited. In addition, they are likely to contain a disproportionately high number of people occupying similar caring roles. As well as sharing broadly equivalent experiences, with these people unlike 'non-carers' the balance of friendship can be maintained as any assistance and help given can be reciprocated. Here need is not one-sided.

Given that neighbour, friend and other non-kin relationships are not normally fashioned to play a major part in caring, it follows that the burden will continue to fall principally on kin. Yet, as we saw in Chapter 2, it will not fall equally on all kin. Like neighbours and friends, secondary kin also seem unsuited for the caring role. They usually know about one another and meet on occasion, but there is little evidence from kinship studies to indicate that this involves any extensive obligation to one another, or consequently any great potential for systematic caring. The relationships are normally too shallow, especially in adult life, and too dependent on the servicing of intermediary kin to provide the basis for long-term care. Of course there are exceptions. A particular grandchild, living locally, may be a very significant social contact for an ageing grandparent. Equally a nephew or niece may take responsibility for an aunt or uncle, especially if the parental sibling bond was particularly strong and the aunt/uncle had no children themselves. Such cases, though, are exceptions and are not ordinarily built into the standard 'rules' of secondary kinship. Normally these ties are purely 'social' and are maintained largely through formal and informal family ceremonies.

In contrast, primary kinship is the one set of relationships which does routinely involve an active, long-term commitment to welfare, a feature long recognized and built on by the state in its social policies. Such a commitment is taken to be the natural outcome of the genealogical bond that by definition exists between primary kin, especially parents and children. As a result, these relationships are largely inalienable in that they typically endure irrespective of any change there might be in either side's circumstances or of the actual level of social contact at any time. Secondly, being inalienable, there is far less pressure for any short-term reciprocity in these ties than is the case with most non-kin relationships. The extent to which the moral obligations that primary kin have for each other's welfare are translated into active caring will clearly depend on the specific circumstances of both parties and the competing domestic and other responsibilities of the potential carers. As noted, the greatest commitment is normally between parents and children, and undoubtedly it is here that the major component of familial caring is enacted, though in different directions at different stages in the family cycle.

While in the abstract these principles apply to primary kin generally, it is worth reasserting that in practice the caring they entail affects females far more than males, as a result of the standard division of responsibilities within domestic life. When care is needed, the burden falls predominantly on mothers, sisters and daughters, supplemented by their equivalent female in-laws. In this sense to talk about family care for the elderly is almost as much a myth as talking about community care: the caring is done not by communities or families as such but by female primary kin — a point that so easily gets lost in general discussions of 'community' care. As well as reflecting the wider division of labour in the family and in society and the dominant principles of our kinship system, the unequal gender distribution of tending in our society plays its part in reinforcing them.

Public policy, the elderly and family care

Now, clearly, the discussion in this chapter has been couched in very general terms. This applies not just to the broadness of the categories of relationship considered but also to the whole concept of 'caring'. The elderly's needs differ, as do the specific relationships that they construct with others. None the less, considering the basis of relationships in these general terms does allow us to gauge the feasibility of attempting to construct a public policy around the ideas expressed through the phrase 'care by the community'. The conclusion that is inevitably reached is that the great majority of informal relationships do not normally entail a sustained caring element, and that generating one within them is unlikely to work in the long run because it would require such a radical alteration to their exchange basis. The only routine relationships in which the majority of people are, as it were, 'naturally' involved that do include the caring element are primary kin ones, as is so clearly indicated by the fact that the enormous bulk of informal caring for the elderly and others in need is performed by such kin, principally female ones.

The 'failure' of other relationships to provide a basis for caring does not mean that they are in some sense pathological or lacking. The organization of informal relationships that has developed historically to meet the requirements of a society whose major institutions emphasize social independence and individuality cannot be modified on demand to produce a range of ties that can provide extensive care. The error lies in the implication of community care models that various forms of relationship can readily be converted into caring ones. This is simply not so: even those which entail an element of 'caring about' are not easily transformed into 'caring for' ones. So rather than their failure to provide 'caring for' being an indication of their deficiency, it is more a consequence of their following social rules in which 'caring for' plays little part. Indeed for many of them, including most friendships, mateships and neighbourhood ties, the lack of reciprocity and the extra involvement of 'caring for' is as contradictory to their nature as other elements are compatible. In consequence, attempting to use existing relationships in this way would not be a natural extension of them, but itself an artificial manipulation.

If these arguments are valid, facilitating and manipulating informal relationships so as to encourage greater support and caring for the elderly is more problematic than some community care theories assume. Relationships generated and sustained for other purposes cannot easily be transformed into caring ones as this involves a major change in their exchange basis. However such arguments do not mean that ways cannot be found to improve the effectiveness of patterns of informal caring – far from it. What it does mean is that we need to be very clear about the ways in which this might be achieved. One avenue, for example, is the use of volunteers, though once more here we need to be conscious of the exchange basis involved and the consequent limits there are in the relationship between volunteers and those elderly in need of support. Volunteers are not directly equivalent to friends even though part of their role may be that of 'befriending' an otherwise isolated individual. Yet being neither friends nor professionals, they may be suited to performing some types of routine, practical service for the elderly like shopping or transport or acting as street wardens who can be called on if help is needed. Having such services done by friends or neighbours on a regular basis places the helped in some degree of debt and is likely to alter the balance of the relationship. Having them done by a 'stranger' for reasons other than their personal obligation to you is a somewhat different matter. Even so the receiver is likely to feel indebted to the volunteer providing regular services, yet have no way of paying back that debt or hence controlling the relationship. In such cases, it may be particularly inappropriate to dress the volunteer relationship up as simply one of (a groundless) friendship. It may be more appropriate to give the receiver some purchase on the relationship by making some of the exchange content explicit, for example by paying the volunteer a small sum for providing the service, as some local authorities now do, or, in the case of the young, emphasizing its 'educational' content.

Similarly it may be possible to encourage the generation of new relationships that would enable the elderly and their families to cope better with their difficulties. Yet this could not be done without some foundation in the relationships for equivalence and reciprocity, factors which tend to be undermined when there is a unilateral need for care. Attempts to generate informal solidarity are consequently likely to be more successful if they involve people experiencing similar circumstances and sharing similar problems. Indeed, increasingly effort is now being directed at facilitating and establishing various forms of clubs or self-help groups for those involved in informal caring. Clearly the potential of the dependent elderly to assist each other is limited, but recent initiatives have shown that it is possible to create organizations for those who care for them, just as contacts between single-parents or those caring for physically or mentally handicapped children can be established. The best known of these is probably the Association of Carers, a national organization which acts as a self-help counselling, information and pressure group for carers. At a local level such strategies are likely to be more effective than ones aiming to help people in need by drawing on less focused friendship networks. Not only will those involved have a greater awareness of the difficulties they face and the support they need but, as importantly, there can be a flow of support and help that does not leave one party continually indebted to another. On the other hand, the involvement in such organizations of carers in most need of their support is likely to be limited by the time and effort their caring entails.

Yet the overriding conclusion to be drawn from this analysis is that the potentiality of informal relationships for providing community care is limited. If community care is to be the basis of policy it will not be through this approach to 'care by the community'. The starting point of a more appropriate and realistic strategy is the recognition that those who normally do the routine caring of others are limited to a few primary kin. Policies need to be built up around this fact rather than seeking to change it by attempting to share the caring amongst a wider network of informal friend and neighbour ties. In other words, given that the great bulk of informal caring is done by female primary kin, then ways need to be found to relieve the burden they bear not by sharing it amongst informal contacts within the community but by increasing the range and number of services − such as day centres, respite care schemes, sitting services, financial assistance − that give some relief from the demands of caring. It is this − providing systematic and practical support for those who are known to be doing the bulk of informal caring − that social care agencies concerned with community care policies should be seeking to develop.

But such support needs to be both systematic and seen as a right by those using it rather than a privilege. This suggests that the state may need to play a more significant role in its provision than voluntary agencies. Certainly many local voluntary groups are ill equipped to provide the form and scale of support required. As Abrams (1979) has shown, a clash frequently exists between the services volunteers, however well meaning, are willing to provide and the support those requiring it in a locality want. The major problem is often the regularity with which support needs to be given and the irregularity with which volunteers are able to provide it. But whether based on official, quasi-official or voluntary agencies, the principal requirement is that the support is organized. Spontaneous or haphazard support for carers is of little help and may even involve them in extra effort. Systematic, reliable support for those doing the caring should be a major priority of community care. This is precisely what we do not have at the moment. Just as neighbours and others often appear least willing to offer support to, say, the elderly if they think that 'family' are helping for fear of interfering, so too, for rather different reasons of economy and rationing scarce resources, do official agencies provide little support for those with informal carers. As Nissel and Bonnerjea (1982, p. 28) note, women had first to define the situation as a crisis, and secondly persuade others that it was: 'if they could present an acceptable definition of a breakdown to the doctor, then help would be provided.' As one of their respondents pointed out '. . . if you're seen to be coping, then you're left alone and there's no help, no share of responsibility. It's very unfair.' Equally telling, in Audrey Hunt's (1970) study of the home help service − arguably the most relevant 'community care' service provided by social service departments − it was found that those receiving informal support from kin were less likely than those without such support to be provided with home helps (see also Charlesworth, Wilkin and Durie, 1984). While this makes sense in terms of rationing a limited resource to ensure that all those at risk in a locality receive some sort of minimum support, it is far from clear that those bearing the greatest burden are the ones receiving help.

The implication of this is clear. Far from being a cheap alternative built around the spasmodic, idealized support of neighbours, friends or volunteers, effective community care policies for the elderly, as for others, call for both an extensive input of resources and effective organization. The various services need to be designed to support the carers as well as those in need of care, and must be systematic in provision and availability. While the creation of such services is clearly desirable, as Finch (1984) has pointed out it is important to recognize that they would do little to alter the gendered character of caring. As with existing schemes like the home help service and the Kent Community Care Scheme, the work they entailed would be seen as particularly suitable for females, be low paid and probably part time. As such, they would employ mainly married women who could combine the work with their domestic responsibilities.

In conclusion, the message of this chapter is that community spontaneity and altruism come a poor second to bureaucratic organization in meeting the needs for care. 'Community care' should be taken seriously and is a proper basis for policy, but only if the nature of contemporary community relations are understood adequately. What it requires is the systematic organization of services designed imaginatively to help both the elderly and those caring for them rather than services which are rationed so that they only appear to act when informal services fail. The problem, in other words, is not that families are failing to care for the elderly. The problem is that they receive so little support from outside in these tasks.

8

Unemployment and Family Life

A major argument throughout this book has been that the conventional organization of marital roles and responsibilities is supported by the gender inequalities of the labour market. Because of their ability to earn significantly more than their wives, husbands are usually defined as the primary income providers while their wives' main responsibility lies in domestic servicing. Even when, as is now usually the case, wives are employed, a husband's wage, being the larger, is none the less accepted as the primary one paying for household necessities like rent/mortgage, food, power and clothing. His wife's earnings, on the other hand, are generally taken to be less crucial and as providing benefits that the family could, if necessary, forego. As a result, wives' employment tends not to alter the basic division of responsibilities within the home very much. Husbands may help more with some childcare and household tasks but the extent of this help is generally limited and responsibility for organizing, planning and co-ordinating domestic servicing normally continues to fall on the wife. Because of this, wives' hours of work – paid and unpaid – tend to be both longer than their husbands' and spread more widely throughout the day and week. They have fewer opportunities for leisure and social participation and tend to have less say in major decisions, instead fitting their activities and personal projects around the short- and long-term requirements of other family members.

Through such mechanisms, male domination of the labour market can be recognized as a key factor in sustaining the structural inequality of marriage. Yet if male economic advantage is significant in the organization of domestic and familial roles, then an evident question to pose is: what happens once this advantage disappears? Will marriage itself become more equal? Will there be a less rigid division of labour within the home? Certainly some of the more optimistic analyses of the relationship have suggested this would be the case as women's earning power approaches that of men. However, there is little evidence that this convergence is occurring at all rapidly for any but a small number of genuinely dual-career couples (for a discussion of such families see Rapoport and Rapoport, 1976). But at the other end of the scale it could be argued that men's superior economic position is being eroded by the rapid increases in unemployment that have occurred in the late 1970s and the early 1980s. If a husband is unemployed, no longer going out to work, no longer providing the primary household income, no longer having fixed hours of work nor therefore of leisure, then the domination he can exercise over his wife through recourse to the ideology of the wage form must be tempered. His wife is, in other words, in a better position to make more demands on him for a more equal sharing of tasks, especially if she is employed. Indeed in these circumstances a genuine role reversal may even seem a possibility.

It is issues like these, together with the broader consequences of unemployment for family life, that form the focus of this chapter. After briefly reviewing current trends in unemployment, its impact on individuals and their families will be examined. This will involve looking not just at male unemployment but also at the rather limited research there is on female unemployment, paying particular attention to the consequences of job loss for married women. The chapter will conclude by examining the type of issue raised above about marital roles, drawing on recent empirical studies concerned specifically with analysing any changes in domestic organization that unemployment might bring about.

Unemployment: the facts

As Pahl (1984) has demonstrated, historically unemployment and/or underemployment have been common experiences for the majority of the working population. Indeed until quite recently much employment, especially though not only for those without recognized skills, was casual and affected by seasonal variations in production, trade and weather conditions. By the middle of this century, and particularly the 1950s and 1960s, this had altered. In these decades a combination of economic growth and Keynesian-style policies resulted in full employment being seen as an achievable state of affairs placed high on the list of priorities of all political parties. However more recent events have once again led to this being questioned. Since the early 1970s unemployment rates have been rising, though the increase has been most dramatic since the early 1980s. Between 1979 and 1983 official unemployment levels more than doubled to over three million in the UK as a whole. Table 8.1 portrays the changes there have been in registered unemployment in Great Britain between 1964 and 1983.

Table 8.1 *Unemployment in GB 1964 – 1983 in thousands and percentages*

	Males		Females		Total	
	No.	*%*	*No.*	*%*	*No.*	*%*
1964	279.6	1.9	92.6	1.1	372.2	1.6
1969	461.9	3.2	81.9	0.9	543.8	2.4
1974	500.9	3.6	98.8	1.1	599.7	2.6
1979	887.2	6.3	346.7	3.6	1,233.9	5.2
1981	1,773.3	12.7	649.1	6.7	2,422.4	10.2
1983	2,133.5	15.6	854.0	8.7	2,987.6	12.7

Source: Employment Gazette, 1975, 1984

These numbers and rates are, of course, official unemployment figures. That is, they represent the numbers of people who are registered as unemployed at any particular time. As a result they underestimate the real level of unemployment as those who receive no financial or other benefit from registering may not bother to do so. While the 'true' number of people currently unemployed is unknown, estimates suggest that at any time there are between 400,000 and 800,000 people wanting employment who are not registered, though equally there are some who register to draw benefit who do not actually want a job (*Employment Gazette*, June, 1983; *Labour Market Quarterly Report*, September 1984). As well as those approaching retirement age, the official figures exclude many married women who want employment. There are a number of reasons for married women not registering. Some will have chosen to pay reduced National Insurance contributions under the 'married women's option' and so be ineligible for unemployment benefit. Others will not have paid sufficient contributions to qualify either because they have been working as full-time housewives over the relevant period or because they have been employed less than the required number of hours per week. Still others will have exhausted their unemployment benefit but be ineligible for supplementary benefit because of their husbands' earnings. Some indication of the extent of non-registration amongst women is given by Martin and Roberts (1984). In their survey they found that as many as a third of those women currently looking for a job were not registered as unemployed.

As is well known, the increases in unemployment that have occurred recently have not been spread equally throughout the population or the country. Firstly, some groups in the population are far more likely to experience unemployment than others. As Elliot Liebow put it, 'Unemployment does not, like air pollution or God's gentle rain, fall uniformly upon everyone . . . it strikes from underneath, and it strikes particularly at those at the bottom of our society' (Quoted in Sinfield, 1981, p. 19). In periods of high unemployment, as at other times, it is those who are already disadvantaged – those without marketable skills, those in low paid jobs, the old and the young in the workforce, those from ethnic minorities, the handicapped and disabled – who suffer unemployment disproportionately (Moylan and Davies, 1980; 1981; Sinfield, 1982). Even in simple class terms, the differences are apparent. For example, figures derived from the General Household Survey suggest that manual workers are twice as likely as white-collar workers to experience unemployment. Within these categories semi- and unskilled manual workers are twice as likely as skilled manual workers to be unemployed, and equally junior/intermediate non-manual workers are twice as likely to be unemployed as professional workers (*Social Trends*, 1980, Table 5.19). Similarly, three-quarters of those interviewed in Colledge and Bartholomew's (1980) national sample of the long-term unemployed were manual workers. Secondly, unemployment is unequally distributed geographically, with some areas being affected far more than others. In particular, the traditional urban centres of heavy industry in Scotland, Northern Ireland, North-east and North-west England, the West Midlands and South Wales have been especially hard hit. So, for example, while in 1984 about one in eight males was officially registered as unemployed throughout the South of England, one in five was unemployed in the North and North-west of the country and in Wales; and more than one in four was registered unemployed in Northern Ireland (*Employment Gazette*, October 1984).

Increasingly it is being recognized that this level and form of unemployment may not be a short-term phenomenon. Rather than simply resulting from a down-turn in the economic cycle from which the economy will recover to re-establish 'normal' levels of unemployment of, say, 5–6 per cent, current levels have been caused, at least in part, by a structural transformation of our society's industrial base. This transformation will not easily be reversed and may prove to be as radical as that occurring at the beginning of the industrial revolution. Because of factors like the introduction of micro-chip technology, the increasing division of labour and consequent deskilling of much employment, and the use industrial capitalism is able to make of cheap third-world labour, employment in the manufacturing industries located in the major urban conurbations is declining rapidly. Indeed the speed with which this is happening is still not widely realized. In the three years between September 1979 and September 1982, the number of people employed in manufacturing industries in this country declined by a full 20 per cent. (*Labour Market Quarterly Report*, February, 1983, quoted in Pahl, 1984, p. 95). This decline clearly has spin-off effects for other occupations in the areas most affected. What new manufacturing developments there are − and it is instructive to note that in the early 1980s net investment in new industry was less than a fifth of the amount spent on beer and whisky (Hawkins, 1983, p. 7) − tend to be located away from the main urban conurbations, but even those based within them often require a different form of labour from that traditionally associated with these areas. Overall the jobs tend to be less skilled, more automated, less arduous and low paid − aimed as often as not at female rather than male labour (Massey, 1982).

Table 8.2   Length unemployed by age, males, UK, July 1984
in thousands and percentages

	Under 25		25−54		54+		All	
	No.	%	No.	%	No.	%	No.	%
Less than 6 months	343	47	358	32	85	29	785	37
6 months − 1 year	153	21	191	17	65	23	410	19
Over a year	239	33	578	51	138	48	955	44
All	735	100	1,126	100	288	100	2,150	100

Source: Employment Gazette, 1984

Given the industrial decline affecting some areas of the country and the consequent high levels of unemployment occurring in them, it is not surprising that many people are remaining unemployed for quite long periods of time. Whereas in 1979 only 29 per cent of unemployed men had been registered unemployed for a year or more, by July 1984 44 per cent had (*Employment Gazette*, 1979 and 1984). The figures for females are much lower − 16 per cent in 1979, 29 per cent in 1984 − but these must be treated with a good deal of caution as many married women who have been unemployed long term may see little point in registering once any unemployment benefit due to them is exhausted. As can be seen from Table 8.2, more than half of all unemployed men over the age of 25 have now been out of work for more than twelve months. This statistic is as important as the total number unemployed for the effects of long- and short-term unemployment for individuals and their families can be quite different.

Male unemployment

A major difficulty in discussing the impact of unemployment on the family is that, like official measures, most studies, especially large-scale ones, treat the unemployed as individuals and pay relatively little attention to the domestic and family relationships of the unemployed. As Hakim (1982, p. 440) notes, for example, there have not been any studies which attempt to examine the total unemployment experience of families or households, though what little evidence there is suggests that 'multiple unemployment' may be more common than is realized. For instance, in his study of the long-term unemployed White (1983, p. 39) found that some 30 per cent of his sample had one or more other members of their families also unemployed. Certainly we know that only about half as many wives of unemployed men are themselves employed compared to the population as a whole, in part because of the disincentives embodied in the national insurance and supplementary benefits systems. While it would seem likely that the consequences of multiple unemployment are greater than when only one family member is out of work, there is little direct evidence available.

But while unemployment is often treated in individualistic terms, it is also predominantly treated as a male issue. That is, the great bulk of existing studies concern themselves with the impact of men's unemployment on men's lives, though they may do this against the back-drop of these men's domestic and familial obligations. As we shall see later, women's unemployment has only very recently come to be seen as an area worthy of concern. This section will aim to summarize the conclusions of research on male unemployment, briefly examining three issues − financial circumstances, psychological well-being and health - which have a bearing on domestic life.

A common theme in virtually all research on unemployment is the sense of stigma and shame that the unemployed feel. In part, this is because unemployment seems to signify personal inadequacy and failure, especially for men whose social identity normally tends to be built around their role in economic production. Even in periods and areas of high unemployment, the image of the unemployed as welfare scroungers who could find jobs if they tried sufficiently hard remains powerful and is difficult to undermine. But in addition to being looked down on in this fashion, the unemployed also tend to be stigmatized through being effectively excluded from much routine social activity. As mentioned in Chapter 3, employment helps integrate individuals socially as well as economically; conversely unemployment limits opportunities for social participation, and so marks the unemployed off as being different. This applies not only in the direct sense that the unemployed have no access to the social relations of employment, but also indirectly. In particular, the limited material resources the great majority of the unemployed have available makes it difficult for them − and their families − to engage in the normal round of social events.

Despite the myths there are to the contrary, there is no question that the majority of the unemployed are in poverty. As Sinfield (1981) notes, without exception study after study demonstrates this. While some of those employed in the short term may not suffer too greatly as a consequence of receiving redundancy payments and tax rebates, these resources are normally exhausted quite quickly. For instance, according to the Social Security Advisory Committee (Second Report, 1982/83), over a quarter of men who had been out of work for six weeks or less were already dependent wholly or in part on supplementary benefit. This figure rose to nearly a half for those unemployed for up to six months. Equally in the DHSS study of men who had been unemployed for at least three months, nearly 50 per cent received benefits that replaced less than half their previous net earnings, and a third had total family incomes that were less than half what they had been when they were in work (Davies, et al., 1982). These figures are likely to underrepresent the current situation because of the withdrawal of the earnings-related supplement in 1982. Those unemployed in the long term face the most severe financial problems. In part, this is because the unemployment benefit system was designed in the belief that unemployment would normally be infrequent and short term, so that the maximum entitlement to unemployment benefit − itself a 'meagre substitute for earnings from employment' (Hakim, 1982, p. 444) − is only 12 months. Consequently with the marked increase in long-term unemployment in the 1980s, nearly 60 per cent of all unemployed men are dependent on supplementary benefit and thus living on the official poverty line, a figure which rises to nearly 80 per cent for those unemployed for 12 months or more (Social Security Advisory Committee, Second Report, 1982/3).

It must be remembered, of course, that it is not just the unemployed themselves who are living at this level. Their families are also surviving on the minimum amount the state regards as necessary. Indeed, unemployed men with families in which there are dependent children are particularly likely to be poor. In 1981, 96 per cent of all unemployed married men with children had incomes within 140 per cent of the supplementary benefit level, compared to only 45 per cent of unemployed married men without children. This involved some 600,000 children in 1981. Since then, the numbers of children in poverty has increased as long-term unemployment has risen. Exactly comparable figures are not available, but in 1983 some 1.25 million children were in families where the head was unemployed and claiming benefit (Child Poverty Action Group, 1984, pp. 9–10). Moreover research has shown that because of the inadequacy of the rates paid for children, families with children who are dependent on supplementary benefit are amongst those suffering most deprivation and hardship (Clark, 1978). In Colledge and Bartholomew's phrase, such families have enough for 'existence rather than living' (quoted in Sinfield, 1981, p. 52). Certainly the majority of families with two or more children find it difficult to manage, particularly in the long run as clothing, furniture and other household equipment wear out and need replacing. One indication of what Sinfield (1981, p. 52) calls 'the wretched position' of these families is provided by Clark. In her study of unemployed men on supplementary benefit, she investigated how many family members had less clothing than that officially considered necessary – a complete change of clothing and footwear and a warm coat. While overall more than half her sample had less than this, three-quarters of those with dependent children had less than the accepted minimum. So too more than half the wives in these families had less than the minimum, and three-quarters of the families had at least one child below it (Clark, 1978, pp. 397–8).

There can be little doubt that most families with dependent children in which the father is unemployed face severe difficulty in budgeting and making ends meet. Many have to economize on basic essentials like food, clothing and heating, particularly when the unemployment is prolonged. Similarly few have the resources to participate in much leisure activity outside the home. As Bakke argued, 'Economic changes are accompanied by social changes in family and community relationships. Economic resources provide not only food and shelter but also the means of establishing and maintaining the satisfying relationships and status of a social nature within the family and community' (quoted in Clark, 1978, p. 401). Again this applies not just to the unemployed but also to their spouses and children. Despite any attempts parents may make to shield their children from the effects of poverty, the absence of resources often means that children in unemployed families miss out on many of the pleasures and pastimes that other children take for granted – pocket money, school outings, fashionable clothes, trips with friends to the cinema or for a burger, and so on. In these respects it can be recognized that the burden of unemployment and financial hardship falls not just on those without work but also on their families. They too are likely to be excluded from full participation in the range of social activities considered normal in our society.

The psychological impact of unemployment is another area that has been researched a good deal, though most studies concentrate exclusively on the reaction of the unemployed and ignores others in their domestic unit. The traditional view, which was first formulated in the 1930s, suggests that four distinct phases can be recognized in the 'psychological careers' of the unemployed. Fagin and Little map out this position succinctly in their study of the impact of unemployment on family life (1984, pp. 40–57). The first phase is one of shock. Those being made redundant feel a sense of disbelief and disorientation at the prospect of job loss. However this phase may only last for a few days and soon gives way to a period of optimism. In this second phase, unemployment is seen as temporary and the benefits and opportunities it offers are appreciated. Unemployment may almost be viewed as a holiday, a short break in which people have the freedom to relax and get on with whatever projects they please. If a new job is not found within a few weeks though, feelings of far greater pessimism and anxiety occur, particularly as money runs short and sacrifices have to be made. In this third phase, which is likely to last a number of months, great efforts are made to find employment, but the individual becomes more irritable and difficult to live with as each new effort fails. Eventually this gives way to a fourth and final stage in which individuals accept their 'unemployed' identity and resign themselves to not finding a job. Frequently their lives become rather empty as they increasingly withdraw from wider social involvement. Much of their time is spent doing nothing in particular apart from sleeping or watching television.

This model of shock – optimism – pessimism – resignation continues to receive support though it is clearly a very generalized picture. Indeed, as Sinfield points out, it is a model which 'has been illustrated and supported rather than tested and validated' (1981, p. 37). Many cases have been found that fit it, but the variations and exceptions to it have probably been underplayed. The point here is that while there are marked similarities in the material and social circumstances of many of the unemployed, there are also numerous differences which mediate the experience of unemployment. Two factors that seem particularly important in this are age/family responsibilities and the previous pattern of employment. Generally, the four stage model would seem to apply best to those in their middle years with family responsibilities who are used to having steady employment and are particularly hard hit by the financial consequences of job loss. It is somewhat less likely to fit the young without many domestic obligations and without a firm occupational identity, or the older worker who may be inclined to treat unemployment as a (possibly undesired) prelude to retirement (Warr, 1983). Equally, those with a history of insecure and temporary employment with previous experience of job loss are likely to react to redundancy rather differently from those who have always had steady employment. They may be more likely to accept it as part of life's pattern without necessarily experiencing the hopelessness and destructive fatalism of the four-stage model (Sinfield, 1981).

Peter Warr and his colleagues have provided an alternative and in many ways more revealing perspective on the psychological impact of unemployment. On the basis of numerous different studies, Warr argues that 'the psychological health of unemployed people is significantly below that of people in jobs' (1983, p. 306). This is not through poorer psychological health leading up to unemployment, but results from the experience of unemployment itself. The effect is neither uniform nor universal, but, overall, unemployment results in higher levels of anxiety, depression, insomnia, irritability, listlessness and nervousness. Warr identifies nine related features of unemployment that help explain this deterioration in psychological well-being following job loss: reduced finances; less varied social participation; fewer social commitments; smaller social networks and interpersonal contacts; reduced scope for decision-making; less opportunity to practise and develop valued skills; the development of an undesired and stigmatized social identity; increased exposure to psychologically threatening situations (e.g. job rejections, negotiating welfare claims); and finally less security and control over the future (Warr, 1983, pp. 306–7). It is not surprising that in combination these various factors have negative repercussions for the unemployed's psychological health. The causal chains involved may be complex, with the different factors interacting with and reinforcing one another to different extents for different people, but overall Warr has no doubt that for the majority they produce a 'very significant reduction in psychological well-being' (1983, p. 306).

Evidence from other studies also support this conclusion. However before leaving this topic, one further point is worth making. It is noticeable in reading through Warr's nine factors that many of them – principally the first seven listed above – are equally descriptive of the situation many full-time housewives and mothers face (see Chapter 3). While there are clearly important differences between these groups, it is interesting that official and semi-official bodies express concern about the impact of factors like these on unemployed men's morale and well-being, while broadly similar social circumstances are seen as unexceptional and quite tolerable for women. In other words, for one group these conditions are recognized as constituting a major social problem; for the other, the tensions and dissatisfactions they create are individualized and often discredited.

As well as psychological health, the physical health of the unemployed has been the focus of much research effort. The overriding conclusion is that the unemployed suffer from poor health a good deal more than the general population. Study after study has demonstrated this, though, as above, it is important to recognize that there is variation in this at the individual level (Fagin and Little, 1984). A minority of people report being in better health since unemployment, often because their work entailed high levels of stress or pollution. But while the link between unemployment and ill-health is generally acknowledged, the reasons for this correlation are less clear. Put simply, the issue is whether unemployment causes a deterioration in health or whether instead it is the other way round with those suffering poor health being particularly prone to job loss. Indeed it is conceivable that both these processes are at work in creating the correlation. The situation is further complicated by the difficulties there are in measuring people's state of health, especially in large-scale surveys. For example, self-reports and indeed frequency of consultation with doctors and other health professionals probably reveal as much about subjective definitions and expectations of well-being as they do about the 'real' level of sickness. Using such measures with respect to the unemployed is complicated further as some may emphasize their health problems as a means of coping with and 'explaining' their failure to find a job. The sick role is, as Fagin and Little (1984) point out, more legitimate and less stigmatized than unemployment.

These considerations must lead to caution in accepting some of the claims about unemployment and ill-health made in the research literature. A further issue is also of relevance here. This concerns the nature of the comparisons that are sometimes made in these studies. While it can be shown that the unemployed have more health problems than the population generally, this comparison is somewhat misleading. To find out the true picture, the unemployed need to be compared with those who are in other respects similar to them. Interestingly, studies which control for age and class background have found that the relationship between unemployment and ill-health is reduced significantly. White (1983), for example, in his study of the long-term unemployed found that once such factors were held constant, unemployed men were only slightly more likely than the employed to be suffering from chronic ill-health. From a different angle, Ramsden and Smee (1981) report that, in the longitudinal study of the unemployed undertaken by the DHSS, overall there was relatively little deterioration in reported health in the first year of unemployment. Some of the sample did experience increasing health problems but these were almost balanced by those whose health improved. As the authors claim, this study suggests that 'if unemployment does adversely affect health the effect appears to be small during the first year of unemployment' (1981, p. 401). On the other hand, some evidence suggests there may be longer-term consequences. Importantly, an unpublished OPCS study based on the 1971 census found that when age and class were controlled for, the unemployed had a 21 per cent higher mortality rate than the employed. This study also found that the wives of the unemployed were similarly at risk. In the ten years after the census, their mortality rates were 20 per cent higher than those found amongst the wives of employed men (*Guardian*, 17/9/84, p. 3) Other reports of this study indicate that the relationship between mortality and unemployment holds even for the 'healthy' unemployed. That is, if those unemployed who are affected by ill-health and registered as sick are removed from the calculations, the remaining unemployed still have a higher likelihood of dying than average (Hakim, 1982; Ramsden and Smee, 1981). Assuming, as seems reasonable, a link between mortality and ill-health, the implication of these statistics is that unemployment does have a direct influence on people's health, notwithstanding the other studies mentioned above.

Clearly our understanding of the effect that unemployment has on people's health is lacking. The same applies with even greater force to our knowledge of the impact that unemployment has on the health of other family members. For example, few studies have paid attention to the impact of unemployment on children's health. As above, the conclusion of those that have is that the effects of unemployment are negative but not necessarily very strongly so. In Fagin and Little's in-depth study, for instance, only three of the 22 families with dependent children in their sample reported a deterioration in their children's health (1984, pp. 202 and 255). Similarly there is some evidence that mortality rates for very young children are increased by unemployment, but the relationship disappears once the children are of school age (Hakim, 1982, p. 448). Overall we would expect the savings that the unemployed are often forced to make on heating and food to affect the health of children. On the other hand, many families try hard to protect and cushion their children from the worst deprivations of unemployment. Indeed there is a suggestion in Fagin and Little's (1984) report that any ill-effects children experience may be due less to unemployment directly than to the increased family tension it creates.

Numerous studies have argued that unemployment increases the level of tension and friction within families. The hardship and lack of finance that unemployment entails clearly contributes to this, as does the psychological stress the unemployed themselves feel. The extra strain unemployment can place on a marriage helps account for the relatively high levels of marital breakdown amongst the unemployed. While unemployment is generally not the sole cause of breakdown, it can, in Hakim's (1982) phrase, often act as the catalyst, exacerbating any difficulties already occurring and pushing the couple that bit closer to separation. However, irrespective of whether separation occurs, the stress and tension that unemployment generally creates in domestic life seems likely to have some repercussions on the well-being of any children in the family, though little research has as yet been specifically directed at this.

Women and unemployment

As already mentioned, very little research effort has been directed specifically at women's unemployment. Until quite recently, female unemployment has simply not been seen as a significant issue, at least in comparison to male unemployment. Marshall's argument that unemployed women 'have appeared only as fleeting shadows in the literature on unemployment' is quite true (1984, p. 237). Not only have many studies been based on exclusively male samples, but, as importantly, those which have included some female respondents have tended to produce a markedly 'male-oriented' analysis which tell us very little about the experiences and consequences of female unemployment. For this reason studies such as those by Cragg and Dawson (1984), Coyle (1984), Martin and Roberts (1984) and Martin and Wallace (1984), which examine the economic and social impact of women's unemployment, are particularly welcome. The reason for this lack of attention is not hard to find. Essentially, despite women's and especially wives', increased involvement in employment, the dominant belief is still that women's major role lies in the family. Employment is consequently defined as an extra, as something which adds variety but is of little real importance. Equally it follows that for the majority of women unemployment is not regarded as crucial. In comparison to male unemployment, female unemployment, as Coyle argues, is not seen as leading to 'the same condition of hardship, either economically or emotionally because women, it is assumed, are supported by the family and occupied within it' (1984, p. 122). Indeed this view is so fully incorporated into our everyday thinking that the notion of married women's unemployment appears to be almost a contradiction − they are either employed or they are housewives.

Yet, as discussed in Chapter 3, employment is far from insignificant for women, both unmarried and married. Even if only the latter are considered, it is clear that employment is now a major and integral factor in the patterning of their lives. Having some sort of job, be it part-time or full-time, in other words, is now a normal and routine experience for the majority of married women for the greater part of their married lives. It is consequently inappropriate and mistaken to regard wives' unemployment as peripheral and unimportant. It may be that because of their domestic obligations most married women have a more flexible orientation to their employment than men (Wood, 1981), and that it is less central to their social identity, but it does not thereby follow that being unemployed has little impact on them or their families. On the contrary, the few studies there are show just how significant the economic and social consequences of female unemployment can be.

Before looking at the consequences of female unemployment, it is worth saying a little more than was said in the introduction to the chapter about its extent and patterning. It is appropriate to begin with Martin and Roberts's (1984) point that the route into unemployment for females is more varied than it is for males. As well as becoming unemployed through redundancy or not finding a job on leaving school, women may stop employment for domestic and childcare reasons and then at a later time find difficulty re-entering the labour market. To put this another way, the pool of 'economically inactive' women is more heterogeneous and fluid than the pool of 'economically inactive' men. It will include some who have no desire for employment in the foreseeable future; others who, while currently not wanting a job, will want one at some future time when their family commitments have altered; and still others who want employment, either full- or part-time, immediately, including some who left their last jobs voluntarily to become full-time housewives and mothers. As Martin and Roberts (1984) emphasize, most women are now employed for most of their adult life, but its patterning involves phases in which they are outside the labour market. It is this which makes drawing precise boundaries between 'unemployment' and other forms of 'economic inactivity' so difficult, especially as some women may not be looking very hard for employment but would accept a job if they were offered a suitable one or if they could make adequate childcare arrangements. Martin and Roberts's national survey provides a good picture of the fluidity involved in this. Nearly one in five of the women in their sample currently without employment wanted a job immediately; a little over a third were not actively planning ever to be employed again; whilst the remainder (46 per cent) consisted of women who thought they would at some future date want employment. A sixth of this last group said they would like a job within a year (1984, p. 81).

For these and the other reasons mentioned earlier, accurate estimates of the real number of women unemployed are impossible to obtain. Certainly the official estimates based on registration are inadequate, and so it is difficult to know whether the current recession is affecting women's or men's jobs the more. However, while comparisons of the absolute number of officially unemployed men and women is meaningless, a comparison of their relative increase over time is more useful, though still problematic.

As can be seen from Table 8.3, despite fluctuations, the broad pattern of increase between 1977 and 1983 is quite similar, though using 1977 as a base the increase in the female rates has consistently been slightly higher.

Table 8.3   *Official unemployment rates 1977–1983 in UK*

	Percentage of workforce officially unemployed		Relative increase on 1977 baseline	
	M	F	M	F
1977	7.3	3.7	—	—
1978	7.0	3.8	−4.1	+2.7
1979	6.5	3.7	−10.9	0.0
1980	8.3	4.8	+13.7	+29.7
1981	12.9	6.8	+76.7	+83.8
1982	15.0	7.8	+105.5	+108.2
1983	15.9	8.8	+117.8	+137.8

Source: Employment Trends, 1984

A similar picture is provided by statistics on the numbers of people in full-time employment. As can be seen from Table 8.4, the numbers of full-time male and female employees have declined by 3.2 per cent and 5.0 per cent respectively between September 1981 and March 1984. However this decline in full-time female employment has been off-set to some degree by an 8.3 per cent increase in the number of part-time female employees. While none of these statistics provide an entirely accurate profile, they do suggest that at least in job terms the recession has not really discriminated that much between men and women, so that unemployment has become as much a problem for females as it is for males.

Yet this is not generally recognized, nor are the problems which female unemployment creates. Thus, the financial implications of women's unemployment are often thought to be relatively unimportant, usually on the grounds that women can always be drawn back into the home and be supported by their husbands if necessary. This claim, common though it is, has little foundation. Firstly it ignores all those single, separated and divorced women who have no husbands or other male to provide support. There is no reason to think that the financial difficulties unattached women face in unemployment are any less severe than those faced by unattached males. Indeed for some the pressures will be greater as unattached women are more likely to be caring for young children. But secondly, the evidence available simply contradicts the claim that women's unemployment does not generally create financial hardship. In Martin and Roberts's extensive survey, for instance, a third of all the women defined as unemployed found it very difficult to manage financially or else felt they were not really managing at all. Less than 10 per cent of women with employment felt this. Similarly nearly half the unemployed women said they worried about money 'often' or 'nearly all the time', whilst only a quarter of employed women did so to this degree (1984, pp. 89–91).

Table 8.4   Employed labour force in UK (thousands)

		Female		
	Male	Full-time	Part-time	All
September, 1981	12,160	5,260	3,810	9,070
March, 1984	11,765	4,995	4,125	9,120
% change	−3.2	−5.0	+8.3	+0.6

Source: Labour Market Quarterly Report, Manpower Services Commission, September 1984

The failure to recognize the financial impact on families of wives' unemployment is clearly linked to the belief that a husband's income normally provides for the necessities of domestic life, like rent/mortgage, heating, food, and so on, while a wife's earnings are used mainly to purchase extras which the family could manage without. As we saw in earlier chapters, this view misrepresents the actual contribution a wife's earnings make to the family's life style. With the increase there has been in wives' labour force participation, the 'normal' family is no longer one with a single, male income earner, but one in which both spouses are employed. As Pahl (1984) has recently argued, new social divisions are emerging based on the number of income earners the household contains. Those with more than one are far less likely to be experiencing poverty. In other words, even accepting the idea that husbands' and wives' incomes are spent in different ways, the so-called 'luxuries' that wives' earnings buy are, in reality, no longer luxuries at all. Rather, they are goods and services which, with changing standards, families have come to expect and which consequently have been incorporated into the routines of domestic life. Certainly many families find it most difficult to manage at all adequately on a single male wage once patterns of behaviour have been built around two incomes, even when that single wage is significantly higher than the one lost.

This point comes out very clearly in Coyle's (1984) research. In her sample of women made redundant by a textile firm in Yorkshire, the married women all had difficulty coping and running the home on a reduced household income. Each family's life style was inevitably affected by the need to cut back and make do on less. One of Coyle's married respondents told her: 'Well my husband's not on a very good wage. I just do without. I don't buy the things I used to buy. When a woman is working I think you put a lot more into the house. We used to eat a lot of meat.. . . When I was working I could do it but I can't now, but they don't moan.' Another said, 'I got so fed up by the end. I missed having a bit of money in my purse that I could call my own. When you've only got one man's wage coming in, it's a terrible worry.. . . you're always scrimping' (1984, p. 106). This last quote also highlights how keenly married women experience the loss of financial independence their unemployment entails. Even though most of their wages get spent on the family, the fact that they are the ones earning the money gives them a greater degree of control over its use. Once unemployed they lose the freedom this income allows and become financially dependent on their husbands, especially if they are ineligible for unemployment benefit. So however 'good' their husbands were, Coyle's respondents disliked having to ask for money and being accountable for its expenditure. As one put it: 'But I missed having my own independence. I did miss that a lot, being able to get ready and go where I wanted and do what I wanted and buy what I wanted.' Another said, 'Sometimes he'll say "Is that your second packet of cigarettes today?" Well at one time I'd have said, "Well who's buying them?" but I can't now.. . . You lose your independence' (Coyle, 1984, pp. 107–8). Cragg and Dawson report that their respondents had similar feelings. One claimed: 'I do want to work. I would like to have a job. Not because of the money. Just because it would give me a little independence of my own. I wouldn't have to rely on my husband for money.. . . And if I wanted anything, I'd be able to get it for myself without having to go to him.' Another said: 'I should want to do something. Although I only get £5 a week it's my independence. I started doing voluntary work, which is satisfying, but it is also important to have a little of one's own money and not have to ask for everything. My husband cannot understand this attitude' (Cragg and Dawson, 1984, p. 21).

From the context it is clear that the loss of independence mentioned by these respondents has a social as well as a financial element. These women could no longer control their lives to the extent they had when employed. Instead they felt all the frustrations many full-time housewives feel, made the worse for most of them both because it was involuntary and because their families no longer needed full-time servicing. For a few women, redundancy and unemployment will more or less coincide with their plans to have children, and so be the start of a period in which it quite suits them to be full-time housewives/mothers. Clearly though, this is only likely to provide a 'solution' for a small number. The changed pattern of married women's employment means that many have finished with child-bearing and have no intention of starting again.

Any suggestion that unemployment matters little to these women as they can readily return to being fully occupied with family matters is plainly unfounded. Initially redundancy offers many a chance to relax a little and catch up on the housework, just as it allows men the time to complete their unfinished projects. Over any length of time though, housework cannot fill the void unemployment creates. Aside from their families no longer needing full-time attention, housework cannot compensate adequately precisely because it is characterized by similar problems to those experienced in unemployment. As we saw in Chapter 3, housework can be monotonous and boring; it offers little structure to the day; it is unpaid so provides few resources; and it generates little social contact outside the home. These are exactly the problems which weigh most heavily on the unemployed, so seeing a return to housework as an answer to unemployment for women is curious indeed.

In summary, any claim that unemployment matters more to men than women ignores the social and economic reality of female employment. While many female jobs are undoubtedly monotonous, low paid and intrinsically unrewarding, they still provide a degree of freedom otherwise missing. In contrast to housework, employment provides an arena for social involvement as well as an income that grants some level of independence. Indeed the very fact that women are willing to do the jobs they do for limited rewards indicates their attachment to employment and its significance in their lives rather than the opposite as is often assumed. As Coyle (1984) argues, employment has provided women with a route out of the social and financial dependence domesticity traps them in. As a result, increased domestic involvement cannot in any real sense act as compensation for unemployment.

Unemployment and the domestic division of labour

It has sometimes been suggested that high levels of male unemployment could lead to some modification in the way in which jobs are distributed in the home. Essentially, the argument is that with increasing numbers of married women in employment, it is likely that some men will become financially dependent on their wives. This may well encourage some form of 'role swap'. As these husbands have no job to occupy them, they would be able to take over the running of the home and any necessary childcare while their wives provided the household income. More sophisticated versions of this thesis have linked these changes with the emergence of what has come to be known as the 'hidden' or 'informal' economy. R. Pahl, for example, in his earlier formulations (1980; 1982a; 1982b;

Gershuny and Pahl, 1979) suggested that in areas with high levels of unemployment, families and households may need to develop new strategies for meeting their needs. This could involve the informal exchange of skills and services between households within the locality either in kind or for cash, or alternatively, it could entail a re-ordering of domestic tasks and responsibilities between household members. While Pahl's recent work has taken him well beyond these ideas into an examination of household work strategies in general (1984), they still provide an interesting perspective on the way unemployment may modify domestic organization. Specifically, if families are regarded as collections of individuals who are trying to achieve a reasonable standard of living through their combined efforts and who organize their individual activities accordingly — which is not to say all benefit equally — then it is at least possible that the strategies families adopt to achieve these aims could change significantly in localities where unemployment is rife. Their division of labour in and outside the home could alter in response to the new conditions under which they find themselves operating. One might expect, for example, greater flexibility than in the past over the allocation of paid and unpaid work and the consequent breakdown of the traditional 'male breadwinner/female servicer' format, especially in areas where female employment opportunities are greater than male ones.

As mentioned earlier in the chapter, most research into unemployment focuses on individuals, usually the unemployed themselves. Relatively little of it concentrates specifically on family or household relationships, so assessing these — or any other — ideas about the impact of unemployment on domestic organization creates some difficulty. None the less, the evidence there is all points in the same direction. It suggests quite firmly that, with or without the development of an informal economy, unemployment has relatively little effect on the normal patterning of domestic roles. Indeed as Bell and McKee (1984) argue, unemployment may well encourage a polarization of male and female activities rather than any convergence between them.

The reasons for this are various. One crucial factor limiting the extent to which unemployment encourages a restructuring of domestic roles is the way the state operates its welfare programmes. As discussed in the next chapter, the regulations currently in force for supplementary benefit and national insurance assume a male income earner/dependent female model, so that with both schemes there is a disincentive for the wives of the unemployed to be in paid work. Given the benefit foregone and the travel and other employment costs incurred, in financial terms it is often not worth their while being employed. Some will continue with their jobs in the short term in the hope that their husbands will soon find work again but in the long run for many the additional income generated by employment, especially under supplementary benefit regulations, is too low to warrant the effort involved. Largely for this reason, wives with unemployed husbands are only half as likely to be in paid work as married women in general.

A further reason why unemployment tends not to challenge the conventional structure of marriage lies in the gender identities created through life-time socialization. As already noted, studies of unemployed men consistently emphasize the loss of identity and self-respect unemployment generates, specifically as a consequence of the unemployed's inability to fulfil their financial obligations to their families. In itself this makes unemployed men – and for that matter their wives – reluctant to countenance any form of marital 'role-swap'. On the one hand, given traditional norms, there is strong opposition to 'living off' wives and relying on them for money as this would threaten their self-identity and social standing the more. On the other, given their failure to perform their acknowledged masculine role, undertaking what are normally seen as female tasks within the home is hardly likely to prove an attractive compensation. In addition though, it would appear that most wives also think it unfair to ask their unemployed husbands to change their domestic performance very much, on the grounds that their masculine identity is already sufficiently undermined. This is certainly a view expressed with great regularity and surprising force in interviews with the unemployed (Morris, 1983; Bell and McKee, 1984; Cragg and Dawson, 1984). Indeed, as Bell and McKee point out, it seems that unemployment more often than not reinforces rather than softens the attitudes to gender roles held by both husbands and wives. From their own interviews with unemployed families in Kidderminster they report that 'a passionate defence of men's right to provide was invariably raised' and that 'very fundamental emotions concerning self-esteem, self-image, pride, views of masculinity, respectability and authority resounded in the expressions of both men and women' (Bell and McKee, 1984, p. 19). As they recognize, the strength with which such views are held makes any significant shift in domestic roles unlikely.

In addition here though, the encroachment of husbands into traditional female activities is experienced by some wives as a threat to *their* own identity. Frequently this is expressed in terms of the different standards expected and achieved by husbands and wives in domestic work, with wives often claiming either that they have to redo tasks to an acceptable standard or that husbands create additional work by interfering in established routines. For example, one of Morris's respondents complained:

He doesn't like housework anyway. I suppose he thinks it's not manly. He'd dust and tidy downstairs but he won't do upstairs because no-one sees it, and he won't clean the front windows in case the neighbours see him. I don't mind housework myself as long as I've got time to do it, but I get irritable at the weekend when there's a backlog of things to do and he won't help. He just tells me to leave it. He doesn't understand that it's got to be done sometime (1983, p. 7).

Similarly one of Coyle's respondents told her : 'I'd rather him go to work and his tea's ready when he comes home, so you're in a routine of your own, but when they're at home you just can't get anything done. You get used to having the house to yourself during the day' (1984, p. 114).

In part, husbands' lower standards are a consequence of their lack of adequate skills and training; in part, they are likely to be a more or less deliberate strategy to reduce the demands their wives make of them. But equally they are a consequence of the different meaning housework has for the two spouses and the different role it plays in their lives. The standards reached matters less to most husbands as, in the end, they are neither held responsible for them nor judged by them. Responsibility is generally taken to rest with the wife, not least in those traditional working-class areas most affected by industrial decline. It is her reputation that is threatened by lower standards, not his; and it is her identity which is undermined if the home is not kept to the approved standard. For such reasons, wives of unemployed men may well resent their husbands' inept domestic contributions.

Lydia Morris's (1983) study of redundancy in Port Talbot demontrates these processes well. While the sample is quite small, the study is particularly interesting because it focuses on the impact of participation in the informal economy on domestic organization. In essence, Morris found that marital roles altered little amongst the 26 couples in her sample in which the husband had been unemployed for a minimum of one month. She identified three distinct patterns of domestic contribution amongst these couples. Firstly, some men, especially those whose wives were employed, increased the contribution they made to domestic work somewhat, though without fundamentally altering the overall balance of responsibility. They gave more help, in other words, but only to a limited degree. There was no suggestion of a major redistribution or reallocation. Secondly, some men, particularly those whose wives were not employed, initially gave increased help in the home, but soon changed back to their former patterns and left domestic work to their wives. This was generally for the reasons discussed above − either their wives found they interfered too much in their own routines and found the additional 'help' counterproductive, or the men tired of making an effort in the face of their wives' criticisms. The third pattern is the most interesting and the one followed by nearly two-thirds of the sample − 16 of the 26. This pattern consisted of 'an extreme reaction against any surrender of the traditional division of labour' (1983, p. 12). The way in which the majority managed this was by finding some form of surrogate work or activity − in other words, by involvement in the informal economy. For example, some spent their time (and redundancy money) improving their homes or helping mates do their's; others managed to find more or less short-term, unpredictable and insecure odd-jobs, 'hobbling' (in the local vernacular) for relatives, neighbours or other contacts. The significant point here is that involvement in informal economic activity did not lead to any new pattern of domestic organization, as some have suggested it might. Rather, spending time looking for work, making contacts and doing jobs not only kept men out of the home but provided them with a justification for not contributing any more to domestic work than they had when they were employed full time. It was a way of maintaining the status quo rather than changing it.

Broadly similar findings are reported by Bell and McKee (1984) in their study of the family life of 45 unemployed men in Kidderminster. Indeed, they argue that while there is variation in the amount husbands contribute to domestic and childcare work, by and large a husband's unemployment intensifies his wife's domestic incorporation rather than reduces it. To begin with, the burden of budgeting and making ends meet − an almost exclusively female responsibility − is increased because of the reduced income available to the household. Wives consequently put even more effort than usual into trying to find a bargain here or save a few pennies there so as to make what little there is stretch that bit further. Equally, while conflict over the allocation of the household income is frequent, in the end it is usually the wife who skimps on her own needs and does without in order to provide more adequately for the other family members.

Secondly, Bell and McKee report that the wives in their study appeared to be 'doubly isolated' (1984, p. 21). While most families find their social activities and relationships curtailed by unemployment, men still have some opportunity to 'escape' into the public domain − looking for work, signing on, chatting to mates, doing odd jobs. Indeed, as Morris's study showed, this can form part of the legitimation for avoiding any modification to domestic loads. Their wives, on the other hand, not only have less access to the public sphere, but may also find that their private domestic world is now under greater scrutiny and surveillance by their husbands. One likely result of this is a further restriction of their social activities, for husbands' presence in the home means that they intervene more − either directly or indirectly − in the way their wives structure their day and use their time. Wives have that much less autonomy over what they do, where they go and who they see than when their husbands are working. So, on top of reduced resources, simply having their husbands around the home much of the day lessens wives' control over their domestic routines and in effect encourages a more privatized, less sociable life style.

In conclusion, it would seem that unemployment does little to encourage any great convergence of domestic roles. For the various reasons discussed above the traditional equations of husband equals breadwinner, wife equals domestic servicer can continue even when the husband is out of work and not bringing home a wage. The ideology of the domestic division of labour is sufficiently embedded into everyday social life for it to be hardly threatened by the male's lack of employment. Indeed the ideology is well enough grounded to contribute to its own continuation, as is seen by wives' own rather conventional responses to their husbands' additional 'free time'. It may be that circumstances will alter to modify this — the state for example may change the principles governing income maintenance policies; in some areas women's employment may be particularly well paid — and so encourage a significant shift in gender roles. However, as yet, there seems little evidence of this happening. One suspects that like the unemployed in Port Talbot and Kidderminster, most men will fight hard to protect their dominant position and find ways to ensure that responsibility for domestic servicing continues to be defined as essentially female.

9

Marriage, the Family and the State

A great deal is said and written about the way in which contemporary family life is changing. Many of these changes have been quite dramatic and so it is not surprising that they are sometimes taken as representing a radical shift in domestic and household organization. Increases in, for example, cohabitation, wives' employment, divorce and one-parent families all seem to undermine the traditional pattern of family life so taken for granted only a generation or two ago. Yet it would be wrong to get such change as there has undoubtedly been out of perspective, for the continuities in both the structure and dynamics of family life are just as marked. As Kiernan (1983, p. 35) rightly notes, it is still the case 'that most young people in Britain will marry, that most marriages will survive, that most married couples will have children and the majority of these children will be brought up by their natural parents'. She goes on: 'In other words, the family based on a married couple with children committed to a permanent relationship is still the norm today.'

Equally, notwithstanding popular claims about the shift to more symmetrical partnerships, the great majority of marriages continue to be built around a firm division of labour in which husbands and wives have discrete responsibilities. Though it is no longer true that wives typically remain at home throughout their marriage, taking care of domestic matters while their husbands go out to work, they none the less retain primary responsibility for domestic servicing. In turn, husbands are still routinely taken as having the main responsibility for income provision, even though in many families domestic budgeting now requires two incomes. The detailed way in which these conjugal responsibilities are carried out have certainly altered, as has the rigidity of the boundaries between male and female tasks, yet at the same time the underlying structure and organization of this division of labour within marriage remains essentially unaltered. The identities of wife as domestic servicer and husband as income earner are as relevant today for most families as they were three or more generations ago.

To quite a large degree, this book can be read as an attempt to depict and analyse the consequences of this continuing division of marital responsibility and labour for the spouses' respective relationships both inside and outside the home. In outline, the argument has been that the nature of the social and economic constraints which operate outside marriage not only serve to make a division of labour within the home rational for the majority of couples, particularly if there are children involved, but also ensures that the form this division of labour takes is systematically patterned by gender. The consequence is that very few couples ever really make decisions about their respective responsibilities. Instead these are governed by the structural realities around which their relationship are built and which have already moulded their expectations through the process of gender socialization. Yet at the same time, these structural realities are reinforced and become the more constraining as each new couple develops its relationship in accord with them.

This chapter is concerned with examining the part the state, in its various guises, plays in sustaining the conventional form of family life and limiting the choices open to couples. Until recently the state's role in this has received relatively little consideration. This lack of concern for the relationship between the state and the family reflects the popular view that the family is independent and separate from state activity. Whereas the state is concerned with regulation, control and coercion, the family is thought of as the arena for love, intimacy and personal fulfilment. So, despite the growth of state involvement in other spheres, it is normally taken as inappropriate for the state's authority to encroach too far into family life. In contrast to the public domain outside, the family is about personal freedom rather than state direction. Yet at the same time, the state is perceived as having a duty to ensure that the family cares properly for its dependent members and socializes its young adequately. When families fail to do this, the state, − or rather its agents, especially police and social workers − are expected to intervene to rectify the situation. Equally, with the growth in social ills apparently attributable to family dysfunction − from delinquency to drug abuse, child battering to school discipline problems − the state is regularly summoned to reinforce family norms.

The state has coped with this contradiction between freedom and direction, between the family being autonomous yet needing policing, by adopting implicit rather than explicit measures. Unlike other European countries, Britain has never had a ministry or department with overall responsibility for family matters, nor a systematic set of family-oriented policies. There are, of course, many social and economic policies which impinge on family life but their aims and objectives are normally expressed in terms other than their impact on the family. None the less, because these various policies are premised on a more or less consistent set of assumptions about the nature of family life, they play their part in sustaining and encouraging a particular form of domestic organization. Much state provision, in other words, is based upon an implicit ideology of the 'normal' family which through its incorporation into standard practice effectively discourages alternative forms of domestic organization from developing. Indeed by sustaining an implicit, taken-for-granted view of family life, such other forms tend to be seen as not simply different but as deviant, and hence potentially damaging. In turn, this allows the state to be flexible and appear non-interfering yet directive at one and the same time. The contradiction, in other words, is solved by tacitly encouraging the standard form of gender and generational relations within families, discouraging others, but only actively intervening against those which are socially defined as pathological and·harmful. In this light, it is noticeable that recent political expositions on family life have been expressed in terms of 'strengthening' the family rather than interfering in it.

Various ways in which the state — taken broadly here to include all public provison and regulation, whether national or local — routinely influences family life have already been raised in earlier chapters. It is none the less worth recapping on them here. To begin with, as discussed in Chapter 4, the state has played a considerable part in improving the physical conditions of domestic life through slum clearance, council house building, the provision of power and water services, building and zoning regulations, and so on. By improving the home's ambience, these measures have fostered a home-centred orientation and an image of domestic matters as separate from, and in some ways oppositional to, the world of industry and commerce. Yet at the same time, these physical changes do not of themselves impose a particular form on the relationship between spouses or between parents and children. Other state activity is of more consequence in doing this.

Particularly important here is the way in which much state provision presupposes a division of labour in the home, and, more specifically, the availability of someone to service other family members. So, for example, as developed in Chapter 2, the specialized institutions the state has created to provide education and health care rely on the flexible and idiosyncratic support that family members can provide. Indeed more than this, these services are based on the assumption that informal carers are available to take over where they leave off. Thus the daily and seasonal timing of schooling is designed to suit educational rather than domestic ends, so that someone needs to be available to look after children outside school hours. Similarly specialized health care is quite limited, with most routine nursing being undertaken informally in the home. There is nothing improper or remarkable in these arrangements – few would want formal, institutionalized care to replace them. However in the absence of accessible alternatives, they do serve to reinforce the very patterns they assume, and consequently are a factor encouraging a domestic division of labour.

Now, in theory, this division of labour need not be gender specific. The range of care that is required can be provided by males as well as females, husbands as well as wives. In practice, of course, it does not work out this way. As with the support that 'families' provide for the elderly discussed in Chapter 7, the burden of informal caring falls principally on females in their roles of wives, mothers and daughters. Life-long socialization into 'natural' gender aptitudes combine with labour market inequalities to ensure that this continues to be so. Consequently the state's assumptions about the family's ability to provide informal care in fact work out as an encouragement of a gender-specific division of domestic roles whereby husbands/fathers are assigned primary responsibility for income provision and wives/mothers that for caring and servicing other family members. Indeed, in some of its other measures, particularly those concerned with family finances, the state assumes this specific division of labour more explicitly.

Hilary Land has shown this to be so in a series of papers on social security and taxation regulations (1978; 1979; 1980; 1983; Land and Parker, 1978). As she demonstrates, the assumption underlying most of these regulations is that a wife is normally economically dependent on her husband, in return providing him with domestic servicing. So, for example, married men are eligible to receive a larger tax-free allowance than single men on the grounds that as they are obliged to support their wives their needs are greater. This applies irrespective of whether or not the wife is herself employed. Similarly, unless a couple choose to be taxed separately, thereby forfeiting the married man's allowance, husbands are normally treated by the Inland Revenue as though they are responsible for financial affairs, with wives' earnings being aggregated with their's for tax purposes (Land, 1983). Equally, the national insurance and supplementary benefit schemes make the same assumptions about husbands' and wives' respective roles. As Land argues 'the social security system is based on the concept of one male breadwinner upon whom the rest of the family rely or should rely for financial support' (1979, p. 144). Consequently, unlike their husbands, wives cannot automatically claim national insurance benefits for their children even when they have paid full contributions. Likewise, they can only claim for a husband if he is incapable of working. He, on the other hand, can claim benefit for her provided she is not employed for whatever reason. Married women are only eligible for invalidity pensions if they are incapable of employment and of doing 'normal household duties'. Men and single women qualify irrespective of their capacity to do housework. Even more remarkably given the predominant pattern of caring, married women are not eligible for the Invalid Care Allowance. It is only available to men and single women. The assumption in this, as elsewhere in the social security system, is that married women's domestic role makes them freely available for caring so that no compensation for lost earnings in required. To quote Land again, 'The British social security system' — and this could be broadened to the state generally — 'does not recognize that most married couples share the economic support of their families and that some may wish to share responsibilities for domestic work: breadwinners are male. Only women care for children, the sick and the old and if they have paid employment this must take second place to their domestic duties' (1979, p. 149).

From all this it is evident that much state regulation and provision assumes a gender-based division of labour within the home, and in so doing reinforces and further encourages the likelihood of its being so. None the less some would argue that the state's view of marriage is slowly altering. The implementation of the Sex Discrimination Act and the Equal Pay Act, for example, in the mid-1970s at least recognized that women's role in society is not solely that of domestic servicer. So, too, changes in divorce procedures and the slightly more favourable treatment of single mothers under supplementary benefit and family income supplement regulations imply that the state's conception of husbands' rights within marriage is gradually altering, as indeed does the special consideration given to physically abused wives in the 1977 Homeless Persons Act. However, even if such arguments are accepted as an indication that the state's view of marriage is neither static nor inflexible, it is hard to believe that these measures represent a particularly radical shift in the way gender relations are conceived. This is the more so given the quite contradictory implications and consequences for domestic life of other recent political action.

One pointer to the likely direction that any political initiative on family policy may take in the next few years was provided in documents leaked to the *Guardian* (17/2/83) about the 'Family Policy Group', a cabinet-level 'think-tank' on domestic and family matters formed in 1982. The group's objective was to find ways in which the family could be strengthened through generating policies that would encourage more caring and responsible attitudes between family members, and so reduce the level of intervention in family affairs of the state's various agencies. As expressed in one of their documents, the group sought to examine 'what more can be done to encourage families — in the widest sense — to reassume responsibilities taken on by the state, for example, responsibility for the disabled, elderly, unemployed sixteen-year-olds' (*Guardian*, 17/2/83, p. 4). Aside from extending parental support for unemployed adolescents, the repercussions of such a policy would in practice be felt mainly in the care of the elderly, an area already heavily dependent on family support, as we have seen. Despite some suggestions aimed at alleviating the burden of this care, any policy encouraging families to 'reassume their responsibilities' in this way is bound to result in their facing even greater problems and pressures in caring for their elderly than they do now. More specifically, as there is little in the policy group's proposals that challenges the gender inequalities occurring outside the family, aside from a suggestion that fiscal discrimination against mothers be removed, it is reasonable to assume that the onus of the increased care and tending required will, as now, be borne by women.

In other words, the likely impact of these measures would be to reaffirm and strengthen the division of roles within the home. In this respect, these suggestions for the elderly are very much in line with another of the proposals made by the policy group — that of encouraging mothers to stay at home rather than be employed. While the desire to see a return to what they take to be the traditional family form in which husbands provide the income and wives the caring is hardly novel, it again indicates the rather limited knowledge that members of the group have of the reality of much family life. If fewer wives were able to take employment and contribute to family income, the consequence would undoubtedly be an increase in the numbers of families in poverty. Yet the contribution that wives' earnings routinely make to the family economy is not recognized in any of the proposals. Instead it is uncritically assumed that families can normally manage on one income, helped perhaps by a little adjustment to tax allowances at the lower range, despite all the contradictory evidence now available.

Though the Family Policy Group's deliberations will not of themselves become policy, their tenor nevertheless indicates the sort of family policy likely to be encouraged over the next few years. Given this it seems extremely unlikely that state activity will do anything other than reflect and reinforce the traditional division of tasks and responsibilities within families, without necessarily making it any easier to meet these obligations. Though policies like these may save the state money, the cost of their so doing will undoubtedly be heavy for those families most affected. It is unlikely that they will perceive their family life to have been 'strengthened'.

Indeed the Government's policies and actions during the current recession give force to this view. There is little in them to suggest that any significant shift in conventional family roles will be encouraged. While attempts to limit public expenditure have taken many forms, a major part has involved cutting back on what, for simplicity, may be termed 'Welfare State' provision. As Edgell and Duke (1983) argue, reductions in expenditure on health care, social services, education and other welfare services are likely to have more impact on women's lives than on men's. Not only do these services employ a high proportion of female staff but they also bear most directly on women's domestic responsibilities.

The second of these points is the more important. Indeed while in theory women's jobs seem the more vulnerable — if only because of the tendency to make savings by cutting back on junior, ancillary and part-time posts which are predominantly female — the evidence is not convincing. For example, nearly half a million male jobs were lost in the public sector as a whole between 1978 and 1983, whereas the number of female jobs remained static in the same period. Even in the 'Welfare Services' — the NHS, education and local authority health and social services — which employ high proportions of female staff, there is little indication that women's jobs have been affected most. Indeed in both the NHS and local authority health and social services, the total number of both full- and part-time female staff increased while male staff numbers have remained the same. Only in education have women suffered a disproportionate job loss, with the number of full-time female posts having been reduced by some 10 per cent compared with only 5 per cent for full-time male posts (*Economic Trends*, November 1979 and February 1984).

These figures are of course only crude indicators of the trends there have been, providing information solely on the numbers actually employed and revealing nothing about changes there may have been in the conditions of that employment. So, for instance, even where jobs have not been lost, savings may be made by reducing rates of pay or hours of employment, sometimes without cutting workloads proportionately. Such strategies are most likely to be implemented with part-time staff, who are nearly all female, because of the absence of any protective legislation and their reduced levels of union membership (Edgell and Duke, 1983).

Whatever the direct implications for jobs, the indirect consequences of expenditure cuts in social provision seem certain to affect women rather more heavily than men. In particular, reductions in the quality of state provision in the fields of health, education and social services will serve to limit the opportunities open to some women by increasing further the level of informal care expected of them. For example, in a period when the numbers of elderly — and very elderly — are increasing quite dramatically, any reduction in actual or proposed residential care facilities, in programmes to provide short-term stays, in home-help services, in day centres, in iniatives in geriatric medicine, and so on, are ultimately going to increase the need for less formal care provision, most of which is, as we have seen, provided by females rather than males. Indeed it is the belief that informal and family care can be stretched that bit further, apparently without too great a cost, that makes cuts in these types of service so attractive to policy makers confronted with reduced resources. Similarly, effective cuts in education, be it in the school meals service or through the 'rationalization' of school periods, either by shortening the school day or rescheduling the dates of terms, clearly have implications for those who are primarily responsible for childcare outside school, though these implications are generally not included in the calculations. So too, despite earlier promises of increased provision, the reduction in available nursery places over the last few years limits the employment opportunities of mothers with young children (Penn, 1982).

In making its savings in these ways, the state is undermining women's economic participation by increasing the pressure on them to replace formal provision with informal care, and thereby reinforcing their domestic role. Whether this response is a deliberate attempt to reinforce gender divisions within the family is difficult to ascertain, but it clearly fits well the Government's declared aim of 'strengthening' the traditional family form. Less overt than the propaganda encouraging wives to relinquish their jobs after the Second World War, the message none the less seems similar. As Lynda Chalker, one of the present Government's more liberal members, put it: 'Maybe in years to come, the country will look at the labour market and decide perhaps it would be better for women with children to stay at home' (quoted by Turner, 1979, p. 646). Certainly some of the ways in which the expenditure cuts are being managed encourages such a view by fostering the ideology of familial responsibility in a way that emphasizes the apparently natural division between male and female labour in and outside the home.

Bibliography

Abrams, P. (1977), 'Community Care: Some Research Problems and Priorities', *Policy and Politics*, 6: 125–51.

Abrams, P. (1979), *Neighbourhood Care and Social Policy: a Research Perspective*, London: Volunteer Centre.

Abrams, P. (1980), 'Social Change, Social Networks and Neighbourhood Care', *Social Work Service*, 22: 12–23.

Allan, G. (1977), 'Sibling Solidarity', *Journal of Marriage and the Family*, 39: 177–84.

Allan, G. (1979), *A Sociology of Friendship and Kinship*, London; Allen and Unwin.

Allan, G. (1982), 'Property and Family Solidarity', in P. Hollowell (ed.), *Property and Social Relations*, London: Heinemann.

Anderson, M. (1971), *Family Structure in Nineteenth-Century Lancashire*, Cambridge: Cambridge University Press.

Antonis, B. (1981), 'Motherhood and Mothering', in The Cambridge Women's Studies Group, *Women in Society*, London: Virago.

Ariès, P. (1962), *Centuries of Childhood*, London: Cape.

Backett, K.C. (1982), 'Images of Parenthood' in M. Anderson (ed.), *Sociology of the Family*, (2nd edn), Harmondsworth: Penguin.

Bane, M.J. (1976), 'Marital Disruption and the Lives of Children', *Journal of Social Issues*, 32: 103–17.

Barclay Report (1982), *Social Workers: Their Role and Tasks*, London: Bedford Square Press.

Barker, D.L. (1972), 'Young People and their Homes: Spoiling and "Keeping Close" in a South Wales Town', *Sociological Review*, 20: 569–90.

Barrett, M. and McIntosh, M. (1980), 'The Family Wage: Some Problems for Socialists and Feminists', *Capital and Class*, 11: 51–72.

Bayley, M. (1973), *Mental Handicap and Community Care*, London: Routledge and Kegan Paul.

Bell, C. (1968), *Middle-Class Families*, London: Routledge and Kegan Paul.

Bell, C. and McKee, L. (1984), 'His Unemployment: Her Problem, The Domestic and Marital Consequences of Male Unemployment', paper presented to the Annual Conference of the British Sociological Association, Bradford.

Bell, C. and Newby, H. (1976), 'Husbands and Wives: the Dynamics of the Deferential Dialectic', in D.L. Barker and S. Allen (eds), *Dependence and Exploitation in Work and Marriage*, London: Longman.

Bernard, J. (1976), *The Future of Marriage*, Harmondsworth: Penguin.

Bernard, J. and Nesbitt, S. (1981), 'Divorce: an Unreliable Predictor of Children's Emotional Predispositions', *Journal of Divorce*, 4: 31–42.

Blau, Z. (1961), 'Structural Constraints on Friendship in Old Age', *American Sociological Review*, 26: 429–39.

Blood, R. and Wolfe, D. (1960), *Husbands and Wives: the Dynamics of Married Living*, Glencoe: Free Press.

Boddy, M. (1980), *The Building Societies*, London: MacMillan.

Bott, E. (1971), *Family and Social Network*, London: Tavistock.

Boulton, M.G. (1983), *On Being a Mother*, London: Tavistock.

Brannen, J. and Collard, J. (1982), *Marriages in Trouble: the Process of Seeking Help*, London: Tavistock.

Britton, M. (1980), 'Recent Trends in Births', *Population Trends*, 20: 4–8.

Brown, A. and Kiernan, K. (1981), 'Cohabitation in Great Britain: Evidence from the General Household Survey', *Population Trends*, 25: 4–10.

Brown, G., Ni Bhrolchain, M. and Harris, T. (1975), 'Social Class and Psychiatric Disturbance among Women in an Urban Population', *Sociology*, 9: 225–54.

Brown, R. (1976), 'Women as Employees: Some Comments on Research in Industrial Sociology, in D.L. Barker and S. Allen (eds), *Dependence and Exploitation in Work and Marriage*, London: Longman.

Burchinal, L.G. (1964), 'Characteristics of Adolescents from Unbroken, Broken and Reconstituted Families', *Journal of Marriage and the Family*, 26: 44–51.

Burgoyne, J. and Clark, D. (1982), 'Reconstituted Families', in R.N. Rapoport, M.P. Fogarty and R. Rapoport (eds), *Families in Britain*, London: Routledge and Kegan Paul.

Burgoyne, J. and Clark, D. (1984), *Making a Go of It*, London: Routledge and Kegan Paul.

Charlesworth, A., Wilkin, D. and Durie, A. (1984), *Carers and Services: a Comparison of Men and Women Caring for Dependent Elderly People*, Manchester: Equal Opportunities Commission.

Cherlin, A. (1978), 'Remarriage as an Incomplete Institution', *American Journal of Sociology*, 84: 634–50.

Cherlin, A. (1981), *Marriage, Divorce, Remarriage*, London: Harvard University Press.

Chester, R. (1972), 'Current Incidence and Trends in Marital Breakdown', *Postgraduate Medical Journal*, 48: 529–41.

Chester, R. (1977), 'The One-Parent Family: Deviant or Variant?' in R. Chester and J. Peel (eds), *Equalities and Inequalities in Family Life*, London: Academic Press.

Child Poverty Action Group (1984), *Poverty, What Poverty?*, London: CPAG.

Clark, M. (1978), 'The Unemployed on Supplementary Benefit', *Journal of Social Policy*, 7: 385–410.

Colledge, M. and Bartholomew, R. (1980), 'The Long-Term Unemployed: Some New Evidence', *Employment Gazette*, 88: 9–12.

Comer, L. (1974) *Wedlocked Women*, Leeds: Feminist Books.

Coyle, A. (1984), *Redundant Women*, London: The Women's Press.

Cragg, A. and Dawson, T. (1984), *Unemployed Women: a Study of Attitudes and Experiences*, Department of Employment, Research Paper, No. 47.

Cromwell, R. and Olsen, D. (1975), *Power in Families*, New York: Wiley.

Cumming, E. and Henry, W.F. (1961), *Growing Old: the Process of Disengagement*, New York: Basic Books.

Dahl, R. (1961), *Who Governs: Democracy and Power in an American City*, London: Yale University Press.

Dalla Costa, M. (1972), *The Power of Women and the Subversion of the Community*, Bristol: Falling Wall Press.

Davidoff, L. (1979), 'The Separation of Home and Work? Landladies and Lodgers in Nineteenth- and Twentieth-Century England', in S. Burman (ed.), *Fit Work for Women*, London: Croom Helm.

Davies, R., Hamill, L., Moylan, S. and Smee, C.H. (1982), 'Incomes In and Out of Work', *Employment Gazette*, 90: 237–43.

Deem, R. (1982), 'Women, Leisure and Inequality', *Leisure Studies*, 1: 29–46.

Delphy, C. (1984), *Close to Home: a Materialist Analysis of Women's Oppression*, London: Hutchinson.

Dennis, N., Henriques, F. and Slaughter, C. (1956), *Coal is Our Life*, London: Tavistock.

Department of Education and Science (1982), *Statistics of Education*, 1979, vol. 4.

DHSS (1981), *Growing Older*, Cmnd. 8172, London: HMSO.

Dixey, R. and Talbot, M. (1982), *Women, Leisure and Bingo*, Leeds: Trinity and All Saints College.

Donzelot, J. (1980), *The Policing of Families*, London: Hutchinson.

Edgell, S. (1980), *Middle-Class Couples*, London: Allen and Unwin.

Edgell, S. and Duke, V. (1983), 'Gender and Social Policy: the Impact of the Public Expenditure Cuts and Reactions to Them', *Journal of Social Policy*, 12: 357–78.

Equal Opportunities Commission (1982), *Caring for the Elderly and Handicapped*, Manchester: EOC.

Fagin, L. and Little, M. (1984), *The Forsaken Families*, Harmondsworth: Penguin.

Farber, B. (1973), *Family and Kinship in Modern Society*, Brighton: Scott, Foresman.

Fast, I. and Cain, A.C. (1966), 'The Stepparent Role: Potential for Disturbances in Family Functioning', *American Journal of Orthopsychiatry*, 36: 485–91.

Ferri, E. (1984), *Stepchildren: a National Study*, Windsor: NFER – Nelson.

Finch, J. (1983), *Married to the Job*, London: Allen and Unwin.

Finch, J. (1984), 'Community Care: Developing Non-Sexist Alternatives',

Critical Social Policy, 3: 6–18.

Finch, J. and Groves, D. (1982), 'Community Care and the Family: a Case for Equal Opportunities?', *Journal of Social Policy*, 9: 486–511.

Finch, J. and Groves, D. (eds) (1983), *A Labour of Love*, London: Routledge and Kegan Paul.

Firth, R. (1956), *Two Studies of Kinship in London*, London: Athlone.

Firth, R., Hubert, J. and Forge, A. (1970), *Families and Their Relatives*, London: Routledge and Kegan Paul.

Garmarnikow, E., Morgan, D., Purvis, J. and Taylorson, D. (1983), *Gender, Class and Work*, London: Heinemann.

Gavron, H. (1966), *The Captive Wife*, Harmondsworth: Penguin.

Gershuny, J. and Pahl, R. (1979), 'Work Outside Employment: Some Preliminary Speculations', *New Universities Quarterly*, 34: 120–35.

Gillespie, D. (1972), 'Who Has The Power? The Marital Struggle', in H.P. Dreitzel (ed.), *Family, Marriage, and the Struggle of the Sexes*, London: Collier-MacMillan.

Giles-Sims, J. (1984), 'The Stepparent Role: Expectations, Behaviour and Sanctions', *Journal of Family Issues*, 5: 116–30.

Ginsberg, S. (1976), 'Women, Work and Conflict', in N. Fonda and P. Moss (eds), *Mothers in Employment*, Uxbridge: Brunel University.

Goffman, E. (1959), *The Presentation of Self in Everyday Life*, New York: Anchor.

Goffman, E. (1964), *Asylums*, Harmondsworth: Penguin.

Goldthorpe, J., Lockwood, D., Bechhofer, F. and Platt, J. (1969), *The Affluent Worker in the Class Structure*, Cambridge: Cambridge University Press.

Goode, W.J. (1959), 'On the Theoretical Importance of Love', *American Sociological Review*, 24: 38–47.

Goode, W.J. (1963), *World Revolution and Family Patterns*, New York: Collier-MacMillan.

Goode, W.J. (1965), *Women in Divorce*, New York: Free Press.

Goode, W.J. (1971), 'A Sociological Perspective on Marital Dissolution', in M. Anderson (ed.), *Sociology of the Family*, Harmondsworth: Penguin.

Griffin, C. (1981), 'Young Women and Leisure: the Transition from School to Work', in A. Tomlinson (ed.), *Leisure and Social Control*, Brighton: Brighton Polytechnic.

Hakim, C. (1982), 'The Social Consequences of High Unemployment', *Journal of Social Policy*, 11: 433–67.

Halsey, A.H. (ed.) (1972), *Trends in British Society since 1900*, London: MacMillan.

Harris, C.C. (1969), *The Family: an Introduction*, London: Allen and Unwin.

Harris, C.C. (1977), 'Changing Conceptions of the Relation Between Family and Societal Form in Western Society', in R. Scase (ed.), *Industrial Society: Class, Cleavage and Control*, London: Allen and Unwin.

Harris, C.C. (1983), *The Family and Industrial Society*, London: Allen and Unwin.

Harris, C.C. and Stacey, M. (1969), 'A Note on the Term "Extended Family" ' in

M. Stacey (ed.), *Comparability in Social Research*, London: Heinemann.

Hart, N. (1976), *When Marriage Ends*, London: Tavistock.

Haskey, J. (1982), 'The Proportion of Marriages Ending in Divorce', *Population Trends*, 27: 4–7.

Haskey, J. (1983), 'Children of Divorcing Couples', *Population Trends*, 31: 20–6.

Hawkins, C. (1983), *Britain's Economic Future*, Brighton: Wheatsheaf.

Hetherington, E.M. (1979), 'Divorce: a Child's Perspective', *American Psychologist*, 34: 851–8.

Hill, M.J., Harrison, R.M., Sargeant, A.V. and Talbot, V. (1973), *Men Out of Work*, Cambridge: Cambridge University Press.

Hobson, D. (1978), 'Housewives: Isolation as Oppression', in Women's Study Group, Centre for Contemporary Cultural Studies, *Women Take Issue*, London: Hutchinson.

Hobson, D. (1981), 'Young Women at Home and "Leisure"', in A. Tomlinson (ed.), *Leisure and Social Control*, Brighton: Brighton Polytechnic.

Hoggart, R. (1957), *The Uses of Literacy*, Harmondsworth: Penguin.

Hole, W.V. and Poutney, M.T. (1971), *Trends in Population, Housing and Occupancy Rates 1861–1961*, Department of the Environment, Building Research Station, London: HMSO.

Hubert, J. (1965), 'Kinship and Geographical Mobility in a Sample from a London Middle-Class Area', *International Journal of Comparative Sociology*, 6: 61–80.

Hunt, A. (1970), *The Home Help Service in England and Wales*, London: HMSO.

Hunt, A. (1978), *The Elderly at Home: a Study of People Aged 65 and Over Living in the Community in England in 1976*, London: HMSO.

Hunt, P. (1978), 'Cash Transactions and Household Tasks', *Sociological Review*, 26: 555–71.

Ineichen, B. (1977), 'Youthful Marriage: the Vortex of Disadvantage', in R. Chester and J. Peel (eds), *Equalities and Inequalities in Family Life*, London: Academic Press.

Jackson, B. (1968), *Working-Class Community*, London: Routledge and Kegan Paul.

Jahoda, M., Lazarsfeld, P.F. and Zeisel, H. (1972), *Marienthal: the Sociography of an Unemployed Community*, London: Tavistock.

Kerr, M. (1958), *The People of Ship Street*, London: Routledge and Kegan Paul.

Kiernan, K. (1983), 'The Structure of Families Today: Continuity or Change?', OPCS Occasional Paper, No. 31, 17–36.

Klein, J. (1965), *Samples from English Culture*, London: Routledge and Kegan Paul.

Kulka, R.A. and Weingarten, H. (1979), 'The Long-Term Effects of Parental Divorce in Childhood on Adult Adjustment', *Journal of Social Issues*, 35: 50–78.

Land, H. (1978), 'Who Cares for the Family?', *Journal of Social Policy*, 7: 257–84.

Land, H. (1979), 'The Boundaries between the State and the Family', in C.C. Harris (ed.), *The Sociology of the Family: New Directions for Britain*, Sociological Review Monograph No. 28, Keele: University of Keele.

Land, H. (1980), 'The Family Wage', *Feminist Review*, 6: 55–77.

Land, H. (1983), 'Who Still Cares for the Family? Recent Developments in Income

Maintenance, Taxation and Family Law', in J. Lewis (ed.), *Women's World/ Women's Rights*, London: Croom Helm.

Land, H. and Parker, R. (1978), 'The United Kingdom' in S.B. Kamerman and A.J. Katz (eds), *Family Policies: Government and Family in Fourteen Countries*, New York: Columbia University Press.

Laslett, P. (1969), *The World We Have Lost*, Cambridge: Cambridge University Press.

Laslett, P. (1974), 'Mean Household Size in England since the Sixteenth Century', in P. Laslett and R. Wall (eds), *Household and Family in Past Time*, Cambridge: Cambridge University Press.

Laslett, P. and Wall, R. (1974), *Household and Family in Past Time*, Cambridge: Cambridge University Press.

Leete, R. (1979), *Changing Patterns of Family Formation and Dissolution in England and Wales 1964–76*, OPCS Studies in Medical and Population Subjects, No. 39, London: HMSO.

Leete, R. and Anthony, S. (1979), 'Divorce and Remarriage: a Record Linkage Study, *Population Trends*, 16: 5–11.

Levitin, T. (1979), 'Children of Divorce', *Journal of Social Issues*, 35: 1–25.

Litwak, E. (1960a), 'Occupational Mobility and Extended Family Cohesion', *American Sociological Review*, 25: 9–21.

Litwak, E. (1960b), 'Geographic Mobility and Extended Family Cohesion', *American Sociological Review*, 25: 385–94.

Litwak, E. (1965), 'Extended Kin Relations in an Industrial Democratic Society', in E. Shanas and G.F. Streib (eds), *Social Structure and the Family: Generational Relations*, Englewood Cliffs, NJ: Prentice-Hall.

Litwak, E. and Szelenyi, I. (1969), 'Primary Group Structures and their Functions: Kin, Neighbours and Friends', *American Sociological Review*, 34: 465–81.

Lockwood, D. (1958), *The Black-Coated Worker*, London: Allen and Unwin.

Lockwood, D. (1966), 'Sources of Variation in Working-Class Images of Society', *Sociological Review*, 14: 249–67.

Lukes, S. (1974), *Power: a Radical View*, London: MacMillan.

Maddox, B. (1975), *The Half-Parent*, London: André Deutsch.

Marsden, D. and Duff, E. (1975, *Workless*, Harmondsworth: Penguin.

Marshall, G. (1984), 'On the Sociology of Women's Unemployment, its Neglect and Significance', *Sociological Review*, 32: 234–59.

Martin, J. and Roberts, C. (1984), *Women and Employment: a Lifetime Perspective*, London: HMSO.

Martin, R. and Wallace, J.G. (1984), *Working Women in Recession: Employment, Redundancy and Unemployment*, Oxford: Oxford University Press.

Mason, T. (1977), 'Intention and Implication in Housing Policy: a Study of Recent Developments in Urban Renewal', *Journal of Social Policy*, 6: 17–30.

Massey, D. (1982), *The Anatomy of Job Loss: the How, When and Where of Employment Decline*, London: Methuen.

McNally, F. (1979), *Women for Hire: a Study of the Female Office Worker*, London: MacMillan.

Medick, H. (1976), 'The Proto-Industrial Family Economy', *Social History*, 1: 291–315.

Mogey, J. (1956), *Family and Neighbourhood*, London: Oxford University Press.

Molyneux, M. (1979), 'Beyond the Domestic Labour Debate', *New Left Review*, 116: 3–27.

Morris, L. (1983), 'Renegotiation of the Domestic Division of Labour in the Context of Male Redundancy', paper presented to the Annual Conference of British Sociological Association, Cardiff.

Moylan, S. and Davies, B. (1980), 'The Disadvantages of the Unemployed', *Employment Gazette*, 88: 29–33.

Moylan, S. and Davies, B. (1981), 'The Flexibility of the Unemployed', *Employment Gazette*, 89: 29–33.

Nissel, M. and Bonnerjea, L. (1982), *Family Care of the Handicapped Elderly: Who Pays?*, London: Policy Studies Institute.

Nye, I. (1957), 'Child Adjustment in Broken and in Unhappy Unbroken Homes', *Marriage and Family Living*, 19: 356–61.

Oakley, A. (1974) *The Sociology of Housework*, London: Martin Robertson.

Oakley, A. (1976), *Housewife*, Harmondsworth: Penguin.

Oakley, A. (1980), *Women Confined: Towards a Sociology of Childbirth*, London: Martin Robertson.

Oxley, H.G. (1974), *Mateship and Local Organization*, Brisbane: University of Queensland Press.

Pahl, J. (1980), 'Patterns of Money Management within Marriage', *Journal of Social Policy*, 9: 313–35.

Pahl, R. (1980), 'Employment, Work and the Domestic Division of Labour', *International Journal of Urban and Regional Research*, 4: 1–20.

Pahl, R. (1982a), 'Family, Community and Unemployment', *New Society*, 59: 91–3.

Pahl, R. (1982b), 'The Pockmarked Road to a Private Life', *New Society*, 62: 12–14.

Pahl, R. (1984), *Divisions of Labour*, Oxford: Blackwell.

Parker, R. (1981), 'Tending and Social Policy', in E.M. Goldberg and S. Hatch (eds), *A New Look at the Personal Social Services*, London: Policy Studies Institute.

Parker, S. (1982), *Work and Retirement*, London: Allen and Unwin.

Parsons, T. (1956), 'The American Family: its Relations to Personality and to the Social Structure', in T. Parsons and R.F. Bales (eds), *Family: Socialization and Interaction Process*, London: Routledge and Kegan Paul.

Parsons, T. (1962), 'Youth in the Context of American Society', *Daedalus*, 41: 97–123.

Pearson, L. (1978), *Non-Work Time: a Review of the Literature*, Research Memorandum 65, CURS, University of Birmingham.

Penn, H. (1982), 'Who Cares for the Kids?', *New Statesman*, 103: 2651, 6–8.

Pinchbeck, I. (1969), *Women Workers and the Industrial Revolution 1750–1850*, London: Cass.

Pinchbeck, I. and Hewitt, M. (1973), *Children in English Society*, Vol. II,

London: Routledge and Kegan Paul.

Pollert, A. (1981), *Girls, Wives, Factory Lives*, London: MacMillan.

Popay, J., Rimmer, L. and Rossiter, C. (1983), *One-Parent Families: Parents, Children and Public Policy*, London: Study Commission on the Family.

Ramsden, S. and Smee, C. (1981), 'The Health of Unemployed Men: D.H.S.S. Cohort Study', *Employment Gazette*, 89: 397–401.

Rapoport, R.N. and Rapoport, R. (1971), *Dual-Career Families*, Harmondsworth: Penguin.

Rapoport, R.N. and Rapoport, R. (1976), *Dual-Career Families Re-Examined*, London: Martin Robertson.

Richards, M. (1982), 'Do Broken Marriages Affect Children', *Health Visitor*, 55: 152–3.

Roberts, K. (1978), *Contemporary Society and the Growth of Leisure*, London: Longmans.

Robinson, M. (1980), 'Step-families: a Reconstituted Family System', *Journal of Family Therapy*, 2: 45–69.

Rosser, C. and Harris, C.C. (1965), *The Family and Social Change*, London: Routledge and Kegan Paul.

Rossiter, C. and Wicks, M. (1982), *Crisis or Challenge? Family Care, Elderly People and Social Policy*, London: Study Commission on the Family.

Rushton, P. (1979), 'Marxism, Domestic Labour and the Capitalist Economy: a Note on Recent Discussions', in C.C. Harris (ed.), *The Sociology of the Family: New Directions for Britain*, Sociological Review Monograph No. 28, Keele: University of Keele.

Safilios-Rothschild, C. (1969), 'Family Sociology or Wives' Family Sociology: a Cross-Cultural Examination of Decision-Making', *Journal of Marriage and the Family*, 31: 290–301.

Safilios-Rothschild, C. (1970), 'The Study of Family Power Structure: a Review 1960–1969', *Journal of Marriage and the Family*, 32: 539–52.

Schneider, D. (1968), *American Kinship: a Cultural Account*, Englewood Cliffs, NJ: Prentice-Hall.

Scott, J.W. and Tilly, L.A. (1975), 'Women's Work and the Family in Nineteenth-Century Europe', *Comparative Studies in Society and History*, 17: 36–64.

Seccombe, W. (1974), 'The Housewife and her Labour under Capitalism', *New Left Review*, 83: 3–24.

Shanas, E. and Streib, G.F. (eds) (1965), *Social Structure and the Family: Generational Relations*, Englewood Cliffs, NJ: Prentice-Hall.

Shorter, E. (1975), *The Making of the Modern Family*, London: Fontana.

Sinfield, A. (1981), *What Unemployment Means*, London: Martin Robertson.

Sinfield, A. (1982), 'Unemployment in an Unequal Society', in B. Showler and A. Sinfield (eds), *The Workless State*, London: Martin Robertson.

Smith, J.H. (1975), 'The Significance of Elton Mayo', in E. Mayo, *The Social Problems of an Industrial Society* (2nd edn), London: Routledge and Kegan Paul.

Sprey, J. (1971), 'Children in Divorce: an Overview', in E.A. Grollman (ed.),

Explaining Divorce to Children, Boston: Beacon Press.

Stacey, M., Batstone, E., Bell, C. and Murcott, A. (1975), *Persistence and Change: a Second Study of Banbury*, London: Routledge and Kegan Paul.

Stone, L. (1979), *The Family, Sex and Marriage in England 1500–1800*, Harmondsworth: Penguin.

Sussman, M. (1959), 'Isolated Nuclear Family: Fact or Fiction', *Social Problems*, 6: 333–40.

Suttles, G. (1970), 'Friendship as a Social Institution' in G. McCall (ed.), *Social Relationships*, Chicago: Aldine.

Thornes, B. and Collard, J. (1979), *Who Divorces?*, London: Routledge and Kegan Paul.

Townsend, P. (1957), *The Family Life of Old People*, London: Routledge and Kegan Paul.

Townsend, P. (1979), *Poverty in the United Kingdom*, London: Allen Lane.

Tunstall, J. (1962), *The Fisherman*, London: McGibbon and Kee.

Turner, J. (1979), 'Women and the Cuts', *New Society*, 50: 645–6.

Turner, V. (1974), *The Ritual Process*, Harmondsworth: Penguin.

Ungerson, C. (1983), 'Why do Women Care?' in J. Finch and D. Groves (eds), *A Labour of Love*, London: Routledge and Kegan Paul.

Wainwright, H. (1978), 'Women and the Division of Labour', in P. Abrams (ed.), *Work, Urbanism and Inequality*, London: Weidenfeld.

Walczak, Y. and Burns, S. (1984), *Divorce: the Child's Point of View*, London: Harper and Row.

Walker, K.N. and Messinger, L. (1979), 'Remarriage after Divorce: Dissolution and Reconstitution of Family Boundaries', *Family Process*, 18: 185–92.

Wallerstein, J. and Kelly, J. (1979), 'Divorce and Children', in J.D. Noshpitz (ed.), *Basic Handbook of Child Psychiatry*, Vol. IV, New York: Basic Books.

Wallerstein, J. and Kelly, J. (1980), *Surviving the Breakup*, London: Grant-MacIntyre.

Warr, P. (1983), 'Work, Jobs and Unemployment', *Bulletin of the British Psychological Society*, 36: 305–11.

West, J. (ed.) (1982), *Work, Women and the Labour Market*, London: Routledge and Kegan Paul.

White, M. (1983), *Long-Term Unemployment and Labour Markets*, London: Policy Studies Institute.

Whitehead, A. (1976), 'Sexual Antagonism in Herefordshire', in D.L. Barker and S. Allen (eds), *Dependence and Exploitation in Work and Marriage*, London: Longmans.

Wilkin, D. (1979), *Caring for the Mentally Handicapped Child*, London: Croom Helm.

Williams, R. (1975), *The Country and the City*, St. Albans: Paladin.

Williams, W.M. (1963), *A West-Country Village: Ashworthy*, London: Routledge and Kegan Paul.

Willmott, P. and Young, M. (1971), *Family and Class in a London Suburb*, London: Nel Mentor.

Wirth, L. (1938), 'Urbanism as a Way of Life', *American Journal of Sociology*,

44: 1–24.

Wood, S. (1981), 'Redundancy and Female Employment', *Sociological Review*, 29: 649–83.

Young, M. and Willmott, P. (1957), *Family and Kinship in East London*, London: Routledge and Kegan Paul.

Young, M. and Willmott, P., (1973), *The Symmetrical Family*, London: Routledge and Kegan Paul.

Zaretsky, E. (1976), *Capitalism, the Family, and Personal Life*, London: Pluto Press.

Index